Teaching English In

EASTERN AND
CENTRAL EUROPE

Robert Lynes

PASSPORT BOOKS
a division of *NTC Publishing Group*
Lincolnwood, Illinois USA

Published by Passport Books
a division of NTC Publishing Group
4255 West Touhy Avenue
Lincolnwood (Chicago), Illinois
60646-1975

ISBN 0-8442-0876-0
Library of Congress Catalog Card Number: 95-68431

First published by In Print Publishing Ltd.
9 Beaufort Terrace
Brighton BN2 2SU
UK

Typeset by MC Typeset
Printed in the U.K. by Bell & Bain

About the author

Robert Lynes went to Eastern and Central Europe in 1988. He taught English in Hungary for six years and has travelled extensively throughout the region. He taught at the University of Economics in Budapest; in companies; privately; and for International House. Up until December 1993 he was Executive Director of International House in Budapest, before which he was Director of Studies.

The advice given in Teaching English in Eastern and Central Europe is gained mostly from first hand experience.

To Márta, Hannah and Laura

Acknowledgements

I would like to thank the many people in each of the countries who contributed to making this book possible. I would especially like to thank all those teachers whose experiences I have drawn on, and without whom this book would not have been possible. Unfortunately because of lack of space it is impossible to name all those who have offered advice, information, comments and contributed in many ways, but sincere thanks go to everyone.

I would especially like to thank the following organizations and people.

British Council, Bell Educational Trust, Central Bureau, International House.

Kaye Anderson, Rachel Appleby, Julia Bannister, Annabel Barber, Carol Berezai, Jim Chapman, Pam Cox, Derek DeWitt, Peter Doherty, Simon Gill, Patrick and Ruth Howarth, Francis Hughes, Roger Hunt, Ania Kolbuszewska, Maria Kropienicka, Hanna Kryszewska, Irena Maskova, Janet Lyons, Elzbieta Lyszkowska, Karen Momber, Douglas Mcfarlane, Andras Nyerges, Liana Popa, Charles Poe, Leslie Papa, David Rowson, Morag Samson, Anna Siko, Frank Smolinski, Joanna Sobczyk, Maciej Wojcseski, Anna Zabrocka.

Note on the text

An (x) after a sentence denotes incorrect or unnatural English: for example,

He go to work (x)

An (x) denotes a sentence which is correct grammatically, but awkward or unnatural:

An accident happened (x)

International House

International House (IH) began in 1953, when John and Brita Haycraft opened a language school in Cordoba, Spain. It has since developed into the largest independent British-based organization for teaching English, with over 100 000 students, 2 000 teachers, and some 90 schools around the world.

The home of the organization is International House in London, a non-profit-making eduational charity whose aim is to raise the standard of English teaching worldwide. Trustees include prominent academics, as well as representatives of the British Council, ARELS/FELCO and BBC English by Radio and Television.

International House in London, based at 106 Piccadilly, operates one of the principal schools of English in the UK, as well as International House Teacher Training. The latter offers a variety of courses leading to the UCLES/RSA Certificate and the UCLES/RSA Diploma, and courses for foreign teachers of English. It also offers specialized training courses – Teaching Business English, Development Course in Teacher Training, Director of Studies Training Course, etc. As well as being responsible for over half of the UCLES/RSA Certificate training in the world, International House Teacher Training is the sole body authorized to offer a Distance Training Programme leading to the UCLES/ RSA Diploma in TEFLA.

International House in London is also the home of the Central Department, headquarters of the IH World Organization. This is an association of independent language schools and teacher training institutes which are affiliated to, but not owned by, the International House Trust. The Central Department supplies the affiliated schools with materials and advice on a wide range of educational and administrative matters, organizes annual conferences, and monitors standards. Through its Teacher Selection Department, IH recruits teachers and senior staff for the affiliated schools and other approved institutes.

The opinions expressed in this book are not necessarily those of IH, and, while every care has been taken to ensure accuracy, IH cannot accept responsibility for any errors or omissions.

Table of contents

CHAPTER 1
INTRODUCTION

CHAPTER 2
POLAND

Part 1. Preparing your trip and finding teaching jobs

CHAPTER 3
THE CZECH REPUBLIC

CHAPTER 4

SLOVAKIA

CHAPTER 5
HUNGARY

CHAPTER 6
ROMANIA

Part 1. Preparing your trip and finding teaching jobs

CHAPTER 7
BULGARIA

CHAPTER 8
TEACHING CHILDREN AND ADOLESCENTS

CHAPTER 9
TEACHING BUSINESS PEOPLE

CHAPTER 10
FURTHER READING

1 | Introduction

This book is designed to provide a much needed source of information for teachers wanting to teach English as a foreign language (EFL) in Eastern and Central Europe. The need stems from the fact that since 1989 (and to a much lesser extent before), thousands of people have been coming to the region, many to teach English, with little if any idea of what to expect. English has replaced Russian as the main foreign language taught in many schools and it is this, as well as other factors, such as closer links with the West, better jobs, and access to Western culture that has created the growing demand for qualified EFL teachers and trainers.

In writing this book I have tried to give the reader a clear picture of what the job opportunities are and where to find them, as well as to give an insight into what it is like to live in each of the countries covered. In addition, I have included suggestions that should help you directly in your teaching. While not wanting to discourage people from coming, I have tried to present a realistic picture, which is not always glowing, in order to help you to make an informed decision about coming here and to be somewhat prepared for what to expect.

The book covers six countries and is ordered geographically running from north to south: Poland, the Czech Republic, Slovakia, Hungary, Romania and Bulgaria. More space is given to the Czech Republic, Hungary and Poland; not because their need for qualified EFL teachers and trainers is greater than the others, but because presently that is where the majority of opportunities to work are, and English language teaching (ELT) in these areas is much more established.

Throughout the book I have indicated the cost of items in local currency, although where I thought it necessary I have also quoted the price in US dollars; this being the most widely recognized and accepted Western currency in Eastern and Central Europe. For each country I have given the exchange rate at the time of printing; obviously these change constantly.

I have divided the information on each particular country into the following parts.

- *Part 1* deals with preparing your trip, finding a teaching job in the country, and gives details about the different teaching opportunities. It includes addresses of useful organizations and a selected list of private language schools.
- *Part 2* deals with the practicalities of living in each of the countries, and gives some background on the country's history, culture and society.
- *Part 3* gives an overview of the education system, specific language problems and an idea of the types of students you will encounter.

In order to make this book as reader-friendly as possible there is a detailed table of contents as well as an index at the back. In addition there are a number of appendices after each country, covering areas such as food and drink, useful words and phrases, case histories, etc.

Many people come to Eastern and Central Europe with a lot of misconceptions. Some still have outdated images of grey, dull cities and people struggling with poverty. Yet, while hardships exist in many areas, the governments are tackling their economies and making them more market-oriented and there is a vibrant spirit among the people. The euphoria which greeted the events of 1989 has long gone, and the region is now shaking off the past and looking towards a better future. I speak here in general, and although the countries share borders, and on the whole have good relations with each other, they are all independent countries in their own right, with their own languages, traditions and cultures. However, 40 years of socialism have obviously left their mark on the region, and you can detect certain similarities, often legacies of the old regimes, in all of the countries. The countries share common problems today which have come with their new found independence, such as inflation, unemployment, pollution and economic difficulties, to name but a few. Nevertheless, each country has its own uniqueness, beauty and interest which many people have yet to discover, and it is these that attract so many visitors.

Eastern and Central Europe is still rapidly going through many changes, and while every effort has been made to make sure the information contained in this book is up-to-date and correct at the time of printing, there will no doubt be errors. Telephone numbers change, places close down and new ones open, prices fluctuate, sometimes weekly, and new government laws are continually being introduced affecting everything from taxes to work permits. Please bear this in mind when reading the book.

The final chapter in the book looks specifically at two areas: teaching business English and teaching children, both of which are very relevant in Eastern and Central Europe and are not always specifically covered on many EFL courses.

I have used the male personal pronoun throughout this book when not directly referring to women. This is for convenience only.

WHO GOES TO EASTERN AND CENTRAL EUROPE?

Since the collapse of communism in 1989, the number of visitors coming to Eastern and Central Europe has risen dramatically, in part due to extensive media coverage of the region. These visitors have included many people wanting to stay for an extended period and teach English as a foreign language. This trend has been encouraged by reports in the West on how Eastern and Central Europe is in need of thousands of native speakers of English. To a large extent this is true, but it is the qualified teacher of English as a foreign language who is most needed.

People who come to Eastern and Central Europe to teach English usually fall into one of the following four categories: in the first group are those who are primarily interested in witnessing the political, economic and social changes happening in these countries; in the second are those who wish to study the language and culture (including a number of people whose parents or grandparents once lived in the region); in the third are those who want to come to Eastern and Central Europe and work in various fields or simply wish to 'experience' being in the region and supplement their income by teaching; and finally a large number wish to offer voluntary help to these countries by teaching English.

It is worth noting here that, because of the recession in ELT in other parts of Europe and the world and the growth in Eastern and Central Europe, many teachers are coming here because this is where a lot of work can now be found.

Pay is poor, especially in the state sector, if you compare it to Western salaries; however, in the private sector at least, employers are generally prepared to pay what are considered high salaries in local terms, so on the whole English teachers usually have a reasonable standard of living. You should be aware, however, that inflation is generally increasing faster than salaries and your living standards will not be the same as those of tourists on a weekend trip.

Generally people who teach English in Eastern and Central Europe are in their early twenties to mid-thirties. There are of course others who are much older. Most usually stay a year, sometimes two, and there are a few who stay much longer. There are also teachers who come out for short periods of one to six months, and others who decide to make it their home, marry and settle down.

There is a lot of work for teacher trainers in all the countries covered in this book. These opportunities can vary from running two-week courses, to stays of up to two years. Within whatever type of school or institute you work there are opportunities for different degrees of teacher training and sharing of ideas for those with the necessary experience and qualifications.

TRAINING

It is now becoming necessary to have had training in EFL to find teaching jobs in Eastern and Central Europe. It is also essential if you want to be effective in the classroom. Competition for jobs at recognized private language schools is getting harder, especially in the more glamorous cities of Prague, Budapest and Kraków, and as a rule employers are now looking only for teachers with EFL qualifications. Many of the organizations recruiting teachers for Eastern and Central Europe are looking more and more to those with EFL qualifications. In a lot of cases this is a legal requirement in order to obtain a work permit.

The most popular course for first-time teachers is the one-month RSA/ULCES CTEFLA course which is run at many centres in the UK, the USA, Canada, Australia and New Zealand. Over the last two years there has been a substantial growth in the number enrolled on such courses, and in 1993 over 6 000 people gained this qualification. This is a practical introductory course in TEFL, usually containing 110 hours of theoretical input and teaching practice. There is no exam at the end of the course, but the grades are given on assessment of teaching over the length of the course, which may be full-time intensive over a month, or part-time spread over three months to a year.

Although expensive (approximately £850/US$1 250) in 1994, the RSA/UCLES CTEFLA course is the first step you should take if you are at all serious about teaching English as a foreign language. Apart from the pedagogical reasons given below, it is a qualification which will go a long way to helping you find work not only in Eastern and Central Europe, but almost anywhere in the world.

As well as helping you find work, training can give you the confidence and credibility to stand in front of a group of students, as well as giving you ideas on what and how to teach. It is not enough just to be a native speaker of English to cope with the problems that come with teaching English. Native speakers are usually quite ignorant of English grammar and have great difficulty in knowing how to go about teaching it without training. Enthusiasm, imagination, common sense and hard work are all qualities you will need in the classroom, but these alone do not make you a good teacher.

Training in the UK

RSA/UCLES CTEFLA courses are run in many centres throughout the UK including large organizations such as Bell, International House and Pilgrims. Because there are so many places now running courses in EFL it is worth reading the literature carefully first to make sure it is the course you want. In the UK, check the *Guardian* on Tuesdays, the *EFL Gazette* or your local library for a list of places which run them (see p 6 for how to obtain a full up-to-date list of centres).

Be wary of one-week courses, or courses containing no teaching practice. They don't really give you a solid foundation, and the course is unlikely to be recognized by recruiting organizations or schools.

It is worth adding here the RSA/UCLES are currently undergoing a review of their TEFL courses which will be completed by 1996.

Trinity College London offers TESOL (Teachers of English to Speakers of Other Languages) courses at both the introductory level and diploma level. These courses are not as well-known internationally as the RSA/UCLES, but are generally accepted as an equivalent qualification. These are usually 100-hour courses which can be taken at about 20 centres throughout the UK. Check the course content first as different centres put emphasis on different areas.

Training in the USA

TEFL/TESL qualifications gained in the USA, Canada, Ireland, New Zealand and Australia are generally accepted by employers as long as the course taken contained a balance between theory and practice. Apart from taking a course at one of only a handful of centres now offering RSA/UCLES courses (see below), most people interested in a career in ELT take a BA or MA in ESL or Applied linguistics, as no other standard equivalent to the RSA/UCLES CTEFLA qualification exists. Courses in the USA vary from one-week introductory courses to full-time MAs.

In the USA the *Directory of Professional Preparation Programs in TESOL* is a guide to the various courses on offer. The same organization publishes a bi-monthly *Placement Bulletin* with information on job vacancies.

These can be obtained from most public libraries or:

> **TESOL**, 1600 Cameron Street, Suite 300, Alexandria, Virginia 22314–2751, USA. Tel: (703) 518 2522. Fax: (703) 518 2525.

Addresses of RSA/UCLES course centres in the USA include the following:

> **New York:** Center for English Studies, International House, 330 Seventh Avenue at 29th St, New York 10001. Tel: (212) 620 0760. Fax: (212) 594 7415.
>
> **San Francisco:** English International, 655 Sutter St (Suite 500), San Francisco, CA 94102. Tel: (415) 749 5633. Fax: (415) 749 5629.
>
> **Washington:** School of Languages and Linguistics, Georgetown University, Washington DC 20057–1067. Tel: (202) 687 6045.

Training in Australia

Addresses of RSA/UCLES course centres in Australia include the following:

> **Cairns:** International House, Queensland College, 130 McLeod Street, PO Box 7368, Cairns 4870, Queensland. Tel: (70) 313 466. Fax: (70) 313 464.
>
> **Perth:** Milner International College of English, 1st floor, 195 Adelaide Terrace, Perth, 6004 Western Australia. Tel: (9) 325 5444.
>
> **Sydney:** TESOL Training Centre (The Australian College of English), PO Box 82, Bondi Junction, Sydney, New South Wales 2022. Tel: (2) 389 0249.

General information sources on RSA/UCLES

A full up-to-date list of centres around the world running RSA/UCLES courses in EFL at Certificate and Diploma level is available free from:

> **University of Cambridge Local Examinations Syndicate (UCLES)**, Syndicate Buildings, 1 Hills Road, Cambridge CB1 2EU, UK. Tel: (01223) 553 311. Fax: (01223) 460 278.

The *EFL Guide* is an annual publication which gives a run down on centres offering various courses from RSA/UCLES one-month courses to MAs as well as other practical information.

> **EFL Limited**, Lightwood, Grove Mount, Ramsey, Isle of Man, UK. Subscriptions tel: (0171) 937 6506.

Further qualifications

The RSA Diploma is primarily for teachers who have usually followed a RSA/UCLES CTEFLA course and have a minimum of two years' recent classroom experience. This course is at a much higher level than the Certificate and goes into the theoretical aspects of language teaching in a lot more detail, although teaching practice plays an equally important role. It can be taken intensively over eight weeks or part-time over eight or nine months. Apart from the many centres in the UK that run such courses, it is currently offered at a few centres in Poland, the Czech Republic and Hungary by International House and the British Council. The cost is usually around £1 200/$1 800.

A PGCE (Postgraduate Certificate in Education) is a UK qualification, and an option for those wishing to move into state education either in the UK or abroad.

Teachers interested in looking into a particular field in more depth may consider an MA course, for example in Linguistics, Teacher Training or ELT Management; although an MA will not necessarily mean a better job or more money. In fact for job opportunities the RSA Diploma can often be a better bet as it is a much more practical qualification. An MA is, however, often required for some positions in the British Council and other organizations and is sometimes necessary if you want to go into mainstream education. As so many universities now offer MAs in ELT it is important to choose your course carefully to be sure it satisfies your particular interests. The current edition of the TESOL *Directory* (see above) lists 178 institutions in the USA which offer MA courses.

Training in Eastern and Central Europe

A number of courses are now being run in Eastern and Central Europe. International House (IH), for example, runs RSA/UCLES CTEFLA courses in: Nove Mesto in the Czech Republic, Budapest in Hungary, and Kraków and Poznań in Poland. IH also runs similar courses for non-native English speakers. The RSA Diploma is offered at IH schools in Budapest, Prague and Kraków.

Applications should be made either to the schools directly or to Central Department, International House (see p 13).

One of the advantages of doing a course abroad is that it is usually a lot cheaper where the cost of living is lower. Furthermore, should you want to teach in that country after the course you will have already had experience with its nationals and an opportunity to see what the possibilities of work are.

CAREER POSSIBILITIES IN EFL

A lot of people initially use TEFL as a means to work abroad and see some of the world for a few years. However there are more and more opportunities now to pursue a career in TEFL and the profession is becoming increasingly diverse. Enormous advances have been made in the field over the last 10 years, and these are likely to develop in the future as English language teaching becomes more professional and demand grows.

It is important to realize that, even after doing a one-month or part-time course, teachers should still consider themselves 'apprentices' until they have had about two years' classroom experience. When considering TEFL as a career you should also bear in mind that while experience is crucial, promotion very much depends on an individual's resourcefulness, energy and adaptability.

Some of the possibilities available after three or four years experience teaching at all levels and after gaining further qualifications include: Director/Director of Studies in a private school or institute; apprenticeship as a teacher trainer; an administrative job in a school; teaching ESL to immigrants; specializing in commercial or technical EFL; English for Academic Purposes (EAP); publishing; writing textbooks; starting your own school; broadcasting; specializing in teaching English to children; and EFL and computers.

It is important that you take advantage of as many opportunities as possible at all stages of your career. When you are in Eastern and Central Europe, for example, learn the langauge of the country you are teaching in. Learn all you can about the educational system and the background of your students. Join local and international teachers' associations, attend any conferences that are organized, give talks at them: anything directly related to your experience will almost certainly be interesting. Read as much as you can about EFL and the country you are in, and assess any textbooks you can get hold of. Observe classes whenever you can and get to know authors and teachers of any nationality. There are often more opportunities to teach a variety of students and levels in Eastern and Central Europe than elsewhere in the world where EFL is much more established.

FINDING A JOB

There are obvious advantages to arranging a job before you go. Accommodation is usually arranged, you will start work as soon as you arrive, and work permits are usually sorted out in advance.

You also have the security of knowing there will be someone to look after you when you arrive and help you find your feet.

There are a number of ways to go about looking for work from your home country. First, you could send a covering letter and CV to any of the organizations, schools, institutes, etc. listed in this book. A good time to start applying is around April, for jobs starting in September or October, although private language schools usually employ all year round.

In the UK, the *Guardian* has a section every Tuesday advertising EFL jobs, as does the *Times Educational Supplement* on a Friday. Other sources of jobs include the *The International Herald Tribune* and the *EFL Gazette* which comes out monthly and can be purchased from major bookshops or by subscription from:

> **EFL Gazette**, 10 Wrights Lane, London W8 6TA. Tel: (0171) 938 1818.

It can be useful to contact the particular embassy in your home country and ask for advice (see Appendices). Some will give you a list of state and private schools along with the phone and fax numbers (some will be out of date), and may even give you a form in order to apply for a position.

In the USA, TESOL (Teachers of English of Other Languages) offers a placement service and publishes a list of available jobs (see p 6). The Citizens' Democracy Corps publishes a *Compendium* which lists jobs in a number of fields including teaching.

Recruitment organizations

The following organizations all recruit English teachers for Eastern and Central Europe. The specific countries they deal with are indicated in brackets after the address. While some recruit primarily for one or more of the countries covered in this book, others recruit for other parts of the world not listed here.

Anglo-Polish Academic Association (PL). The association was set up to encourage and promote contacts and exchanges between nationals of Poland and the UK. Opportunities exist to teach English on a semi-voluntary basis in holiday locations belonging to Polish universities, medical schools and the Ministry of Education. Contracts are usually only for short periods over the summer. For further details write to:

> **Anglo-Polish Association**, Att: The Hon Secretary, 93 Victoria Road, Leeds LS6 1DR, UK. Tel: (01532) 758 121.

Bell Educational Trust (CZ, HU, PL). Bell currently has two schools in Eastern and Central Europe, in Budapest and Prague, plus an associate school in Kraków. It recruits a number of qualified teachers each year either on full- or part-time contracts. Terms and conditions are generally good.

> **Bell Educational Trust**, Overseas Department, Hillscross, Redcross Lane, Cambridge CB2 2QX. Tel: (01223) 246644. Fax: (01223) 414080.

The British Council (BL, CZ, HU, PL, RO, SL). The British Council recruits for a variety of posts in Eastern and Central Europe each year, mainly specialists on behalf of government agencies and institutions. Posts are usually at university level institutions and are mainly in teacher training, curriculum design, English for special purposes (ESP), EFL and British Studies. There are also a number of positions for classroom teachers in dual-language schools and English medium schools.

At present three DTOs (Direct Teaching Operations) have been set up in Eastern and Central Europe; in Budapest, Bratislava and Prague.

For detailed information on opportunities with the British Council write to the address below. Posts are usually advertised in the Tuesday's *Guardian* and the *Times Educational Supplement*. Most British Council posts offer a sterling supplement plus local salary. Accommodation is also usually provided, as well as medical cover and airfares:

> *For information on DTOs:* Recruitment Section, Central Management of Direct Teaching, The British Council, 10 Spring Gardens, London SW1A 2BN. Tel: (0171) 389 4931 Fax: (0171) 389 4140.

> *For information on other posts:* Overseas Appointments Services, The British Council, Medlock Street, Manchester M15 4AA. Tel: (0161) 957 7383. Fax: (0161) 957 7397.

CFBT Education Services (HU). CFBT is an independent non-profit making organization established in 1968 which provides a wide range of services from consultancy and project management to direct teaching. Applicants must be graduates with minimum of two years' teaching experience. Contracts are for two years and teachers work up to 25 hours per week.

Rates depend on country, qualifications and experience. Travel costs are provided and accommodation and board included in some contracts. Placements are primarily in Hungary.

> **CFBT Education Services**, Quality House, Gyosei Campus, London Road, Reading RG1 5AQ. Tel: (01734) 756 200.

Central Bureau Language Assistants (BL, CZ, HU, SL). The Bureau was set up in 1948 by the UK government as the national office for the provision of information and advice on educational visits and exchanges. Assistants are aged between 20–30 and must be native speakers of English. Most applicants are graduates. Assistants are assigned to state schools or colleges, where one of their roles is to help teachers of English. Contracts are for a minimum of one academic year and teachers work 12–20 hours a week. A monthly allowance is paid in the local currency and accommodation is provided. Teachers must pay their own travel costs. Placements are primarily in the Czech and Slovak Republics and Hungary. *Readers should note that Central Bureau has merged with the British Council. From June 1995, all queries should be addressed to the British Council at 10 Spring Gardens (see above).*

Central Bureau for Educational Visits & Exchanges, Assistants Department, Seymour Mews House, Seymour Mews, London W1H 9PE. Tel: (0171) 486 5101.

Central Bureau, 3 Bruntsfield Crescent, Edinburgh EH10 4HD. Tel: (0131) 447 8024.

Central Bureau, 1 Chlorine Gardens, Belfast BT9 5DJ. Tel: (01232) 664418.

Charter 77 (CZ, SL). Charter 77 is an organization formed in the 1970s by a group of dissidents, including Václav Havel, to monitor human rights in former Czechoslovakia. Among its other activities today, it brings EFL teachers over to work in different schools and institutes in the Czech Republic and Slovakia.

Charter 77, Suite 609, 1270 Avenue of the Americas, New York NY 10020, USA. Tel: (212) 332 2898. Fax: (212) 332 2890.

Charter 77, Washington 17, 113 00 Prague 1, Czech Republic. Tel: +42 (2) 2358 572.

Charter 77, Zuzana Szatmary Staromestska 6, 811 03 Bratislava, Slovakia. Tel: +42 (7) 316 341.

East European Partnership (BL, CZ, HU, PL, RO, SL). EEP is a branch of VSO (Voluntary Service Overseas), and was set up to contribute to the development of Eastern and Central European countries. It operates in the following sectors: health, education, business advice, social welfare and environmental protection. Teachers of English/ESP are needed for high schools, teacher training, agricultural and commercial colleges and Universities while other volunteers are placed in hospitals, Ministries, Chambers of Commerce and NGOs. A degree and/or appropriate professional qualification and two years practical experience are necessary. As with VSO, EEP volunteers are paid a local salary and receive free accommodation while EEP provides a benefits package which includes travel expenses, an equipment grant, relocation allowance, NI Contributions, medical insurance, language training and professional support. Posts are for one or two years:

EEP, Carlton House, 27a Carlton Drive, London SW15 2BS. Tel: (0181) 780 2841. Fax: (0181) 780 9592.

Education for Democracy (CZ, SL). Set up in Canada in 1989 and shortly after in the UK (branch now closed) and the USA, EFD currently recruits over 300 volunteers in schools and universities and in government and commercial enterprises. Volunteers usually teach 'conversation classes' on average four hours a day. Contracts are usually from one to six months. Accommodation is provided either with a family or in a university dormitory and a local allowance is paid by the Ministry of Education. EFD's Prague office is at 16 Revolunci.

Education for Democracy, PO Box 40514, Mobile, AL 36640–0514, USA. Tel: (205) 434 3889. Fax: (205) 434 3731.

EFL Fellow Program (BL, CZ, HU, PL, RO, SL). For teacher trainers and ESP specialists, positions are offered in the state sector or working with businesses. Usually for mid-career professionals with an MA in TEFL or Applied Linguistics and several years' experience, some of it outside the USA. Open to US citizens only. Countries subject to change.

> **Council for International Educational Exchanges (CIEE)**, EFL Fellow Program, 205 E 42nd Street, New York, 10017. Tel: (212) 661 1414.

Fandango (CZ, HU, PL). An organization involved in recruiting qualified teachers for various parts of Eastern Europe. There is a placement fee of around $500.

> **Fandango,** 1613 Escalero Road, Santa Rosa, CA 95409, USA. Tel/Fax: (707) 539 2722.

Fulbright Teacher Exchange, Fulbright Program and English Teaching Fellow Program. The Fulbright Teacher Exchange is a programme designed to bring qualified secondary school teachers over to Eastern and Central Europe, in exchange for sending a teacher to the USA. The teachers usually live in each other's home. Not all the teachers teach English. Teachers of other subjects are also accepted.

Under the Fulbright Program, lecturers work in a university and teach such subjects as American Literature. Positions are open only to well qualified applicants.

The English Teaching Fellow Program offers opportunities for people who have recently completed an MA in TEFL or Applied linguistics to work as teachers in secondary schools.

All three programes run for a year with the possibility of renewing. For more information contact:

> **USIA (United States Information Agency)**, E – CE Room 304, 301 4th Street, SW, Washington DC 20547.

GAP Activities Projects (PL, RO). Offers work opportunities for school leavers aged 18–19 in Poland and Romania. Posts are for at least six months. There is a fee to join the scheme (over £300) and air fares are not usually paid.

> **GAP**, 44 Queens Road, Reading, Berks RG1 4BB. Tel: (01734) 594 914. Fax: (01734) 576 634.

Georgetown University (BL, CZ, HU, PL, SL). Georgetown has a fee-paying programme which selects and trains college graduates to teach for a minimum of one year in a number of countries in Eastern and Central Europe.

> **Georgetown University**, PO Box 2298, Hoya Station, Washington, DC 20057–1011, USA. Tel: (202) 298 0200/(202) 298 0214.

ILC Recruitment – International Language Centres (CZ). ILC is an affiliate of International House (see below) and its Recruitments and Contracts Division has a TEFL Register, free and open to all qualified (degree plus TEFL) native-speaker teachers from around the world.

ILC Recruitment, Palace Court, White Rock, Hastings, Sussex TN34 1JY.

International House (CZ, HU, PL, RO). IH is a non-profit educational charity which was founded in 1953. It is now the largest UK-based organization for teaching English with nearly 100 schools worldwide. It is also a major teacher-training institute.

IH was a pioneer in Eastern and Central Europe and now has teaching operations in the Czech Republic, Hungary, Poland and Romania.

International House employs native-speaker teachers from a number of countries. Teachers are usually graduates with a good grade in a recognized TEFL qualification. IH has job opportunities ranging from newly qualified teachers to teacher trainers. For detailed information on particular countries and schools:

International House, Teacher Selection Department, 106 Piccadilly, London W1 9FL. Tel: (0171) 491 2598. Fax: (0171) 495 0284.

Jan Hus Foundation (CZ, SL). This is not a recruitment organization but will help to put teachers in contact with schools in the Czech and Slovak Republics looking to employ native teachers. The Foundation tries to match teachers with appropriate vacancies; however the teacher and educational establishment are responsible for the final agreement, and each individual must make the final decision. Placements are normally in state secondary schools in the country or small industrial towns.

Jan Hus Foundation, 4 Offord Road, London N1 1DL. Tel: (0171) 609 2703. Fax: (0171) 607 0725.

Jan Hus Foundation, Radnicka 8, PO Box 735, 663 35 Brno, Czech Republic. Tel: +42 (5) 4221 2314. Fax: +42 (5) 4221 2084.

Language for Eastern European Development. LEED offers placements in secondary schools and institutes of higher education, usually for a minimum of one year. Placement fee required.

LEED, 41 Sutter Street, Suite 510, San Francisco, CA 94104, USA. Tel: (415) 982 5333. Fax: (415) 982 3726.

Language Link (CZ, HU, PL, SL). Language Link is a private company with many schools in various parts of Eastern and Central Europe. It employs qualified EFL teachers and pays a local salary. Contracts are usually for six to nine months.

Language Link, 181 Earls Court Road, London SW5 9RB. Tel: (0171) 370 4755. Fax: (0171) 373 4179.

Nord–Anglia International (CZ, HU, PL, SL). Nord–Anglia International is a licensed recruitment agency which puts teachers in contact with employers abroad. Applicants must be UK nationals and native speakers with TEFL qualifications and six to twelve months' previous experience. Contracts are usually for one academic year and teachers work 25–30 hours per week. Terms and conditions depend on individual positions.

Nord–Anglia International, 10 Eden Place, Cheadle, Stockport, Cheshire, SK8 1AT. Tel: (0161) 491 4191.

Peace Corps (BL, CZ, HU, PL, RO). The Peace Corps recruits volunteers, usually for two-year contracts, to work in many different types of state educational establishments. Nearly all the positions are in small towns in the provinces and teachers are paid a local salary. There is a three-month training programme prior to starting work which contains language training, culture and history. A certain amount of training in EFL is given to volunteers without any experience.

> **The Peace Corps**, 1990 K Street NW, Box 941, Washington, DC 20526, USA. Tel: (202) 800 424 8580 (ext 2293)/(202) 606 3780.

RLC International (HU). This is a commercial recruitment agency which has placed a number of teachers in Hungary, primarily in the private sector.

> **RLC International**, 27–28 George Street, Richmond, Surrey TW9 1HY, UK.

Services for Open Learning (CZ, HU, PL, SL). SOL is a non-profit-making educational charity set up in 1990 to support the teaching and learning of English in a wide variety of ways. Its main emphasis is on the countries of Eastern and Central Europe.

> **SOL**, North Devon Professional Centre, Vicarage Street, Barnstable, Devon EX32 7HB, UK. Tel: (01271) 327 319. Fax: (01271) 76650.

Solidarity Eastern Europe – Canada. This organization has an office in Poland:

> Centrum 'C' 9/56, 31–931 Krakow. Tel/Fax: +48 (12) 44-91-14.

Soros Foundation and Soros English Language Programme (BL, CZ, HU, RO). The Soros Foundation sponsors many teacher trainers to run training courses in Eastern and Central Europe. These are mainly in the former Soviet Union and Romania.

The Central European University based in Prague and Budapest occasionally has openings for English teachers, although these are usually only for those with English for academic purposes (EAP) experience.

Teachers normally have to be well qualified (MA in Linguistics or TESOL) and experience is essential.

> **The Soros Foundation**, 888 Seventh Avenue, Suite 1901, New York, NY 10106, USA. Tel: (212) 757 2323. Fax: (212) 974 0367.

In conjunction with International House Soros has opened up schools in various parts of Eastern Europe including Timisoara in Romania (see IH above). The organization also arranges short-term teacher training contracts, especially in Romania and the Baltic states.

Students for Czechoslovakia (CZ). This is a programme organized by US students and supported by the Czech Ministry of Education. It places teachers in educational schools and institutes as well as in business establishments.

> **Students for Czechoslovakia**, c/o Dum Zaharanicnich, Styku, Minis-

terstva Skolstvi, CSR, Namesti M. Gorkeho 26, 11121 Prague 1, Czech Republic. Tel: +42 (2) 267 077.

Teach Hungary (HU, RO). Teach Hungary was set up in 1991 and recruits teachers for state schools, mainly secondary, although there are placements in primary schools and colleges. Placements are also offered in Transylvania (Romania). There is a fee of around $500 to join the programme, and for this you are placed in a school, with an English-speaking contact person, given an orientation course on arrival in Hungary and your work and residence papers are also sorted out. Contracts are initially for a year but renewable, and there are currently over 70 people working on the programme. Hungarian language courses are offered at Beloit College in summer.

> **Teach Hungary,** Att: Lesley Davis, Beloit College, Box 242, 700 College Street, Beloit, WI 53411, USA. Tel: (608) 363 2619. Fax: (608) 363 2689.

Teachers for Poland (PL). Teachers for Poland is a voluntary organization established in 1990 which recruits teachers to assist with teaching of English in schools and colleges in Poland. Most of the posts are filled by fully-qualified retired teachers, but they do consider qualified teachers of all ages.

> **Teachers for Poland,** Hereford Education Centre, Blackfriars Street, Hereford HR4 9HS. Tel: (01432) 353 363. Fax: (01432) 276 969.

United Reform Church (HU, RO). Opportunities exist for volunteers to work in church institutions and teach 'conversational English'.

> **United Reform Church,** Att: The Personnel Secretary, World Church and Mission, 86 Tavistock Place, London WC1H 9RD. Tel: (0171) 916 2020. Fax: (0171) 916 2021.

World Teach (PL). Opportunities exist to teach English in primary and secondary schools, as well as in colleges and universities or non-profitmaking organizations. A programme fee is required to cover airfare, health insurance, and training and support throughout the year.

> **Worldteach,** Att: Director of Recruiting, Harvard Institute for International Development, 1 Eliot Street, Cambridge, Massachusetts. Tel: (617) 495 5527. Fax: (617) 495 1239.

ENQUIRIES AND CVs

When making enquiries to any of the above organizations or to schools listed in this book, it is advisable to include a CV. Obviously letters which are typed or neatly handwritten will leave a better impression.

As well as including the usual information on your CV, it is essential to highlight your teaching experience, however little it may be. In doing this describe the level and ages of students taught, type of materials and course books used, etc. Other information such as business English teaching experience, monolingual/multilingual classes is particularly useful. If you have had previous business experience in a particular field this should also be highlighted as demand for ESP is growing.

INTERVIEWS

It is probable that you will be interviewed in the country in which you want to work, unless you are applying through one of the organizations listed above. Whatever the case, be very wary of a school or organization that wishes to employ you without a proper interview.

Apart from the usual advice about interviews, such as arriving a little early, dressing smartly and taking along relevant certificates, you should consider the following:

First of all, be prepared to be asked about your teaching experience, ages and levels taught, books you have used, the reason for wanting to work in that particular country and your future plans in EFL. Also be prepared to be asked something directly associated with teaching, for example, how you would teach a certain structure or particular item of vocabulary.

You may be asked to do a demonstration lesson. If so, then see if you can observe the class first, and talk to the teacher. Don't go over the top to impress both the students and observer. A good solid lesson will go down much better. Be prepared to discuss the lesson with the observer afterwards, and offer your thoughts on how it went.

After the interviewer has asked you questions to determine your suitability, there are a number of questions you should ask to ensure that you have reasonable conditions of employment. These are not in any particular order and they may have been covered already during the interview.

- *'How many hours a week will I work?'* You want to be looking for a maximum of 25 hours per week, and a further 15 hours of administration and preparation, making a total of 40 hours. NB A teaching 'hour' is usually 45 or 50 minutes, but check this first. In state schools full-time contracts are usually for 18 to 20 'hours' a week, but determine what 'extracurricular' activities you are expected to do.
- *'How will these be arranged?'* You want your work to be as well 'blocked' as possible, and not in a 'split shift', spread over a long day. In addition, it is preferable for the period each day to be similar, so you are not teaching late into one evening and then

early the next morning.

- *'What about weekends?'* This is worth asking as some schools teach on Saturday mornings.
- *'Where will I be teaching?'* If you have to work in different places, what will the travelling time be? It can be substantial.
- *'Will I receive travelling expenses?'* If not, will you be compensated for time spent travelling, or simply have your transportation costs covered?
- *'What is the salary?'* Is it guaranteed? Will you receive a fixed salary? If not, is there a guaranteed minimum, either in terms of hours or money? Is there an increment system, do all teachers get paid the same? What is the overtime rate? Will you get paid more for teaching special classes, eg exam classes? If you are teaching by the hour what is the hourly rate? What about tax and social security? What happens if a class is cancelled – will you be paid all or part of what you would have been paid for teaching? When do teachers receive their pay? Do you receive an advance?
- *'Do I receive any holidays?'* If so, are they paid? Are there any restrictions on when you can take them – either the dates or the maximum period you can take off at one time? If the position is part-time, will you be paid for public holidays? What are the term lengths?
- *'Who will I be teaching?'* What kind and what size of classes will there be? What levels? How far apart are the levels lumped together to form a class if numbers are low? Will students be business people? Will you be expected to teach business English? Will you have to teach children? If so, how young? Will you be teaching one to one? Will you have to share any classes with another teacher?
- *'What is the academic set-up?'* What books/syllabus/tapes/other facilities are there? Do the students have copies of books? Are there photocopying facilities? What are the classrooms like, ie what is the seating arrangement; is there a whiteboard or blackboard; is a taperecorder provided, etc? Who are the other teachers – native English speakers or other? Will you receive any educational support in terms of help in lesson preparation, educational seminars or workshops?
- *'Are there regular staff meetings?'* What happens in them? Will the school encourage and pay for you to go to educational conferences? Does the school subscribe to any publications such as the *EFL Gazette*? Will you be observed? If so how often? Will you be obliged to use a certain teaching method or textbook, if so what will it be?
- *'Does the school make any provision for learning the local language?'* Is this free?

- *'Does the school arrange work and residence papers, etc?'* What documents do you need? Will you be covered for health? Is there a school doctor?
- *Does the school provide accommodation or give help in finding it?*

Contracts

Whatever contract you are asked to sign, make sure you understand it. If it is not in English (which is probable) ask for a translation or get someone who knows about these things to go through it with you thoroughly. Also ask for a copy for yourself. It is important to establish terms and conditions *before* you start work so there is no misunderstanding at a later date. This is best done in writing.

PREPARING YOUR TRIP

What to take

Although you do not want to take too much with you (as you will undoubtedly come back with a lot more), apart from the essentials you might want to consider taking along a few home comforts. This may simply be a jar of marmite or peanut butter, or a taperecorder and your favourite tapes. If you are stuck out in the middle of nowhere then you will be surprised how these little things can make a difference to your mood when you are feeling low.

On a practical level it is advisable to take the originals and a number of copies of your university degree, educational qualifications, EFL certificate, and birth certificate.

If you possess one, take your driving licence, as well as an international driving licence if possible. It is also a good idea to take along any references you have, and several copies of your CV if you are going out on spec. Pack a number of passport size photos (minimum 10) which you will need for work papers, travel pass, etc. If you have an international student's card then bring that along as well. Take some smart clothes along with you – you might need them for interviews, teaching and the school dance!

Check how much you are allowed to take before getting to the airport otherwise you might find yourself paying an enormous sum in excess luggage. Sometimes if you phone the airline and tell them you are going for a long period of time they waive the charges as long as you aren't too much over the limit. Finally, take along a small medical kit, which should include bandages, plasters, TCP, hay fever tablets and some painkillers, eg aspirin, as you never know when you will need it.

For specific information on each country see essentials.

Teaching materials

First of all it is worth trying to find out as much as possible about what is available in the school you plan to go to. In many parts of Eastern and Central Europe, especially outside the major cities, teaching materials are very thin on the ground. You may, for example, have to take your own taperecorder and listening material including some blank tapes. Whether it is possible to find this information out or not, the following materials are always very useful: some flash cards (small pictures mounted on card) and magazine pictures (A4 size mounted on card); blu-tack; Prit (glue); a good grammar book (eg *Practical English Usage* by Michael Swan (OUP), or *A Practical English Grammar* by Thompson and Martinet (OUP)); photos from home (or even slides); songs on tape plus lyrics; a good dictionary (eg *The Collins COBUILD English Language Dictionary*); a set of cuisennaire rods (box of coloured rods of different sizes); and, if possible, a few videos of material from TV (NB videos from the USA are not compatible with European machines). If you write to your local tourist board they will usually supply you with lots of useful material. Authentic materials such as menus, brochures, magazines, photos are always useful, as is a map of your country.

A book on classroom activities will always be useful – eg *Grammar Practice Activities* by Penny Ur (CUP) or *Grammar Games* by Mario Rinvolucri (CUP), as well as *Discussions That Work* by Penny Ur (CUP).

If you have already been teaching then you will of course have your own favourite books and supplementary material which you will want to take along. Finally it might also be a good idea to arrange some pen-pals before you go. Students usually love writing to people in another country, and if you organize this before leaving it will save you a lot of effort trying to arrange it from a distance.

Health and insurance

It is worth taking out some health insurance before you go, especially if you are not going to a pre-arranged job. Once you have a full-time contract with a reputable school they will normally pay your health and social security contributions (although this is not guaranteed), which will entitle you to use the local health service, although this does not cover repatriation.

For those recruited prior to going, check with the organization, school, etc what the situation is. Dental treatment is not usually included. If you are working part-time, it is probable you will have to sort our your own health insurance and social security payments.

One reason to take out insurance would be to cover you should something serious happen requiring you to be flown home. It is also worth checking out travel insurance which will cover your luggage.

Teachers from the USA should consider the International Youth ID Card. If you are under 26, for a very small fee this card covers medical evacuation and emergency travellers' assistance:

> **International SOS Assistance, Inc,** One Neshaminy Interplex, Suite 310, Trevose, PA 19058, USA. Tel: (800) 523-8930.

Endsleigh Insurance has considerable experience in insuring teachers working overseas. Their main London branch is at:

> **Endsleigh Insurance Services Ltd,** 97–107 Southampton Row, London WC1B 4AG. Tel: (0171) 436 4451. Fax: (0171) 637 3132.

Money

At the time of going to press not all currencies in Eastern and Central Europe were convertible, therefore any money you earn in local currency cannot technically be taken out of the country and you cannot bring local currency into any of the countries. It is a good idea to bring as much money as you can with you, to finance any trips you should wish to make, and to tie you over until you are settled in a job. If you have debts back home then leave enough money to pay these, as you are very unlikely to be able to send money back.

Although not essential, a credit card may occasionally come in handy in the major towns and cities. They can be useful for paying for train/air tickets or drawing money. American Express has offices in most of the capitals and will be able to give you hard currency, as opposed to most other credit cards which can only provide local currency.

Traveller's cheques are sometimes difficult to cash, especially in Poland, although they are the safest way of carrying money. Another good option is Eurocheques. The US dollar and the German mark are the preferred currencies, but there is usually no problem changing sterling. A certain amount of cash should be in small denominations; often people don't have change for large notes and therefore small bills are especially useful when travelling from one country to another in the region.

As you may well be quoted a price in another 'international' currency, here are some exchange rates at the time of going to press (early 1995). It will be worth keeping these in mind to avoid getting ripped-off:

£1 = $1.58	$1 = £0.63	1DM = $0.67
£1 = DM2.35	$1 = DM1.48	1DM = £0.42

2 | Poland

Poland has seen an enormous growth in the teaching of English as a foreign language since 1990, and it is now one of the biggest markets for ELT (English Language Teaching) in Europe. English has replaced Russian as the main foreign language taught in schools, creating an ever-increasing demand for more teacher trainers and qualified teachers. This demand cannot currently be met by Polish teachers of English graduating from universities and colleges alone, and a growing number of native speaker teachers of English are helping to bridge the gap. In the private sector there has been an explosion in the number of new schools in all major cities throughout the country. Large foreign language institutes have already established themselves, with International House leading the way with eleven schools in various cities and towns including Kraków, Poznań, Katowice, Bydgoszcz, Wrocław and Łódź. Bell has an associate school in Kraków and the British Council is now expanding its teaching and teacher training programmes. In addition there are established schools set up in all major cities, including Warsaw, Gdańsk and Wrocław. UK and American based organizations such as the Peace Corps, Teachers for Poland, EEP, World Teach and others also recruit teachers for different parts of the country, often for state schools and institutes of higher education (see organizations pp 9–15).

The Institute of Polish Culture in New Cavendish Street, London sells Polish newspapers which advertise for EFL teachers as do Polish papers in the USA.

Many of the native English speaker teachers working in Poland up until recently have been unqualified, or newly qualified, and came out to gain valuable experience. With competition between private language schools growing, this trend is clearly changing. Learners have higher expectations now regarding quality teaching, and native speakers of English are no longer the novelty they once were. There are more applicants than positions for some of the better posts and schools are now looking more and more to employ local qualified teachers before native English teachers whose costs are a lot higher.

However, whereas unqualified teachers will now find it difficult to find work, especially in places like Kraków and Warsaw, qualified teachers will still have little difficulty. Many opportunities exist throughout the country, in both the private and state sectors.

Poland is still making the transition toward a market economy and teachers coming to Poland should expect a drop in their standard of living. Bureaucracy is still a problem, especially if you are working in the state sector, and anyone coming to Poland should come with an open mind, patience and attitude that, while you are able to contribute something to help Poles learn English and understand a little bit about your culture, you are not going to change the country overnight. Realistic goals should be set as to what can be achieved within each school or institution. Wherever you work you will find living and teaching in Poland a rich and rewarding experience and one you are not likely to forget. Interestingly, many teachers who originally intended staying in Poland for a short period of time have remained, and others who left at the end of their contracts have returned.

PART 1
PREPARING YOUR TRIP
AND FINDING TEACHING JOBS

Before you go

Essentials

It is now possible to buy almost anything in Poland, and although some Western products are as expensive as in Western Europe, cheaper Polish equivalents are generally available. It is a good idea to bring a supply of any prescribed drugs you may be taking, including the pill and condoms, which are not always readily available, or for that matter reliable. Your favourite toiletries and cosmetics won't go amiss either, if you prefer using particular brands. Electricity is 220 V/50 cycle and plugs are of the two-pin variety so an adaptor will be needed if you are bringing any electrical appliances.

Be sure to pack a warm jacket or coat and a good pair of boots for winter, as it can get very cold, especially in the east of Poland. You may also want to consider bringing some skiing equipment as there is excellent skiing in the Tatras. See pp 18–19 for further suggestions on items to bring with you.

Teaching materials

Most of the major EFL publishers have agents in Poland (see p 19), and an increasing number of teaching materials are now available in the big cities, although they are less easy to find in the country, where resources in state schools are scarce. For this reason you are as well to bring a few useful books with you (see pp 73–74), your own supplementary materials, and a variety of authentic materials. Anything that will give the students a taste of life and culture in your country will be useful.

Facilities very much depend on where you are working, so obviously the more you can find out about your particular school before you come the better. However, it will probably be worth bringing a taperecorder and a selection of listening material with you just to be on the safe side. Photocopying will probably be difficult. Even if your school has a photocopier, you may find yourself paying for every copy you make. Alternatively there is usually somewhere in the town to get photocopies done. Polish stationery is easily obtainable and relatively cheap; western-style stationery is less easy to find and expensive. Again, pack some Blu-Tack which always comes in handy for sticking pictures on the board, etc.

Health and insurance

If you are coming to a pre-arranged job check whether the school will pay your health and national insurance contributions (ZUS), as not all places will. If it does, you will be covered under the Polish health care system and entitled to the usual benefits. Should you be coming without a job to go to, it is advisable to take out travel and health insurance before you leave (see p 19) and again check with any future employer how you will be covered locally. The UK has a reciprocal agreement with Poland which covers emergency health care. However the USA does not. Private health care in Poland, should you need it, is relatively cheap (see p 52).

Language

Polish is a Western Slavic language like Czech, Slovak and Serbian. It is largely phonetic, ie one letter of the alphabet corresponds to one sound, and in almost all Polish words the stress falls on the penultimate syllable.

It is not a particularly easy language to learn for English speakers, with the many consonant clusters and unfamiliar sounds.

Indeed it is quite daunting at first. The grammar is also quite complicated, with seemingly more exceptions than rules. However, Polish is a beautiful language, and an effort to learn a few basics before you come will help you enormously, especially as outside the cities English is still not widely spoken. You will discover that your quality of life will be greatly enhanced with even a little knowledge of the language.

There are numerous books around for Polish learners. One of the better ones is *Colloquial Polish*, published by Routledge, which comes with accompanying cassettes. You will also be able to find a number of locally published books in Poland, including a selection of dictionaries.

For those who want to study the language in more depth, Lublin University holds summer courses for foreigners, as does Warsaw University (addresses can be obtained from embassies), and in the larger cities language schools offer courses in Polish. In Warsaw these are often advertised in the English language paper, the *Warsaw Voice*.

Money – expenses and how much to take

Poland is no longer the incredibly cheap country for Westerners it once was. For tourists here on a short visit, it is still relatively inexpensive, but for teachers living here on local salaries, some money in reserve is essential.

Initially you need enough money to settle in and find accommodation, which will be your most expensive single outlay. If your employer is providing accommodation count this as a big advantage.

Of course, how much you will need to tide you over will depend to a large extent on where you are going to be working, and what sort of rent agreement you will have. A recommended minimum is $500; more if you intend to work in Warsaw.

In addition, you will want to have some money available should you wish to travel to any neighbouring countries, and at least have access to funds should you have to return home suddenly.

Although traveller's cheques are the safest form of carrying money they can be a hassle to change in Poland. This can usually only be done in certain banks in major cities. It is therefore a good idea to take a certain amount of cash with you, ideally US dollars or deutschmarks. Alternatively bring Eurocheques which can be cashed in most banks. Be aware that you will be charged a high commission (up to 10%) for changing a Eurocheque or traveller's cheque.

Poland is very much a cash society, and although credit cards are being accepted at more and more places, these are mainly in the cities. It is worth noting that cash in local currency can be withdrawn from banks with a credit card.

The złoty is 'partially' convertible and can also be exchanged for dollars, pounds, DMs, etc at banks or *Kantors* (exchange bureaus), although some places will not perform the transaction without proof that you have already exchanged some hard currency.

Finally a note on the black market; it is now all but obsolete, and the only people using it nowadays are criminals. Wherever you are, look after your money and valuables, as all Westerners are a target for potential theft.

The unit of currency is the złoty, which is pronounced 'zwoty' and means gold. It will be indicated from now on as zł.

Exchange rates (early 1995) – see p 51:

$	24 000 zł (old)	2.4 zł (new)
DM	16 000 zł (old)	1.6 zł (new)
£	37 000 zł (old)	3.7 zł (new)

Visas

UK, US and Irish citizens do not need a visa to enter Poland and are allowed stays of up to 90 days. However, visas are still required by citizens of Canada, Australia and New Zealand.

Visas are issued at embassies and consulates abroad (see p 81) and may be used for up to six months from the date of issue for periods of up to 90 days. Visas can be obtained at most border crossings, but as they may be more expensive there than at an embassy or consulate, and are generally only issued for a month, you are better off getting one before you come. Visas can be extended in the country, or alternatively you can leave the country for a few days and return with a new stamp in your passport. Problems can occur if you overstay your 90 days!

Work permits

If you are going to a pre-arranged job, work permits (*zezwolenie na pracę*) are relatively easy to get, and are generally sorted out by the employer. Check this out if possible before you go, and if not, on arrival.

Some places, although offering advice on the procedure, will leave it up to you to sort out your papers and may not be unduly concerned whether you have them or not. It is a legal requirement for the employer to apply for the papers on your behalf, and in your interest to have the correct documents, so do not take the risk of working without them.

Work permits are issued for a specific period (usually the length of the contract) and have to be renewed every year. Permits are not necessary for short-term contracts up to three months. There are numerous forms to be filled in, plus two passport-sized photos and an official translation of the original, or a copy of your EFL certificate or equivalent. Some local labour offices in the bigger cities want proof that you are a university graduate and that your major was in something related to English teaching, but it is rare for people to be refused. It usually takes about six weeks to sort everything out (though it can take longer), after which you will receive the all important stamp in your passport. Technically you should have your work permit sorted out by your employer before you come to Poland and applied for at the consulate in your home country; however, the authorities usually turn a blind eye to this and issue them to applicants already in the country.

In Warsaw the employment office is at ul. Czierniakowska 44, 00-717.

Residence permits

Obtaining a residence permit (*prawo pobytowe*) is usually straight-forward once you have your work permit sorted out; however be aware that laws regarding work and residence papers do change, so get an update on arrival. How rules are applied can sometimes vary depending on whether you wish to work in a state or private school, or simply on the whim of the authorities. Apart from the numerous forms to be filled in for your residence permit, you will need to provide proof of accommodation, ie a letter from your landlord/landlady, which is not always as easy as it may sound.

Arriving and finding your feet

Travel to Poland

Flights from the UK. Both British Airways and LOT, the Polish Airline, run daily direct flights to Warsaw from London's Heathrow Airport, with weekly flights to Kraków and Gdańsk. Domestic flights from Warsaw operate on a daily basis to the other major cities. There are also flights from Manchester in summer.

Apart from the normal Apex flights, you can usually pick up student reductions with certain operators. Prices fluctuate depending on the time of year, and, in summer especially, it is worth checking out the bucket shops advertised in *Time Out* and national newspapers for cheap deals. Alternatively look for cheap flights to Berlin and travel overland from there. (See p 89 for details of STA and Council Travel.)

The following airlines and agents deal with flights to Poland:

British Airways, 75 Regent Street, London W1. Tel: (0181) 897 4000.
LOT, 313 Regent Street, London W1. Tel: (0171) 580 5037.
Fregata Travel, 100 Dean Street, London W1. Tel: (0171) 734 5101.
Polorbis, 82 Mortimer Street, London W1. Tel: (0171) 636 2217.
Travelines, 154 Cromwell Road, London SW7. Tel: (0171) 370 6131.

Flights from the USA and Canada. There are direct flights to Warsaw from New York, Chicago, Los Angeles, Montreal and Toronto on LOT or Delta Airlines. Generally though it is cheaper to fly other European carriers such as KLM and British Airways to destinations such as London or Berlin and take a connecting flight, or make your own way there by train or bus.

In Chicago and New York where there are large Polish communities, travel agents advertise in the local Polish papers offering reasonable deals.

Fregata Travel, 250 W 57th Street, Suite 1211, New York, NY 10107. Tel: (212) 541 5707. Fax: (212) 262 3220.

By train. Trains leave from London's Liverpool Street station to Warsaw via Berlin, every day except Sundays. You can change in Berlin if you need to take a train to Poznań or down to Kraków. Trains also operate from Victoria to Warsaw via Ostend. Tickets, however, are about the same price as an Apex flight, and with the journey to Warsaw taking over 30 hours, flying is probably a better option. If you are under 26 you may want to take advantage of student reductions or buy a Eurorail ticket which is valid in Poland. Eurotrain tickets can be bought from Campus Travel:

Campus Travel, 52 Grosvenor Gardens, London SW1. Tel: (0171) 730 3402.

By coach. The coach is cheap, but it is not a particularly comfortable way to get to Poland.

Several companies operate regular services from London, including Eurolines whose tickets (around £80 one way) can be purchased at any National Express office in the UK. The journey to Warsaw takes about 36 hours. Coaches also go to other major cities such as Gdańsk and Kraków. Take some food and drink for the trip and a few DM for coffee stops in Germany. It is worth checking out the national papers and *Time Out* for other offers. Campus Travel also act for Eurolines:

Campus Travel, 52 Grosvenor Gardens, London SW1. Tel: (0171) 730 3402.
Fregata Travel, 100 Dean Street, London W1. Tel: (0171) 734 5101.

By car. Should you decide to take a car and drive, it takes around 18 hours from Ostend to the Polish border. You will need to bring all your car documents including registration papers, green card (car insurance) and driving licence.

Bringing a car into Poland duty free is no problem. Providing you are legally employed you can purchase a car in Poland. Note that outside the cities not all petrol stations will sell lead-free petrol and the speed limit in built up areas is 60 km/h and on open roads 90 km/h.

In order to register your car in Poland it is first necessary to hold a residence permit. The car will have to go through a roadworthiness test and other such formalities and the bureaucracy often does not warrant the effort.

If your car is registered in the UK or any country outside Poland, and you wish to keep your British or foreign plate, as long as you have insurance to cover you and have all the necessary papers, there seems to be little problem.

You cannot sell your car in Poland unless you have paid the duty on it (or had it in Poland for seven years) and it would be illegal for a Pole to drive it. Insurance can be purchased in Poland.

Renting a car in Poland is expensive. You will need a full driver's licence, an international licence, valid passport and enough money to pay the usual hefty deposit!

While having a car in Poland may at times be useful, it is definitely not a necessity, and those thinking of taking one should weigh up exactly what the advantages are before deciding.

Arrival

Transport from the airport. Flying to Warsaw you will arrive at Okęcie airport which is only 10 kilometres from the city centre. Most international flights arrive at Terminal 1 with Terminal 2 serving domestic and East European flights.

To get to the city centre the cheapest way is to take the 175 or 188 bus. Both leave at regular intervals throughout the day. If you arrive at night there is the night bus 611. Tickets can be purchased from a kiosk at the airport.

Be wary of taking a taxi from the airport; you can easily be heavily overcharged. If you prefer to, then make sure it is a registered one with a number, and Warsaw's emblem (a golden mermaid) is on the door. Agree on an approximate price before setting off (see taxis p 49).

By train. Warsaw has three stations, but the central station (Warsaw Centralna) is where all international trains arrive. Most trains will also stop at Warsaw's Western and Eastern stations should you need to go to another part of the city. A word of warning to those who plan to come by train. Some organized gangs work the trains, and a number of people have woken up to find their valuables stolen. You should be especially wary of people in the corridors pushing past you when you are getting off or on.

In the main hall you can get information on all train and coach (PKS) services, as well as on purchasing tickets, which you can book up to 60 days in advance. Left-luggage and post office facilities are available, as is an array of shops, including places where you can eat, buy maps and change money. A number of buses and trams stop outside the station, and taxis can be found at the front, although again these should be avoided.

Accommodation

A wide range of accommodation is available in all major cities, from classy hotels to private rooms (*kwatery prywatne*), although the standard outside the more expensive places may seem rather poor. Prices for rooms at the big hotels are the same as in the West, but you can find some small hotels offering reasonable rates. If your resources are limited, cheap places to stay include hostels and private rooms.

Urgent accommodation

If you need urgent accommodation on arrival in Poland, the PTTK (Polish Tourist Association), has offices in most cities and offers hostels called *Dom Turysty* or *Dom Wycieczkowy* throughout the country providing simple but cheap places to stay.

For a private room, find a *Biuro Zakwaterowania* or *Biuro Kwater Prywatnych*. They act as agents for landlords, and have offices in most cities. Buy a map and check the location before you take a room, otherwise you could end up miles away from the centre. One of the problems with this sort of accommodation is you don't know what you are getting until you see it. Be cautious of people approaching you at the station offering rooms. While these may be all right do not hand any money over until you have seen the place.

Warsaw. Warsaw is the most expensive city in Poland for just about everything, including accommodation, but it is still possible to find cheap places to stay in the short term.

About 20 minutes walk from the station, a good agent for private rooms in Warsaw for around $10 (single) $15 (double) a night is at:

ul. Krucza 17. Tel: (022) 25-72-01/28-75-40.

Information on hotels and hostels in Warsaw can also be obtained from the Information Centre on Plac Zamkowy.

The Polish Youth Hostel Society (PTSM) has two places in Warsaw at ul. Smolna 30, which is very central and ul. Karolkowa 53a. Beds are around $6 a night and there are reductions for students of up to 50%.

Gdańsk. The main tourist information office for maps, etc is on ul. Heweliusza 8. The Almatur office Długi Targ 11/13 provides hostel accommodation and for private rooms go to the:

> **Biuro Zakwaterowań**, ul. Elzbietanska. Tel: (058) 31-94-44/(058) 33-88-40.

Kraków. The main tourist office for maps and information is on ul. Pawia 8 (near the station) and next door is a place organizing private rooms. The Almatur office is at Rynek Głowny 7/8 (in the courtyard), Tel: (012) 22-63-52 and deals with student hostel accommodation. For cheap hostels try:

> **PTTK Dom Turysty**, ul. Westerplatte 15/16. Tel: (012) 22-95-66.

Łodź. The tourist office is at Biuro Obsługi Cudzoziemców ul. Piotrkowska 104, and provides information on accommodation and the city. The cheapest and most central place is:

> **Central Youth Hostel**, ul. Zamenhofa 13, Tel: (042) 36-65-99.

Poznań. The main tourist office is Stary Rynek 77, Tel: (061) 52-61-56. The Almatur office for hostel accommodation is Al. Aleksandra Fredy 7, Tel: (061) 52-36-45. For private rooms try the Biuro Zakwaterowania near the station: ul. Głogowska 16, Tel: (061) 60-313. Hostels can be found at ul. Berwińskiego 2/3, Tel: (061) 66-36-80.

Wrocław. For urgent accommodation at the bottom of the market try the tourist office at ul. Pilsudskiego 98 which organizes private rooms. There is a hotel at the same address.

Long-term accommodation

One of the big advantages of having a pre-arranged job to come to is that it is more likely that accommodation will have been sorted out for you. If, however, you are having to look yourself, then this can prove both a frustrating and tiring experience. Some schools will help you to find somewhere, but some won't be interested where you live.

Long-term accommodation in Warsaw is the most difficult to find as well as the most expensive. Flats at rents which are affordable also tend to be quite a distance from the centre. In other major cities the situation is not as bad, although nowhere is hunting easy.

The best way to start looking for a place is through any Polish or Western contacts you have made, asking them if they may know of anyone who has a flat or room to rent. If this proves unsuccessful, you may have to go through an agency, although this will undoubtedly be more expensive.

Before taking a flat, try and get some sort of official contract. A number of landlords/landladies will be unwilling to give you one, as this normally means the money has to be declared for tax purposes. On the one hand this may make the flat cheaper, but on the other it gives you no security whatsoever. It may also prove a problem when you apply for a residence permit.

For addresses of agencies look in the telephone book under *Biuro Pośrednictwa/mieszkań or mieszkaniowego*; alternatively look through the newspaper under *lokale* for rented accommodation. Note that flats advertised can be either furnished or unfurnished. Unless you speak Polish with some confidence you will need a Pole to help you. It is often better getting a Pole to do the initial negotiating as $ signs usually appear in the landlord's eyes if he knows you are a foreigner.

The type of accommodation you can get will vary to some extent on where you are working, and who for. Most teachers find themselves living in small one-room flats, known as *kawalerka* (bachelor's flat) or sharing a two-room flat in a block. The type of accommodation most teachers can afford is, on the whole, fairly basic; furniture in most cases is sparse and flats usually contain the essentials, but other than that little more.

It is very rare, for example, to find a washing machine in a flat, and phones are not very common. Sofa-beds seem to be standard, and gas cookers are the norm for cooking. If the flat has a phone then you need to be extremely careful about using it. International calls are very expensive and even the cost of local ones soon adds up. Cases of teachers receiving extortionate bills for calls they never made are not uncommon; having a phone can be a mixed blessing!

One thing you can be sure of is there is little chance of your getting cold at night as flats are centrally heated and windows double-glazed. Although teachers should not come with any high expectations regarding accommodation, flats can be made to feel 'home' and remember the average Pole will be living in more cramped conditions than you.

Problems with the landlord/landlady or neighbours are not uncommon, and getting things fixed usually takes time. Plenty of patience, understanding and an easy going attitude are needed.

On average in the large cities the rent per month is around 2 million zł ($80) to 3 million zł ($120) for a one-room flat, and between 3 and 4 million zł ($120–160) for two rooms. Rent is often indexed to the US dollar to keep up with inflation and you should expect to pay more if you live in Warsaw and less in smaller towns.

Finally, you may be asked to pay rent in advance, which can be anything from three to twelve months.

Bills

Check the situation regarding bills with the landlady or landlord, ie who pays for water, gas, electricity, etc. Flats are rented either including bills *plus płatności* or without bills *bez płatności*. (This of course does not include the telephone.) Bills can be substantial and need to be taken into consideration. They usually come either every month, as in the case of the telephone bill, or every two months, and can be paid in at the post office. Pay them on time otherwise you run the risk of being cut off; often without warning.

Arriving without a job

If you arrive in Poland without a pre-arranged job, finding work should not pose too much of a problem provided you are a qualified EFL teacher. There is still a shortage of trained English language teachers, especially in the state sector, and in the private sector there is still an upward trend in the number of schools opening or expanding. In this area in particular though, the market is becoming more saturated. You may not be offered full-time work straight away, and you will probably find yourself teaching at more than one place initially, in addition to doing some private work on top.

The Polish secondary school year starts in September and universities begin in October. After the winter break the second semester usually starts in the second half of February for both schools and universities. There is generally work available throughout the year in the private sector.

Starting points

You may have a particular preference as to the type of institution you wish to work in, for example a state school or a private language school, or you may simply prefer to work freelance. Without contacts the latter is particularly difficult. If you are interested in jobs in the private sector, contacting language schools, or better still going there in person and speaking to the Director or Director of Studies, is the best way to start.

If there are British Council or USIA offices in the city then they will be worth contacting for any local or national information. They may be able to advise you on which schools are reputable and which are not, or at least give you an up-to-date list of addresses and phone numbers. The British Council in Warsaw (p 42) for example, keeps a file on schools which are looking for teachers or where you may leave your personal details, and is open to anyone.

Selected private language schools for a handful of cities are given here (pp 36–38), but for a more comprehensive list of addresses check the telephone book under *szkoły*. Another source is a publication called *Languages '94* which gives a complete list of both private schools and state institutions in every major Polish city. For a copy write to:

> **Wydawnictwo Perspektywy Press**, 00-511 Warsaw, ul. Nowogrodz-ka 31 Vp. Tel: (02) 628-58-62. Fax: (02) 29-16-17.

If you are interested in working in the state system, you should either contact schools directly or go through the District Educational Authority for primary and secondary schools, the so-called *kuratorium*. Alternatively you can contact the Ministry of National Education, which can often help teachers directly, or at least give them details of local people to get in touch with. Send a copy of your CV and EFL certificate, together with a covering letter to either or both of:

> **Ministry of National Education** (Ministertwo Edukacji Narodowej), Ms Joanna Sobczyk, Department of International Co-operation, Al. Szucha 25 00-918, Warsaw. Tel: (02) 628-41-35. Fax: (02) 628-85-61.
>
> **Kuratorium Oświaty i Wychowania**, Dzial Językyów Obcych, Al. Jerozolimskie 32, Warsaw, Poland.

Finally, personal contacts, whether Polish or Westerners, are invaluable in helping you find work. You always have a better chance of getting a job if you come personally recommended.

City v country

Poland is a country of nearly 40 million people and has several large cities where there are sizeable native English-speaking communities. However, there are many smaller towns that teachers get sent to, devoid of both native speaker company and the usual entertainments provided in the cities. Life in such places suits some and not others. Away from the cities Poland's rural landscape offers a more peaceful and intimate way of life. As an English language teacher you will be regarded as a celebrity and your company will be very much sought after. Even so it is easy to feel lonely; the language often providing a stumbling block to anything other than the superficial conversation, and a lack of English newspapers may make you feel out of touch with what is going on in the world. Teachers have also complained of being bored living in small towns, and, unless you take the initiative to do things, it is easy to feel this way. The long cold winters tend to exacerbate the situation and a good supply of books is often comforting at such times. A lack of support within the school can be frustrating and some teachers feel there is nobody to help them in everyday life. How teachers cope with such situations very much depends on the individual, but expect to go through some degree of culture shock initially when you first arrive, although this soon goes if you adopt the right attitude.

One of the benefits of living in a small town is you have more chance of getting to know the Polish people, language and culture. You will generally be made to feel very welcome, and will find it easy to make friends. The more you integrate with the local community the more at home you will feel. While everyone can expect to go through ups and downs, teachers generally look back on their time wherever they were in Poland as an enjoyable and invaluable experience.

Where to teach English

There are a number of different types of institutions employing native English speakers as teachers, and each has its advantages and disadvantages, as well as its own terms and conditions. The best time to start looking for work if you are applying through an organization is in April or May to start in September. If you are coming out on spec then towards the end of August is a good time to arrive in order to give yourself a few weeks to find work before term starts.

Most native teachers, like their Polish colleagues, have more than one place of work. For example, state school teachers will often supplement their low incomes by teaching privately at home or doing a few hours in a private language school.

Wherever you teach you should be aware that information within the school or institute is often far from forthcoming. If you want to find out anything, you will constantly have to ask for it, and never expect to be fully informed, even then. This can be frustrating and to some degree infuriating, but it is something you will have to learn to live with if you want to stay sane! Rather than constantly complaining and getting yourself worked up, try a little resourcefulness to find out what you need.

Private language schools (*Prywatne szkoły językowe*)

Private language schools in Poland range from 'cowboy operations' to highly professional, well-run organizations such as International House, British Council Studia and Bell. Most are run locally by Poles and employ both Polish teachers of English and native speaker teachers. A number of schools are still not particularly bothered whether you have experience or any EFL qualifications, but as competition increases this is becoming less so. For schools such as Bell, International House and several of the more established local schools the necessary qualifications are essential. Recent moves to regulate the quality of private language schools have got off the ground, initiated under PASE (see p 43).

Most private language schools teach general English to both children and adults, although there is a growing demand for business English. Special courses in business English are either run at the school or in the company itself. General English classes are often held in rooms in the local secondary schools which are rented out for that purpose.

Nearly all teaching takes place in the afternoon and evening, with classes finishing as late as 9pm, but you may get the odd class in the morning (sometimes from 7am) for those who study before going to work. Students generally attend two 90 minute classes a week, although this may differ from school to school.

Pay varies from place to place, but in most cases you will be paid substantially more than in a state school. Normally you will be paid by the hour for the number of lessons you teach (which can range from 120 000 zł to 200 000 zł net per hour), although some schools will offer contracts for a minimum quota per week. For these purposes, one hour is equal to 45 minutes and for one and a half hours you will be paid for two real hours. Resources on the whole are adequate, but some schools may require you to use their own materials and methods.

Apart from the established schools, few offer anything in the way of in-service teacher training or teacher support.

Below is a selected list of private language schools city by city.

Gdańsk
Best, ul. Pestaloziego 7, 80-153 Gdańsk. Tel: (058) 41-29-02 (ext 6).
English Unlimited, ul. Podmłyńska 10, 80–855 Gdańsk. Tel: (058) 31-33-73. Fax: (058) 31-33-73.
English Language Services (ELS), ul. Polanki 11, 80-308 Gdańsk. Tel: (058) 52-47-81.
Hayes English, ul. Zaruskiego 28, 80-299 Gdańsk. Tel: (058) 52-75-44.

Katowice
International House, ul. Gliwicka 10, 40-079, Katowice. Tel: (032) 59-99-97. Fax: (032) 59-84-04.

Opus, ul. Dworek 13b/33, 44-200 Katowice. Tel: (032) 244-28.

Eurolingua, ul. J. I. Kraszewskiego 2b, 42-550 Sosnowiec, Katowice. Tel: (032) 63-74-63.

Europe 2000, ul. Dąbrowskiego 24/4 40-032 Katowice. Tel: (032) 155-10-53.

Kraków

American Language Center, Rynek Glowny 34/23, 31-101 Kraków. Tel: (012) 21-31-89.

British and American English School, ul. Konarskiego 2, 30-071 Kraków. Tel: (012) 36-13-50.

Celt (Centre of English Language Training), ul. Konarskiego 2, 31-227 Kraków. Tel: (012) 36-13-50.

Gama-Bell School of English and Teacher Trainer College, ul. Smoleńsk 29, 31-112 Kraków. Tel: (012) 21-26-43. Fax: (012) 21-73-79.

International House, ul. Czapskich 5, 31-110 Kraków. Tel: (012) 21-94-40/(012) 22-64-82. Fax: (012) 21-86-52.

Pro-Lingua, Rynek Główny 7/8, 31-013 Kraków. Tel/fax: (012) 21-74-93.

Łódź

Headway, ul. Tokarzewskiego 29, m 1091-842 Łódź.

International House, ul. Zielona 15, 90-601 Łódź. Tel: (042) 30-00-26/27. Fax: (042) 30-00-28.

Linguarama, ul. Malczewskiego 37/47, 93-154 Łódź.

Success, ul. Bat. Chlopskich 14/50, 94-058 Łódź. Tel: (042) 86-91-32.

Poznań

American English Konwersatoria, ul. Berwinskiego 1, 60-765 Poznań. Tel: (061) 66-07-13.

'Lektor' International House, ul. Fredry 2, 61-701 Poznań. Tel: (061) 51-61-71. Fax: (061) 51-61-71.

The English Language Centre, ul. Słowackiego 20, 60-823 Poznań. Tel: (061) 41-72-52 (ext 34). Fax: (061) 53-65-36.

Program, ul. Fredry 7, 61-701 Poznań. Tel: (061) 53-69-72.

Warsaw

American English School, Rynek St. Miasta 2, 00-272 Warsaw. Tel: (022) 17-11-12. Fax: 19-27-74.

Berlitz Poland, ul. Nowowiejska 56, Warsaw. Tel: (02) 628-76-85.

Greenwich School of English Poland, ul. Nowoiejska 5, Warsaw. Tel: (022) 25-29-53.

Greenwich School of English Poland, ul. Zakroczymska 6, 00-225 Warsaw. Tel/Fax: (022) 25-26-54.

Premiere Training Company, ul. Żurawia 2/20, 00-503 Warsaw. Tel: (02) 625-76-00. Fax: 628-03-22.

Surrey Business and Language Center, ul. Gwardzistów 20, 00-422 Warsaw. Tel: (02) 625-66-56. Fax: (02) 625-67-31.

Wrocław

International House, ul. Ruska 46A, 50-079 Wrocław. Tel: (71) 356-73.

Language Education Centre, ul. Pilsudskiego 74, 50-020 Wrocław. Tel: (71) 383-68/44-37-32.
School of English, ul. P. Skargi 29, 50-082 Wrocław. Tel: (71) 360-17.

State school sector

Primary schools (szkoły podstawowe). Children normally attend primary school from seven to fourteen and have not usually had any English prior to this. More children are starting to learn from an earlier age, often after pressure on the school from parents, but in primary schools especially there is a dearth of qualified English teachers and hence many opportunities.

Secondary schools. These are divided into three main types:

- General secondary schools (*liceum ogólnokształcące*) where students attend four-year courses leading to college or university entrance. Here students have to study at least one foreign language.
- Vocational and technical schools (*technika zawodowe*) which offer five year courses which provide both general and vocational training. All students have to study a foreign language, and they may also go on to higher education.
- Basic vocational schools (*szkoły zasadnicze*) where the courses are three years long and offer both theoretical and practical training, with an element of general studies.

The majority of native English speaker teachers in the state sector tend to work in general secondary schools where the teaching load is around 18 teaching units (45-minute periods) a week and the salary low, around 2 500 000 zł ($100) – 3 500 000 zł ($140) a month depending on qualifications and experience. In some cases native speakers of English get paid up to 30% more than their overworked Polish colleagues. Classes normally start at 8am (but can start as early as 7.15am due to the shortage of classrooms) and finish in the early afternoon or at around 5pm.

On top of your regular classes, some schools may offer more teaching units called 'extra hours' (*nadgodziny*) and pay a bit more, but there is no rule. You may also be expected to take part in extracurricular activities.

Teachers in the state sector, whether employed individually or through a scheme or voluntary organization such as the Peace Corps, EEP or Teachers for Poland, are generally offered accommodation with board or its equivalent, eg set meals in the school canteen.

Resources in schools are limited and students and teachers may often be without course books. Photocopying is often difficult and you may find that there is a lack of educational support. Sometimes there is even no syllabus. While your Polish colleagues will generally be happy to offer advice and appreciate a native speaker in the staffroom, they will all too often be too busy. An ability to work to a large degree independently is necessary. A lot of pressure is put on children to do well at school and one of the consequences of this is cheating in exams, which unfortunately is quite common (see p 66).

Classes are usually about 20 students, but can be larger, and 12 is the smallest group you could realistically hope for.

The school year starts around the beginning of September and finishes in June, after which you will receive six weeks paid summer holiday. Other holidays include: two weeks at Christmas, three weeks at the end of January/beginning of February, when everybody seems to go skiing, and one week at Easter plus public holidays.

Private school sector

Private primary and secondary schools (szkoły prywatne). The last few years have seen an increase in the number of new private primary and secondary schools. These are monitored by the state and the Roman Catholic Church and on top of the usual subjects they offer courses outside the curriculum. These schools usually pay teachers better than the normal state secondary schools, and the working atmosphere can often be more relaxed.

Parents' co-ops (szkoły społeczne). These are schools set up and controlled by parents and again they operate on a private basis. Normally there is at least one in every town, although the quality varies. These schools are particularly keen to provide good language training, hence job opportunities are common.

Universities and colleges (Uniwersytety i kolegia)

Apart from *studia* (see below) a number of posts at universities and colleges for both teacher trainers and general EFL teachers crop up each year. Anyone with an arts degree and EFL qualifications may apply for a teaching position, although competition for jobs is getting stronger.

There are 11 universities in Poland and, although pay is poor if you are recruited locally, you are normally required to teach only about 12 hours a week. This will leave you time to take on private students or work part-time elsewhere. The British Council recruits for *Lektor* posts where the pay is high and accommodation is provided. Contracts are usually for a year. For information on positions apply either directly to the university or college, or through the Ministry of National Education (see p 34). Addresses for universities and colleges can be obtained from Polish embassies or consulates.

Teacher Training Colleges (Nauczycielskie Kolegia Języków Obcych)

Around 50 teacher training colleges (NJKOs) have been set up in nearly all major cities throughout the country offering three-year courses to prospective teachers. There are opportunities for both teacher trainers and language teachers in these institutes. Applications can be made directly to the colleges, through the Ministry of Education or through the British Council PACE project (see p 42).

Polish governmental institutions

Occasionally there are posts offered at Polish governmental institutions such as ministries. Recruitment is carried out by the British Council.

Studia

The British Council, in partnership with certain Polish universities and technical universities, recruits qualified and experienced teachers for their *studia* programme. Up until recently this only involved teaching English to the academic staff and research assistants, many of whom went on to take one of the Cambridge exams, usually the First Certificate. However, as well as the teaching staff, courses are now offered to the general public, although as yet only to adults and university students. Teachers are employed, not by the British Council, but by the university or technical university, and therefore receive Polish salaries in złoty. Jobs are advertised in the *Guardian*, although people are recruited locally. The centres are regarded as 'pockets of excellence' and the local staff are generally highly respected.

There are currently centres in Warsaw, Poznań, Łódź, Wrocław, Kraków, Gdańsk, Katowice, Lublin and Szczecin. For a full list of addresses contact the British Council in Warsaw (see p 40).

Companies

With the increasing need for company employees to speak a foreign language, especially English, there are opportunities for those with a business background and EFL experience to teach in companies.

If you are interested in teaching business English the options are: to approach companies directly; to use contacts; or simply to look for a school which specializes in business English. Pay is usually high by local standards, although the work may be more demanding as some of the courses will need to be specifically designed, and teaching hours are usually early in the morning, from 7am or after work. The majority of students studying in companies tend to be low-level, although this is changing rapidly. The teaching is general English with a business slant.

You may find a lot of students are middle-aged, and not used to communicating in a foreign language. In general younger employees adapt and progress more quickly.

Groups are mainly small, but can range from classes of 14 to one-to-one teaching.

Take along a supply of business materials to such classes, but do not be surprised if your students are more interested in learning social English which they regard as being very important (see pp 264–273 on teaching English to business people).

Teaching privately

Private students are relatively easy to find and a lot of teachers take them on to supplement their income. The price varies from 150 000–200 000 zł. an hour for conversation classes (some people ask more, especially in Warsaw) but is partly based on the financial means of the student. Having a phone is a great benefit when it comes to arranging (or cancelling) private lessons.

Exchange lessons

You may be offered Polish-for-English exchange lessons, but unless you have a qualified teacher or your Polish is already good enough to converse be careful; you could end up giving free English lessons for little in return.

Summer camps

For people looking for short-term work in summer, a number of camps are organized by UNESCO. Teachers are recruited through the Central Bureau for Educational Visits and Exchanges (see p 11) and usually receive free board and accommodation and pocket money.

There are a lot of other summer courses, many organized by private language schools, and these jobs are often advertised in the

UK and US press. On such courses the majority of students will be teenagers and the work can be very demanding.

British Council

The British Council has a number of ongoing projects in Poland in conjunction with the Polish Ministry of Education. Posts are very competitive and salaries are high, usually with a sterling and local salary plus accommodation. They are also tax-free. Teachers must be well-qualified and an MA is often required.

One of the schemes is the Polish Access to English (PACE) project. This is part of the UK government's support for three-year Teacher Training Programmes, specifically to the 52 English language Teacher Training Colleges. Jobs are advertised in the UK papers but applications can be sent directly to the British Council in Manchester (see p 10).

Useful organizations and addresses

The American Center/US Information Service. Within the Center there is a well-stocked library and reading room with a good selection of books, up-to-date magazines, journals and newspapers. The USIS housed in the same building keeps a selection of EFL books for teachers.

> **The American Center/USIS**, ul. Senatorska 13/15, 00-075 Warsaw. Tel: (022) 26-70-15/18. Fax: (022) 26-13-34.

The British Council. The British Council Office in Warsaw is opposite the central station.

> **The British Council**, Al. Jerozolimskie 59, 00-697, Warsaw. Tel: (02) 628-74-01/03. Fax: (022) 21-99-55.

International Association of Teachers of English as a Foreign Language (IATEFL) – Poland. IATEFL currently has well over 400 members in Poland, and as well as a newsletter, organizes an annual conference, and monthly local events. It is officially based on Kraków, although the committee is spread around the country. For further information write to the secretary:

> **IATEFL Poland**, c/o Instytut Anglistyki UW, Nowy Swiat 4, Warsaw.

Peace Corps

> **Peace Corps**, Associate Peace Corps Director, Education/TEFL, United States Peace Corps – Poland, ul. Bukowińska 24, 02-703 Warsaw. Tel: (022) 43-50-11. Fax: (022) 43-42-00.

Polish Access to English (PACE). This is a British Council project to train English language teachers and re-train Russian teachers. See British Council (above).

Polish Association for Standards in English (PASE). PASE was established in 1993 by a group of Polish specialized language schools committed to excellence in teaching English as a foreign language. The PASE Recognition Scheme carried out its first inspections in spring 1994.

> **PASE**, ul. Polanski 110, Gdańsk. Tel:/Fax: (058) 52-47-81.

Polish Association of Teachers of English Primary and Secondary Schools (PATE).

> **PATE**, Ewa Osiecka, President, Centralny Ośrodek Doskonalenia Nauczycieli, Al. Ujazdowski 28, 00-478 Warsaw. Tel: (022) 21-30-31 (ext 51).

Polish Teacher Trainer. A practical journal for foreign language teacher trainers and teachers.

> **Polish Teacher Trainer**, Alistair Maclean, ul. Dąbrowskiego 5/91, 38-411 Krosno, Poland.

PART 2
LIVING IN POLAND

How expensive is Poland?

Poland is still not expensive compared to many Western countries, but prices are forever increasing and many teachers find they have to supplement their incomes with private students. The cities, and espcially Warsaw, Kraków and Poznań are considerably more expensive than smaller towns in the country.

Living costs

On an average teacher's salary working in a private language school, you can expect to pay up to a third on accommodation including bills. On a state school salary this would be much higher, but accommodation is usually provided. On a day-to-day basis you can get by on around $10 a day, excluding accommodation and cooking primarily at home.

Eating, drinking and nightlife

You can find reasonable inexpensive food, ranging from $2 at a snack bar for a soup and meat dish, to around $6 for a good two course meal in a restaurant. Drinking out varies, but on average expect to pay around $1–$1.50 for a beer. Spirits, especially vodka, are cheap. Wine is imported, usually from Bulgaria, and is relatively expensive. Eating out for vegetarians is difficult, although less so in big towns, but eating at home can save you money if you shop at the markets (see pp 50–51).

Discos and clubs

Although by Western standards Poland's nightlife still lags some way behind, in the larger towns and cities it is possible to stay out partying until the early hours. A cover charge is usually required to get into clubs, and drinks (especially imported brands) are more expensive than in the local bars.

Taxes

Poland has a progressive tax system which is relatively high. Currently you pay 20% on a salary of up to 6 million zł a month and 40% above that. Note that the tax laws change every year so get an update from your employer. Taxes are deducted automatically from your pay. All foreigners not employed on a contract with a school are taxed at 20%, and they are responsible for filling in their tax returns at the end of the year.

Citizens from the USA and UK are exempt from paying income tax in Poland for the first two years if they pay taxes in their home country.

How far does money go?

How quickly you spend your millions of złoty will of course depend on what sort of lifestyle you lead. If you buy Western goods on a regular basis you will find your money doesn't go very far. Again if you regularly drink imported beer in up-market places this will soon bite into your pocket, but in general teachers who spend sensibly enjoy a reasonable standard of living. Cinemas, theatre, etc are cheap, as is public transport, but remember you are not going to save any money in Poland, at least not without substantial sacrifices, and definitely not enough to think about taking money home.

An average salary for a full-time (25 hours a week) teacher working in a private language school is around 8 million zł net ($320) a month. Out of this you will have to pay for your accommodation, and this should leave you around 5 million zł ($200) to spend. You will need to be earning that to have a reasonable standard of living.

A final point here is that, while efforts are being made to cut inflation, it is still relatively high at 30% (1994).

A guide to costs

Large loaf of bread 5–6 000zł
Litre of milk 10 000zł
Glass of wine in a pub ... 25 000zł
Cinema.......................40 000zł

Litre of mineral water ... 12 000zł	Month travel pass
Jar of coffee (100gms) .. 40 000zł	(Warsaw) .. 200 000–300 000zł
Packet of tea 20 000zł	Packet of cigarettes
Bottle of beer	(Western) 20 000zł
(in a supermarket) 15 000zł	Packet of cigarettes
Bottle of wine 70 000zł	(Polish) 10 000zł
Glass of vodka 15 000zł	Cover charge for club..... 10 000zł
Meal in a restaurant 60–100 00 zł	Opera/concert ticket
Beer in a pub 20 000zł	from 50 000zł

These prices were generally correct at the time of writing, but should be treated with caution. They are intended as a guide only.

Tipping

There are no specific rules regarding tipping, but 10% is a basic guide. People tend to give a tip only when they feel they have had special service. In restaurants service is generally included in the price of a meal, although it is the custom to round the bill off to the nearest 5–10 000 zł.

Tipping taxi drivers is not common. Note that if you say 'thank you' as you hand your money over this is accepted to mean you do not want any change!

Everyday living

Eating

Polish cuisine is generally rich with a tendency towards meat and sauces, yet heavy with a lot of potatoes and dumplings. Although the food in restaurants lacks imagination, home cooking is considerably better. The main meal of the day for Poles is dinner (*obiad*), which is in the afternoon or early evening, and they will then usually have a light supper later in the evening. Pickled food is popular, especially in winter, and can be exceptionally good.

Polish specialities. Soup is a popular starter in Poland, for example beetroot (*barszcz*), sour rye meal mash (*zurek*), mushroom (*grzybowa*), or chilled beet soup (*chlodnik*), which is served only in summer. The national dish is sauerkraut with pieces of meat and sausage (*bigos*); although it is not always served in restaurants and anyway homemade *bigos* is far superior. Pork chops in bread crumbs (*Kotlet schabowy*) are also very common both at home and in restaurants. Other Polish specialities include pork knuckles cooked with vegetables (*golonka*), pasta stuffed with meat or cheese (*pierogi*), big dumplings made from yeast (*pyzy*), rolled stewed beef (*zrazy*), and the famous Polish sausage (*kielbasa*).

Restaurants. Over the last few years a lot of private restaurants have opened in most cities. Under communism Poles didn't often dine out, preferring to eat at home; even now despite the wider choice, the increase in prices makes eating in restaurants prohibitive for a lot of people. Western-style fast-food outlets are becoming common, as are ethnic restaurants, and these compete with the more traditional Polish establishments, which in turn have had to improve their quality and service. Restaurants usually close at 9pm or 10pm, although in the larger cities some will stay open later.

Eating out cheaply. For a cheap meal, go to one of the fast-service bars (*bar szybkiej obsługi*) or 'snack bars' that provide simple food in rather basic surroundings, many of which are self-service. Milk-bars (*bar mleczny*) which until recently were popular places for inexpensive, mainly vegetarian type food based on dairy products, are disappearing and becoming fast-service bars.

Another alternative is to eat at a student canteen attached to a university or college, and often open to anybody. The food here is basic but very cheap.

Vegetarian. It is unusual to come across a Pole who is a vegetarian, and the idea of someone not eating meat still raises eyebrows in this country.

Apart from the *bar mleczny*, where tasty vegetarian food is guaranteed – for example, dumplings stuffed with cottage cheese or mushrooms (*pierogi*) or pancakes with various fillings (*naleśniki*) – the vegetarian will find little choice on the menu in an average restaurant. Ask the waiter for something *bezmiesne* (without meat).

Salad bars are becoming more popular, and in the larger cities you can always find a pizzeria. A good supply of fruit and vegetables makes it possible to have a balanced diet when cooking at home, although home cooking can be an inconvenience if you are teaching late.

'Nowe Miasto' is a restaurant in Warsaw which sells vegetarian dishes, organic products and health foods. Very good but not cheap!

Nowe Miasto, 13, Rynek Nowego Miasta. Tel: 31-43-79

Cafés, coffee and cakes. Cafés (*kawiarnie*) serve tea and coffee, as well as spirits, beer and cakes. Poles love to drink tea (*herbata*) which is normally served in a glass with a slice of lemon and lots of sugar. If you want milk you will have to ask for it specially. Coffee (*kawa*) likewise is usually drunk black, and is made by pouring boiling water on coffee granules or crudely ground coffee which often floats in the glass and gets stuck in your teeth. Expresso coffee and cappuccino are becoming more common, although they are available only at the more up-market places. Instant cappuccino is widely available and is not bad.

Cakes and pastries can be bought from the local cake shop (*cukiernia*) as can ice cream (*lody*), another popular delight eaten throughout the year!

Drinking and nightlife

The Poles enjoy a drink, and alcohol consumption is more or less a national pastime. It does not help that large quantities of spirits are drunk over and above any beer, and this is one of the causes of the alcohol problem. It is believed that the problem is improving because people cannot afford to drink as much now and the problem is being taken seriously in the workplace where it has affected production. A lot of drinking goes on in restaurants, especially in the villages, or in cafés and beer bars (*pijalnia piwa*).

New pubs similar to those in the West have sprung up recently, especially in the cities, and are frequented by the wealthier younger Poles and Westerners. Bars close at various times, and some will stay open until the last person has left or fallen asleep!

The national drink is vodka which comes straight and in numerous flavoured varieties. It is usually served with food, eg pickled gherkins (*zakąski*). It is best drunk chilled and neat, and, although some Poles like to knock it back in one go, to fully appreciate Polish vodka it should be sipped! For most people a couple of glasses are enough to make you lose any inhibitions you may have had, and good vodka won't leave you with a hangover!

Beer (*piwo*) is popular and is often the preferred drink with meals. There is an assortment of imported beers, mainly German and Czech which tend to be more expensive than the local Polish brews. Guinness and Fosters are also available in a few places. Check the price before ordering, as Guinness is especially expensive. Although most local beers are not quite on a par with those from the Czech Republic and Germany, there are a few which aren't bad. Popular brands, which are brewed mainly in the south include Zywiec, Okocim and Warka. 'EB' is a new beer from the north which can now be found everywhere. All wine is imported and therefore can be expensive.

Nightlife. Poland is not noted for its great nightlife, and even in the major cities it is somewhat limited. You can usually find a disco which will stay open late or if you are lucky bars which will stay open until the small hours. Occasionally you will find places with live music and other places offering a 'floor show'. If you are tempted by the latter, be aware that drinks at such places are extortionate, and the cover charge usually high. In Warsaw, Kraków and Poznań the nightlife is a lot livelier than in small towns in the country, where finding somewhere to go after 11pm is virtually impossible. New places are regularly opening up and your students will normally know what's going on.

Transport

The public transport system is old and not always reliable, especially in the country. However, it is still more than adequate, and, as a lot of people still do not have cars, buses, trams and trains and in places trolley buses remain the most popular form of transport. In most cities monthly season tickets can be bought from a special office or individual strips from the many *RUCH* kiosks.

Tickets are valid for one journey irrespective of the distance, but a new one must be punched every time you change. Transport normally runs from 5am to 11pm, after which a night service operates in the larger cities.

Trains. There are three types of train in Poland. The local slow trains (*osobowe*) which stop at every station, the faster direct trains (*pospieszne*) which stop only at larger towns, and the express (*expresowe*) trains, for which you must reserve a ticket, and which stop only at major cities.

Wherever possible take the express trains which come with a reserved ticket. There is an extensive train network which covers most of Poland and for overnight and long distance domestic trains there is a couchette and sleeper service. All tickets are either first or second class except on suburban trains. The best trains are the named trains which run from Warsaw, these usually have WARS dining cars and are quite luxurious, especially in first class. One thing to be aware of when travelling by train is that signs telling you what station you are at are difficult to see. You therefore have to keep your wits about you and ask if you are not sure.

If you teach for a state school you are entitled to 50% reduction on train travel and in some cases to travel free (ask at your institute). When travelling to other countries by train you can save money if you buy a ticket to the border and then another ticket from there. You will need small amounts of the respective currencies in order to do this. For international trains you will normally have to buy a seat place. Ask when purchasing your ticket whether you have to do this.

International trains operate to the following cities from Warsaw: Berlin (6–8 hours); Budapest (12 hours); and Kraków (3 hours).

Buses. The bus service is run by the PKS and serves nearly every town in Poland, operating more in the mountainous regions in the south. It is divided into 'regular' and 'fast' and for long-distance buses seats can and should be booked in advance, but only from the place of origin. Tickets can be purchased from bus terminals and some ORBIS offices as well as from the bus driver. Usually there is no charge for baggage up to 20 kg, but check with the driver first.

Public transport within Warsaw. Warsaw has an efficient and well-developed public transport system of trams and buses (the metro is under construction), which is still relatively cheap. It gets very busy at peak times when traffic jams are common.

Tram routes cover a large portion of the city and start running as early as 5am and stop around 11pm. Tickets valid for both buses and trams must be bought beforehand from one of the *RUCH* kiosks or newspaper stands and punched both ends once on board. They can be used for one journey only. Inspectors occasionally come round and issue instant fines for invalidated tickets.

Ordinary buses have black numbers and fast buses that stop only at selected places have red numbers. A number of night buses operate after 11pm, as in most major cities.

Taxis. The last few years have seen a growth in the number of taxis on the streets with a large proportion being illegal and charging exhorbitant prices. As a rule find out what the situation is in your area and ask locals which taxi companies to use. Taxis should be metered but, apart from radio taxis where you pay what is indicated, you have to multiply what is shown on the meter with another number. Always ask the price per kilometre and approximate cost of the journey before setting off. If you know how much it should cost, it could work out cheaper agreeing on a figure and having the meter switched off. Taxis tend to charge more in the evening after 10pm and sometimes at the weekends. If you have problems ask for a receipt (*rachunek*) and take the number of the taxi. Taxis ordered by phone are often less expensive than those picked up at a taxi rank.

Hitch-hiking. Hitch-hiking is popular in Poland and a good way to meet people and practise the language. As in any country though, caution is needed, and it is always safer to hitch with someone else.

Air. International air travel from Poland is becoming competitive as more travel agencies open up and an increasing number of Poles travel abroad. Check the local papers and shop around for the best deals.

Shopping

Shopping has improved tremendously since 1990, but can still take a bit of getting used to. Grocery stores are open from 7am–7pm and everything else from 11am–7pm or 10am–6pm. Smaller shops close earlier. On Saturdays shops open at 9am or 10am and close at 2pm. You won't find anything open on a Sunday, except in major towns where there are a few 24-hour shops. While you can buy most products, knowing exactly where to find what you want can be frustrating.

New shops open literally every week (and sometimes close just as rapidly) so you need to keep your eyes open. Service can still be surly, especially in some of the old state shops, but is gradually improving. In most shops you pick up a basket on entering and pay at the *kasa*; in other places you tell the assistant what you want, pay at the *kasa* and return to the counter for your goods. Buying clothes off the rack is not always easy as quality is variable and sizes are not standard. Words you will quickly get to know are *otwarty* (open), *zamknięty* (closed), *pchnąć* (push), and *ciągnąć* (pull).

Here are some of the types of shops you will find in your neighbourhood.

- 24 hour shops (*całodobowy*). There are plenty of 24 hour shops, especially in the cities where you can buy essentials such as bread and milk plus of course alcohol.
- Baker's (*piekarnią*). Usually open from 7am to 7pm Monday to Friday.
- Barber's/hairdresser's (*fryzjer męski, fryzjer damski*). You can get quite a reasonable haircut in Poland very cheaply. It is not normally necessary to make an appointment, although weekends are busy.
- Butcher's (*mięso*). These usually sell most types of meat, although the cuts are different. Meat is expensive and you are advised to always check it is fresh. Lamb is difficult to find.
- Fruit and vegetables (*owoce i warzywa*). Local grocers sell a good selection of fruit and vegetables, but make sure you wash them thoroughly before eating.
- Stationery (*papierniczy*). Literally a paper shop selling pens, paper, notepads and other paper products such as toilet paper at relatively cheap prices.
- Supermarket (*Supermarkety*). Supermarkets come under a variety of names, but you will find you can purchase most things here, although generally not a lot in the way of fruit and vegetables.
- Markets. The open air (*plac targowy*) or indoor (*hala targowa*) markets are the best place to do your shopping where fruit and

vegetables in season are cheap. Out of season they are expensive, as are any imports. Apart from fruit and vegetables you can usually purchase dairy products, flowers, meat, etc. They open early around 7am and close around 6pm.

- General store (*spożywczy*). Most neighbourhoods have one, and here you can buy your staple products such as milk, flour, coffee, bread, etc. Check times on the door as they can sometimes change.
- Drug store (*kosmetyczny*). Not the place for medicines (go to an *apteka*) but a shop selling soap, shampoo, toothpaste, condoms and cleaning liquids.

Banks and financial matters

There are currently two types of currencies in circulation in Poland. The 'old' currency with its frightening number of noughts on the banknotes, is being replaced over the next two years by the 'new' less intimidating złoty. The 'old' Polish currency is all paper money, not all of which you will see on a day-to-day basis. The 100, 500, 1 000, 5 000, 10 000 notes are the most common, although they are not worth very much and considered as change. The notes that really matter are 50 000, 100 000 and 500 000 zł. To make matters worse they are all the same size and some are of similar colour, eg 1 000 and 100 000. The highest banknote is 2 million zł. The 'new' currency (introduced November 1994) has simply knocked four noughts off the old, and the 'new' złoty is made up of 100 'grosze' (gr) coins. Therefore 10 000 'old' złoty = 1 'new' złoty. 1 'new' złoty = 100 grosze (gr). Prices in this chapter are in 'old' złoty.

Banks are generally open Monday–Friday 8am to 12.30pm and in some large cities they stay open until 5pm or 6.30pm. Poland is very much a cash society and traveller's cheques are only accepted in banks, some Orbis offices and some of the larger hotels. It is difficult to change them in small towns in the country. If you do find a bank that will change them they will probably charge a high commission and give you a low exchange rate. *Kantors* found on every corner are the popular place to change money. They only accept cash.

Unless you are legally employed, you will be unable to open a złoty bank account. You can open an account in hard currency although there is usually a minimum deposit, around $3 000. If you intend to open a hard currency account you will need to have a declaration form (obtained when entering the country) stating how much money you are bringing in. (Ask for one as they are not automatically given out.) Money can be sent through American Express which has an office in Warsaw.

Health

While Poland does not carry a health warning, you should be aware of the problem of pollution and take care in certain areas. It is, for instance, not advisable to drink tap water unless it has been boiled. Bottled water is readily available. Poland has a high incidence of AIDS and condoms although available are not always reliable. It is safer to bring your own supply.

Not all employers will pay your social security payments which are high, at 48% of the gross salary, in which case you will not be covered under the Polish health system.

Once you are covered you must fill in a form with a photo and you will be given a health book. You must then register with your local doctor. This does not cover dental treatment, and private dentists, although cheaper than in the West can be expensive. Polish hospitals are underfunded and although the quality of the doctors is high they often lack the necessary facilities and equipment. Polish hospitals are not places you would wish to spend any length of time in!

For anything minor go along to the local chemist (*apteka*) where they will probably speak a little English and can supply over the counter medicines for a small fee.

Launderettes and dry cleaners

Launderettes (*pralnia*) are few and far between, and the scarcity of washing machines in flats means a lot of washing gets done by hand in the bath.

Dry cleaners (*pralnia chemiczna*) are more common, although you might have to wait two weeks to get your clothes back. There are express places which will do it in a few hours for an extra fee. Three western style launderettes have opened in Warsaw but are expensive.

Libraries and book shops

You won't come across too many bookshops (*księgarnia*) selling books in English, especially outside the large cities, therefore take a few with you. In Warsaw the American Center (p 42) has a well stocked library and reading room. The British Council has well stocked libraries in the following towns, Warsaw, Białystok, Gdańsk, Katowice, Kraków, Łódź, Lublin, Poznań, Szczecin, and Toruń. For the addresses check the local telephone directory or contact the British Council in Warsaw (address on p 42; see p 73 for ELT books).

Post

The main post office in towns is generally open from 8am to 8pm on weekdays, but closes around 3pm in smaller towns. Post offices are closed on Saturdays and Sundays, although there is always a post office open 24 hours in major cities, especially for telephoning and faxing. In Warsaw the post office at Świetokrzyska 31/33 is always open. Mailboxes are green for local mail (within the city) and red for other cities within Poland and foreign correspondence. Postcards and postage stamps can also be purchased from *ruch* kiosks. Post from the UK can take from four days to a week and from the USA from 10 days to two weeks. Parcels and packages are expensive to send by airmail, but if you send them surface mail they can take anything up to three months to arrive.

Addresses and telephone numbers

Polish addresses are written in the following way: name first, followed by the street, which always precedes the number; then the post code/zip code; and finally the city or town. Often the word for street (*ulica*) is abbreviated to ul., and avenue (*Aleja*) to Al. These come before the name of the street.

The correct way to address an envelope is:

Name	David Ronson
Street name followed by number	ul. Bronieckiego 22
Post/zip code followed by town	30-034 Kraków
Country	Poland

Telephone numbers for Poland listed in this book include the local code but not the country code which is (48).

Public telephones

The telephone system is improving with the introduction of new technology and even making long distance calls is getting easier. To make a phone call you require *zeton* tokens or a phonecard, both of which can be purchased from the post office or newsstands. Some telephones for local calls accept only (A) tokens, while telephones for both national and international calls require a (C) token. It is, however, a lot easier to make international calls from the post office or a hotel but more expensive. For calls outside Europe you may need the assistance of the operator. Alternatively you can use a phone credit card such as an AT&T card. Local calls when made from public call boxes are cheap, but phoning abroad is expensive. Phonecards are rapidly being introduced, although they are still mainly confined to the major cities.

Useful telephone numbers in Warsaw include the following: operator-assisted international calls (901); operator-assisted domestic long distance calls (900); long-distance and international area codes (913); and directory assistance for numbers in other cities (912).

Helplines are as follows: police (997); fire (998); ambulance (999); the speaking clock (926); telegrams (905); telephone and address information (913); customs office (54-42-06, 59-42-44); and medical information (155-31-78, 54-41-29).

International dialling codes are as follows: Australia (0061); UK (0044); and USA (001). When making a direct call to a foreign country dial 0 and wait for the tone. Then dial 0, the country code and the number you want.

For calls within Poland, pick up the receiver, listen for a continuous tone, dial 0, wait for the continuous tone again and then dial the rest of the number.

Media, culture and sport

Television and radio. Polish television has three to four channels, depending on the area, none of which is very exciting. Many Western programmes are shown but all are dubbed or have voice-overs. Poles nowadays are tuning into satellite and cable TV showing MTV, Sky, etc which is springing up everywhere. It is possible to pick up the BBC World Service and Voice of America on a shortwave radio, although reception varies depending on the time of day. World service is on 12.095 Mhz (24.08 M) or 9.141 Mhz (31.88 M).

A daily morning news programme (Central Europe Today) covering news and stories from around the region is broadcast from Warsaw in English at 7.30am on 103 FM or 72.3 FM. Local networks often broadcast English language programmes.

Newspapers. International newspapers and magazines can generally be found, often on the day of issue in the afternoon at most of the larger hotels and some bookshops in major cities. These include the main US and UK dailies.

Only one English language newspaper is published in Poland, the *Warsaw Voice*, which comes out weekly and contains news on business, politics and culture in Poland, as well as listings of what's on in Warsaw. It is not widely circulated outside Warsaw. A Polish newspaper, *Nowa Europa*, carries a page of news in English which is usually quite good.

Classical music. Poland's most famous composer was undoubtedly Chopin, and the music tradition continues today with a host of international and local music festivals throughout the year, including the Warsaw Autumn festival of contemporary music and the Spring festival in Poznań. Most cities have their own concerts and opera. Tickets are popular and should be purchased in advance, either from the venue or the local tourist office. Tickets from the venue are often cheaper. In Warsaw the central ticket office is on Al. Jerozolimskie 25, Tel: 21-93-83.

Jazz and popular music. Jazz is popular, although only really in the cities, which play host to a lot of the big names. Western pop music is popular among the young people and more and more places now hold live concerts. 'Dinosaurs' concerts are also currently in vogue, with bands popular 20 years ago having revival concerts. Poland has not hosted any of the big names doing their world tours, and the Aerosmith concert in 1994 was the largest by a rock group in Poland since the Stones in the 1960s. Folk music is no longer as popular as it used to be.

Cinemas and theatre. Arguably the most famous contemporary Polish film maker is Krzysztof Kiéslowski who made *Three Colours Red, White and Blue*, although Andrzej Wajda (*Man of Marble, Man of Iron*) is also well known in the West. The heart of Polish cinema is in Łódź where Roman Polanski was just one of the many famous and talented people to go through the film school. Today, however, lack of money has meant fewer Polish films are being made, although ironically more Western companies are coming to Poland to make films, mainly because it is cheaper. Probably the most well known film to be made in Poland by a Western director is Steven Spielberg's *Schindler's List* which was filmed in and around Kraków in 1993.

More and more films from the USA and the UK are being shown in Polish cinemas, often shortly after their release in the West. Many are not dubbed and are shown in their original language with Polish subtitles. Fortunately the cinema is still cheap. Note that on Mondays museums and theatres close.

Sport. There are opportunities to participate in many different types of sport in Poland, from skiing to horseback riding.

The Tatras are an excellent place to go skiing, Zakopane is probably the best centre, although it is the busiest. Even if you don't ski, this is an excellent area for walking. There are some beautiful places to go hiking, especially in the mountains along clearly marked trails, and it is probably the most popular outdoor activity among Poles. Other popular activities include tennis, canoeing on the many rivers, and sailing on the Masurian Lakes.

The national sport is football and during the 1970s Poland had one of the best teams in the world. Although the national team is now going through a bad period some of the local teams are worth watching.

City-by-city

Gdańsk. A major port and trading centre for centuries, Gdańsk was once controlled by Germany and known as Danzig. It forms part of what is known as the Tri-city with Sopot and Gdynia. Totally destroyed in the second world war, it has been carefully rebuilt over the years. It is the home of Solidarity.

There are several established and well run private language schools in the area with quite a number of native English EFL teachers working in both the private and state sectors.

Katowice. A city of 350 000 people set in Poland's industrial heartland, Katowice is surrounded by a number of other towns, making it a densely populated conurbation. The region is infamous for its high level of pollution and has major health problems. It has a number of private language schools as well as a university and the surrounding countryside is easily accessible. Teachers who have worked in Katowice have on the whole enjoyed their time there.

A popular place for ex-pats is the Longman Bar, situated under International House (see p 36), which sells Guinness and serves food with live music on some nights.

Kraków. Once the royal capital, this historic city survived the destruction many others suffered during the second world war. Its many monuments and ancient buildings, sadly blackened by pollution from the surrounding industrial landscape, make it a popular tourist centre. Although it is a large city, getting around is easy and everywhere in the centre is within walking distance.

The old blends in with the new in Kraków's cultural life and it draws a lot of EFL teachers each year. Most of the bars where the ex-pat community hang out are situated in and around the main square, Rynek Głowny.

Łódź. Once the most important textile city in the world, this largely industrial city is the second largest in Poland with a population of over 850 000. It is also famous as the centre of the film industry in Poland, and has a large university giving the city a youthful feel. The EFL scene here is thriving, with a number of private language schools. A popular place to meet teachers is the British Council Resource Centre.

Poznań. A major industrial centre with a population of over 650 000, Poznań has a thriving educational and cultural community. It holds the most important trade fair in Poland, and has easy access to Berlin. Its beautiful architecture and growing EFL market make it a popular place for teachers.

Foreigners tend to hang out in the bars around the old market. The British Council library is also a meeting place.

Warsaw. The capital Warsaw, with a population of over 1.6 million, has a history going back centuries, although the destruction this fine city suffered during the second world war means there is little evidence left of its past splendour. Most of what stands today has been built over the last 40 years, including the reconstruction of the old city *Stare Miasto.* The centre of the city is dominated by a monolithic Stalinist building built in the 1950s and given to Poland as a gift from the former USSR. The city is divided by the river Vistula.

The following bars are popular with teachers and other expatriates:

> **Akwarium Jazz Club**, ul. Emilii Plater 49 (behind Palace of Culture)
> **The Guinness Pub**, ul. Koszykowa 1 (near Łazienki Park)
> **The Irish Pub**, ul. Miodova (close to the castle)

Wrocław. The fourth largest city in Poland, with a population of 650 000, Wrocław was almost razed to the ground during the second world war. The city has slowly been rebuilt and is now the major industrial and commercial centre of south-western Poland. Its numerous institutes of higher education give the city a youthful feel and with several theatres, a concert hall and a opera house, it has a good cultural life.

The country and the people

Poland has a rich and diverse history going back over 1 000 years and maintains traditions today which have existed for centuries. The second world war had a significant effect on the country and people, as did the subsequent Soviet-led government.

Since Solidarity enforced the collapse of communism Poland has begun to re-establish itself in Europe and rebuild its economy. Initial austerity measures affected most of the population, but the natural entrepreneurship of the people has kept Poland moving towards economic stability.

History

375	Invasion of the Huns. Slavs settle in what is now present day Poland.
966	The Polish court and Count Mieszko I adopt Christianity. Polonian tribes unite with Slavs.
1000	In Gniezno the first Polish church province is established.
1025	Boleslaw I, son of Mieszko I, is crowned King of Poland and receives blessing from the Pope.
1226	Duke Konrad of Mazovia calls for help from the Teutonic Knights, (a German religion and military order), to help in his battle against the Prussians.
1241	Tartar invasions devastate southern Poland and Kraków is destroyed.
1364	Kraków University is founded, one of the first in Europe.
1386	Princess Jadwiga marries the Grand Duke of Lithuania, Jagiello uniting the two countries.
1410	Polish, Lithuanian and Ruthenian forces defeat Teutonic Knights at the Battle of Grunwal giving Poland access to the Baltic ports.
1525	Teutonic knights pledge allegiance to Polish state.
1543	Copernicus publishes his book on planetary motion proposing the earth moves round the sun.
1569	Poland and Lithuania officially become one country.
1600	War with Sweden.
1618	Start of Thirty Years' War.
1655	Swedish invasion (which lasts until 1660).
1772	First partition of Poland.
1793	Second partition of Poland. Russia and Prussia take control of vast areas of Polish territory.
1795	Third partition of Poland. Austria, Prussia and Russia occupy the country and Poland ceases to exist for next 123 years.
19th century	During the 19th century there were numerous uprisings which failed to liberate the country.
1919	Independent Polish state formed by the Treaty of Versailles.
1921	Upper Silesia divided.
1939	Second world war starts after German attack on the Polish garrison at Westerplatte near Gdańsk followed two weeks later by an attack from the Russians. The war has a devastating effect on Poland. Millions of Polish jews lose their lives in Nazi concentration camps and a further 2.8 million non-Jewish Poles also die in the war.
1944	Warsaw uprising.
1945	Oder-Neisse line is established as the border with Germany.

1952	Poland becomes 'people's democracy'.
1955	Founding of Warsaw Pact. Palace of Culture in Warsaw, symbol of Soviet friendship opens.
1956	Strikes and unrest in Poznań. Gomulka takes leadership of country.
1970	Willy Brandt, Chancellor of West Germany, signs recognition agreement.
1976	Widespread civil unrest after price increases.
1980	Strikes in Gdańsk spread throughout the country. Solidarity is formed.
1981	Martial law proclaimed by General Jaruzelski.
1989	Round table discussions lead to first democratic elections in over 40 years.
1990	Lech Wałęsa elected president.
1992	Hanna Suchocka become Poland's first woman prime minister.
1993	Parliamentary elections see return to power of the Socialists.

Geography

Poland covers an area of 312 683 square kilometres and stretches 650 kilometres north to south and 690 kilometres from east to west. It is mainly a lowland country with a beautiful mountainous region in the south and long stretch of coastline in the north bordering the Baltic Sea. The northern area of Poland, around the Mazury region, is filled with thousands of lakes and forests. The country's two main rivers are the Vistula and the Oder.

Climate

Poland's climate, although changeable, has four distinct seasons. Winters are long and can be very cold with temperatures dropping to −30C, often with intermittent periods of snow from December to March (lasting even longer in the mountains). It is usually still cold when spring arrives around March, but the summer months June to August are generally hot with temperatures reaching 30C. Autumn tends to be dry but by November it is usually cold and damp.

The environment

Like other East and Central European countries, Poland has a problem with air and water pollution in many of the big cities after years of neglect of the environment. Heavy industrialization in the past, without any concern for environmental damage, has left many areas suffering from smog and contaminated rivers. This is especially apparent in winter. There has been investment, from the government, private industry and abroad, to help relieve this problem, for example fitting filters on chimneys, but this has not yet had a marked effect. If you suffer from respiratory problems you should think carefully when deciding where you want to go, and find out as much as you can about the local situation before making a decision.

Crime

Crime has risen in recent years, but is mainly confined to the cities and Warsaw in particular. Most offences are connected to money and violent crime is still rare. The streets are on the whole safe to walk at night and the only hassle women are likely to come across is from drunks. As a rule avoid rough looking bars. If you have a car never leave valuables inside. Finally look after your handbag, wallet, etc especially in crowded areas such as markets or on buses and trams.

Politics and religion

Politics. The first elections for over 40 years took place in 1989, and Solidarity came to power, handsomely defeating the Communists who had ruled Poland with an iron fist for the previous 44 years. Tadeusz Mazowiecki, a journalist, became the prime minister. Solidarity's initial programme of reforms included reforming the legal system and writing a new constitution; establishing a local administration; abolishing censorship; guaranteeing independent trade unions, freedom of opinion and religious denominations; establishing equal rights for minorities; and restructuring health, finance, environmental and economic policy.

Drastic economic reform initially created huge price increases, but lead to the złoty becoming the first 'partially' convertible currency of the former Soviet satellite countries.

Six years later and after several prime ministers, Poland today has an array of political parties and Solidarity is no longer the major force it was. In the elections in 1993 the reformed Socialists gained power, forming a coalition government with the peasants' party.

While there were initial fears that the new government would slow down the changes, they have surprised everyone by adopting fairly liberal policies.

The president, currently Lech Wałęsa, whose popularity has been gradually waning, is elected in a direct vote for a five-year term as head of state and nominates the prime minister. The next Presidential elections are scheduled for the fall of 1995.

Parliament consists of two houses, the 460-seat lower house, the *Sejm* or Diet and the 100-seat upper house, the *Senat* or senate. The latter was created only in 1989.

Religion. Christianity was introduced in Poland in the 10th century and today about 90% of the population is Roman Catholic. Other religions include Protestants, Methodists, Baptists, Muslims and Buddhists. The church has always played an important role in Polish society and this was clearly demonstrated through the Solidarity years. The current Pope, John Paul II, is Polish and his visits to his homeland in 1979 and 1983 had an enormous uplifting effect on the people.

Nowadays, however, the church is losing some of its authority, especially with the young people, who are becoming more liberal and less devout than their parents. The church's apparent attempt to secure more political power since the fall of communism has also come in for heavy criticism.

The people

Poles are warm, friendly and extremely hospitable people, if rather emotional. Their moods may change from being placid to argumentative quickly and there is a saying in Poland that where there are two people there are three different opinions. If they come across as being rude at times, this is not normally their intention. Part of this problem is the different stress patterns in the two languages which sometimes lead to Poles sounding rude or bored when speaking English. In fact Poles are on the whole incredibly polite.

Poles like to talk a lot and can come across as being rather intolerant. On the other hand they are very open and although a very proud people they don't often show it. Largely because of their strong religious beliefs they can be quite conservative, and do not like novelty. They are also staunchly individual.

As a nation they are survivors and will unite in a crisis, quickly splintering up once the worst is over. Their sense of individualism and faith in the Polish spirit has helped them to fight for their freedom, often in the face of adversity, making them a determined people. Wherever there is hope they will sacrifice themselves to the greater cause. Polish history, fraught with occupation and subsequent uprisings, bears this out.

Conversation nowadays often focuses around money and many Poles have a feeling of insecurity and fear of the future. Politics has also become a common topic of conversation, although many Poles appear to be sensitive about their personal political beliefs. In day to day life they never seem too bothered about being on time for anything and deadlines often get passed. At the same time they promise more than they can deliver, and often judge people on what they can do for them.

Should you ever need help, a Pole will do everything possible for you until he or she is satisfied you are all right.

Habits and customs. Eating and drinking lie at the heart of social life – Poles will lavishly wine and dine you in their homes, and once there it isn't long before the vodka is out of the freezer and on the table. As a rule never eat anything before going to a Polish home!

Poles say *smacznego* (bon appetit) before eating and *na zdrowie* before drinking. It is customary to take along some flowers (*kwiaty*) or chocolates for your host when invited for dinner as well as a bottle of vodka or wine. Flower sellers, many of them old women, can be found on most street corners and out in all weathers.

Poles greet each other by shaking hands, but if you are a woman don't be surprised if a man should kiss your hand. This custom is common among young people as well as the older generation.

Namedays are as popular as birthdays and if you are invited to a celebration party be sure to take along some flowers for a woman and some alcohol for a man.

Typical lives. In many respects the life of the average Pole has changed since 1989 and it has become apparent that the gap between the rich and poor is widening. Furthermore, life in Polish cities is very different from that in the villages. Nevertheless, it is still possible to draw on certain patterns to give an overview of the typical life of a Pole.

The size of the average Polish family is four and families will usually live in a small flat or a house, often shared with the parents or grandparents. Poles are family-centred and outside the family everyone seems to be connected to a larger web of people; it seems everyone will know someone who can solve any problem that occurs.

About 50% of flats are privately owned, although buying a flat is difficult. Some people join a flat association where they can borrow money and pay the money back over a number of years.

In an average family both parents will generally work. This is necessary in the current economic climate in order to survive although growing unemployment can leave only one bread winner. Wages cannot keep up with prices.

Work starts at around 7am and finishes at 3pm or 4pm. One Saturday a month is also a working day. A lot of Poles will take on a second job to make ends meet and they are well known for their entrepreneurial skills. This often means children spend a lot of their time alone.

Free time is spent on allotments growing vegetables or watching TV. Poles rarely go out and, whereas in the past it was popular to entertain at home, even this is now becoming less common.

Polish society can be roughly divided into two groups, the educated middle-class and the workers. There is also a new group emerging, the 'upper middle-class' who live in villas, have summer houses and drive around in big cars. In these families the wife does not usually work.

Although men are deferential toward women, sexism exists and women are expected to carry out the typical role and duties of wife and mother. Divorce rates in Poland are low, mainly due to the Catholic religion, and many couples simply 'live together'. However, divorce is on the increase. People tend to get married at around 20–21 or 25–26 for the middle class.

Women retire at 55 and men at 60, although early retirement through illness is possible. However, the sickness pension is very low.

PART 3
TEACHING ENGLISH

The Polish education system

- Kindergarten (*Przedszkole*), 3–6 years;
- Primary school (*Szkoła podstawowa*), 6/7–15 years;
- Secondary school (*Szkoła średnia*), 15–18/19 years; and
- University/technical colleges (*Uniwersytety i politechniki/Szkoły wyższe*), 18/19 years up.

The whole Polish education system is currently going through changes, and although there has been heavy investment, especially in EFL, cuts in government spending mean it could be a long process.

Over 96% of children attend pre-school educational establishments and compulsory education lasts for eight years from ages seven to fifteen and is free at all levels. In addition to state schools there are a number of fee-paying private schools, administered under state supervision and other schools run by the Roman Catholic Church.

The first stage of education is the eight-year school (*szkoła podstawowa*). Secondary education is free, starts at 15, and is open to all pupils who pass the entrance exam. Most students continue with secondary education which is divided into three main types:

(1) vocational and technical schools (*technika zawodowe*) which provide five-year courses combining general education with vocational training, with the option of obtaining qualifications leading on to higher education; (2) basic vocational schools (*zasadnicze szkoły*), which run three-year courses made up of three days theoretical classes, including some general studies, and three days practical training per week; and (3) general secondary schools (*liceum ogólnokszatałcące*), where four-year courses lead to college or university entrance. Poland has 11 universities and many more colleges.

Well qualified Polish teachers tend to choose to work in private schools where the pay is better, or colleges or teacher training colleges where they may be better paid and the social status is higher. In 1994 it was estimated that only 50% of the teachers working in secondary schools were qualified to teach English.

Some kindergarten schools have English tuition (based around songs and rhymes) although this is rare. In primary schools one foreign language is compulsory and in secondary schools two. Polish parents now tend to choose schools that have English programmes.

Methods used in classrooms

Although the situation is fast improving, the basic methodology used in the classroom is the 'grammar translation method'. Students are accustomed to rote learning with an emphasis on memory. Reading skills tend to concentrate on summarizing, and texts are used to introduce new vocabulary which is usually taught through translation. Listening involves repeating dialogues and is used mainly as a pronunciation test. Classes are very teacher-centred.

However, with the establishment of teacher training colleges throughout the country, Western books and, more importantly, teacher trainers, the situation is definitely getting better.

There are many excellent Polish teachers of English, and in most cases they have undergone a number of years' training, which involved learning a lot of theory. However, this has not always been transferred to the classroom. Teachers today are hungry for new ideas, and teaching is becoming more communicative and less rigid.

The kind of language needed

Because of the more traditional methods used over the years, students today need a lot of functional language as well as colloquial expressions and everyday language. In universities, for example, up until recently students have studied from old fashioned books, and have tended to transfer their academic language into conversation. It is therefore important to make students sensitive to different teaching and learning styles. Communicative activities are important, but not to the total detriment of grammar.

There are of course issues such as size of class, age, level, etc. which will lead you to adapt your approach to the constraints of your particular class or classes.

Increasingly students need to be prepared for exams such as the TOEFL and Cambridge First Certificate.

Grading

From primary school through to secondary school students are graded on a scale of 1 (indicating a serious problem) to 6 (excellent). Grades are recorded in the registers and play an important part in a student's life. For example they are taken into account for entrance into university. At the end of term students receive grades only and unlike some countries there is no written report.

Exams

Since the state English exam has been abolished, the University of Cambridge Local Examinations Syndicate (UCLES) examinations have become increasingly important in Poland and are used as reliable and internationally recognized evidence of language proficiency. The British Council and its network of university partnerships *studia* are the administrative and registration centres in Poland. The Cambridge First Certificate (grade A or B) is also enough to qualify a Polish teacher to teach English in a primary school up until 1995, after which they must have the Cambridge Advanced. (This is in addition to undergoing a methodology course.)

TOEFL is becoming increasingly popular as more people look to study or work in the USA.

The final school exams (*matura*) are taken in a number of subjects and Polish and a modern language are compulsory. The English exam for the *matura* is similar to the Cambridge FCE, and comprises written, grammar, listening and oral components. Two different exams are set depending on whether the student has been studying for 2–3 hours a week or 6 hours a week. After successfully passing the *matura* exam, a certificate is awarded which gives the students the right to take higher school entrance examinations.

Polish students

In general Polish students are keen and highly motivated to learn English, which they see as increasingly essential for good job opportunities as Poland forges closer links with the West. The level of English is quickly improving as Poles are learning younger, have access to cable TV and can travel abroad more freely.

In the state sector expect to have mixed ability classes, but basically bright kids, a large number of whom will be gifted towards languages. Poles generally have a good ear for picking up pronunciation. As many of them will not have been exposed to communicative methodology, they may appear quite passive at first. They will, for example, expect the lessons to be teacher-centred, and as a result they may initially be reluctant to take part in activities involving pair or group work. This reluctance soon passes, and as long as the learners understand the rationale behind an activity they are usually happy to go along with it.

In the private sector, although learners are motivated, adults are often not able to put in the time outside the classroom owing to work and family pressures. Nevertheless, they expect a lot from the teacher, especially as the cost of an English course is very high in comparison to the average salary.

Cheating

Do not be surprised to come across cheating among your students in the form of whispering, copying and other methods. Cheating is universally discouraged by Polish teachers, although you may have a hard job convincing your students not to do it.

Discipline

Students in general maintain a lot of respect for their teachers and serious discipline problems are virtually unheard of. You may get the odd student disrupting pair or group work or even doing work related to other subjects in your lessons, but if you keep everybody interested and busy, varying your activities and materials, you should be able to keep order. With disruptive students, if you give them roles as leaders with a sense of responsibility, this often calms then down. As a teacher if you let students get away with certain things then this will only encourage them more, and will create problems later on. It is better to start off being firm rather than lax. In private schools, as in state schools, students are on the whole well disciplined and well behaved in the classroom, although young learners coming to study after a full day at school are often tired and restless.

Business people

More and more business people are having to learn English as ties with the West develop. The majority of English teaching to business people is still general English, although ESP is beginning to take off (see 'Teaching business people' pp 264–273).

Specific Polish problems

While many of the problems Polish learners experience when learning English are shared with learners from other countries, it is worth highlighting areas where particular difficulties occur. A lot of the problems come from interference from the native language, and an awareness of these differences may help you to predict and possibly prevent mistakes. Poles do have a habit of wanting to translate everything, and often run into difficulties when no exact equivalent exists or when negative transfer leads to mistakes.

Grammar

Tenses. There are fewer tenses in Polish than English and this can lead to a tendency to extend the use of 'favourite' tenses to all situations. Omission of one or more auxiliaries is the commonest type of mistake:

> **Peter reading a book. (x)**
> **Where he live? (x)**

The Polish learner will have a lot of problems distinguishing between the various situational subtleties and corresponding verb forms in English.

Continuous tense. Present and past continuous tenses express actions in progress at a given present or past moment in time. Such actions are not expressed in Polish by any special grammatical devices, but usually by adverbials such as today, now, etc. Polish learners will have difficulties in seeing situational justification for using the continuous tense and may use the simple tense instead or vice versa.

Perfect tense. The present perfect is used to express an action that has taken place at some indefinite time in the past. The action is finished and we are not interested in when it took place, but in its relation to the present. In Polish there is no concept of the perfect tense and hence it causes a lot of problems.

It is a common mistake, for example, for the Polish learner to use the simple past tense instead of the present perfect when expressing completed actions. In many cases the sentence will still be grammatical, but could be misunderstood by the listener. Thus instead of 'I've done my homework' a student may say:

I did my homework (*x*)

To express uncompleted actions the simple present tense may be used instead of the present perfect.

I live here for five years. (x)

Another problem is that both the present perfect continuous and the present continuous translate into the Polish present tense.

The past perfect tense has no correspondent in colloquial modern Polish. The Polish learner will have difficulties in recognizing contexts where the past perfect tense should be used.

Future tense. There is only one future tense in Polish, and this leads to learners overusing the future simple where 'going to' or a continuous tense would be more appropriate. In Polish the present tense is often used to express a future action.

Conditionals. There are three basic conditionals in English expressing whether we think the outcome is likely to happen or will happen: possible but unlikely; or has happened and cannot be changed:

(1) If it snows, I'll go skiing.
(2) If I won a lot of money, I'd buy a house.
(3) If she had worked hard, she would have passed her exams.

Problems with the first conditional are usually related to form, with learners wanting to use 'will' after the 'if' clause.

If I will finish the housework, I'll go for a walk (x)

With the second conditional problems occur when learners want to use the present simple after the 'if' clause or after 'would'.

If I am rich, I'll buy a house (x)
If I would be rich I'll buy a house (x)

There is no third conditional in Polish and problems with the third conditional are usually related to structure, which is very long and difficult to remember. Mixed conditionals, ie a conditional with elements of, say, first and second conditionals, cause endless difficulties.

Passive voice. The passive voice is not difficult for learners when it is used in the same way as in Polish. Difficulties begin when verbs which are not transitive in Polish are used in the passive voice in English. There are a lot of expressions in the passive voice which cannot be translated directly into Polish. Verbs that cause difficulties include: given, told, ordered, listened, depended, and allowed.

To have somebody do something and to have something done structures can lead to mistakes. A visit to the hairdressers can end up as:

I cut my hair. *(x)*

If a sentence has direct and indirect objects there is a possibility of two passives.

Articles. In English there are two articles, the definite (the) and the indefinite (a, an). As the Polish language contains no articles this is an area that causes problems for students when learning English. Apart from mixing up indefinite and definite articles, there is sometimes a tendency to omit them altogether.

This is car. (x)

Reported speech. Direct speech is when the exact words being said are used: She said 'I like your hair'. Reported or indirect speech is when the meaning but not the exact words are reported: She said she liked his hair.

When changing direct speech to reported speech, a number of things happen. For example, 'I' becomes 'he/she', 'my' becomes 'his/hers', 'now' becomes 'then' etc.

These changes are similar to those that occur in Polish and therefore do not pose too many problems. The real difficulties occur with the change of tense which is different from Polish. In English the general rule is the tense goes back one in the past.

He said 'I live here'. (Direct Speech in the present simple tense)
He said he lived here. (Reported speech in the past simple tense)

Reported questions also cause difficulties. The rule of tense shift is the same as above, as well as reinverting as for indirect questions: eg 'Where do you come from?' becomes She asked her where she came from.

Questions. In Polish questions are formed with intonation rising at the end of a question or with the word 'czy' at the beginning of the sentence.

Learners have problems with inversion:

He is married. Is he married?
She lives here. Does she live here?
Play you a lot of tennis? (x)

Questions relating to subject ('who' questions) also cause difficulty:

Where do you live?
How old are you?

Reported questions often prove difficult for learners because they have to be moved back one tense and reinverted.

'Do you love me?'
She asked him if he loved her.

Confusion can arise between when to use 'how' questions versus 'What is it like?' and 'what does it look like?' questions.

How does he look like (x)

Gerund v infinitive. The gerund, ie the noun formed by adding -'ing' to the verb is sometimes mistaken by learners as a continuous tense. For Polish learners the problems are: (1) when to use the gerund; (2) when to follow a verb by a gerund or an infinitive or both.

Use of prepositions. The main problems occur through translation from Polish:

I'm going on the seaside (x)

Modals. Unlike English modals, Polish modals can be preceded by 'will' or 'shall'. This can lead to sentences like:

We shall must see you. (x)
She will can swim. (x)

The Polish learner will have difficulties in distinguishing between 'can' and 'may' as there is only one equivalent word in Polish (*móc*).

There may be a slight tendency for the Polish learner to overuse the modal 'must' since its synonyms 'have to', 'have got to', etc do not exist in Polish or are used very rarely.

Double negation is another common error:

I don't have no money. (x)

Word order. In English the word order is rigid, ie subject +

predicate + object. In Polish, however, the elements of the sentence may be arranged in a different order and for learners mistakes occur when Polish word order is followed:

I shall spend with you the whole weekend. (x)

In Polish unlike in English adjectives are marked for numbers. This may cause problems with beginners:

Four greens pens. (x)

Reflexive pronouns. There are certain verbs which are reflexive in Polish but not in English.

I wonder myself. (x)

Vocabulary

Polish does not have as wide a vocabulary as English and may have one word to describe something, whereas English will have two or three. This is something to be aware of especially when teaching higher levels when vocabulary extension is important.

False friends. These words look similar to words in Polish but have a different meaning. Polish learners may sometimes use them in the wrong context (eg a student may say 'he was very sympathetic' when he means 'he was very nice'):

actual – at present
agony – dying
eventually – perhaps
original – unique

pathetic – grandiose
sympathetic – nice
colleague – friend

Overused words. Polish learners overuse 'can be':

It can be anybody. (x)

and

I think so that . . . (x)

'Too' is often used instead of 'either' in negative sentences:

I don't like football.
I don't too. (x)

'Make' v 'do'. In Polish there is only one word *robić* to cover the verbs 'make' and 'do'. The basic difference in English is that 'make' describes the result (what you make) and 'do' describes the action (what you do).

To make the bed.
To do the shopping.

'Go' v 'come'. While both 'go' and 'come' describe the action of movement, 'go' is away from the speaker while 'come' is towards the speaker. The two are commonly confused by Polish students.

'Used to doing' something v 'Used to do' something.
    (1) I'm used to getting up early.
    (2) I used to play tennis.

In (1) 'used to' means being or becoming familiar with a new experience. In (2) 'used to' means it happened in the past, on more than one occasion, or over a period of time and it has now stopped.

'Speak' v 'say' v 'tell'. 'Speak', 'say' and 'tell' can be translated into Polish by the same work (*mowic*) and are therefore often misused. 'Speak' normally refers to the action, eg She speaks quietly. 'Say' is usually used when the actual words are spoken: He said 'I can't find my coat'. 'Tell' involves a third person: He told her to leave.

Phrasal verbs. A phrasal verb (verb plus preposition) often means something unconnected with either of its two component parts. For example 'tie up' has nothing to do with 'tie' or 'up'. Students often do not understand phrasal verbs when they hear them, and have difficulty in production. They are not comfortable using them, preferring to use full verbs. They should be treated as vocabulary items and taught in context.

Phonology

The following phonemes have no equivalents in Polish at all: /θ/, /ð/, /æ/, /a/, /o/, /ə/, /r/, /n/, /l/, /h/. Polish learners often confuse:

    /æ/*bat*/e/*bet*
    /θ/*thin*/s/*sin*
    /θ/*thimble*/f/*fimble*
    /ð/*then*/d/*den*

/ŋ/ in contrast with /n/ and /nk/ sing:sin;sink

    It should be stressed that /p,t,k/ before a stressed vowel should be aspirated and that /r/ may be trilled.

    Devoicing is common (eg ship v sheep) and /sib/ /rid/ /dig/ may become /sip/ /rip/ /dik/.

    In Polish the majority of words carry the stress on the penultimate syllable, and the Polish learner will encounter difficulties learning the correct stress of polysyllabic words in English.

Poles tend to have a flat intonation and to have problems with connected speech and weak forms especially the 'schwa' /ə/.

For a more detailed comparative analysis of Polish and English try to get hold of a copy of *Teaching English to Polish Learners* by Tomasz Krzeszowski.

Published EFL material available and addresses of EFL publishers

Poland has been flooded with Western ELT material over the last couple of years and all the major publishers have representatives in the country. Most private language schools now use familiar books such as the Cambridge English Course, the Headway Series, Blueprint and various First Certificate materials.

In the state sector too, Western published material is now being used in the schools. Each school can decide on what coursebooks to follow, selected from a Ministry approved list, so what is used varies widely from place to place. However, the Headway series and the Cambridge English Course are both popular, as are Project and Hotline for younger learners. Books are often the same price as in the West and in some cases more, making them expensive for Poles. For this reason not all students will necessarily have their own books.

Distributor

Cambridge University Press (CUP), ul. Dzika 6/225, 00-172 Warsaw. Tel/fax: (02) 635-61-30.

Heinemann, ELT Books, ul. Polanki 110, 80-308 Gdańsk. Tel/Fax (058) 52-47-81.

Longman ELT Poland, Al. Jerozolimskie 53, 00-697 Warsaw. Tel: (02) 628-44-71, ext 95. Tel/Fax: (02) 625-55-97.

OXPOL Oxford University Press Office, ul. Traugutta 21/23 p.1012, 90-113 Łódź. Tel: (042) 33-16-20. Fax: (042) 32-87-13.

Penguin Adviser for Poland, ul. Wawrzyniaka 28/30 m 4, 60-504 Poznań. Tel/Fax: (061) 47-43-63.

Nelson, Lektor Poznań, ul. Fredry 2, 61-701 Poznań. Tel: (061) 51-61-71. Fax: (061) 51-61-71.

SARA, 00-724 Warsaw ul. Chelmska 19/21. Tel: (022) 41-12-11, ext. 479, 247. (Distributors for Cambridge University Press, Macmillan, Oxford University Press, Collins, Cobuild, BBC English. Can also supply Mary Glasgow Publications.)

Selected list of ELT Bookshops
Warsaw

Atlas, 00-133 Warsaw, ul. Jana Pawła II 26. Tel: (022) 20-36-39.

Bookland, 00-697 Warsaw, Al. Jerozolimskie 61. Tel/fax: (02) 625-41-46.

Linguae Mundi Salon Językowy, 00-828 Warsaw Al. Pawla II 13. Tel: (022) 20-70-68. Fax: (022) 24-35-65.

Polanglo, 00-643 Warsaw ul. Zurawia 24a. Tel: (02) 628 49 94.

Gdańsk

English Book Unlimited, 80-885 Gdańsk ul. Podmlynska 10. Tel/fax: (058) 31-33-72, ext 6.

English Books Unlimited, 81-368 Gdynia, ul. Swietojanska 14.

English Plus, 80-287 Gdańsk, ul. Nalkowskiej 9a/10. Tel: (058) 47-99-35.

Kraków

BEBC Poland, 30-363 Kraków, ul. Kobierzyhska 23a, paw 105 i 106. Tel/fax: (012) 36-07-86.

Elefant, 31-118 Kraków, ul. Podwale 6

International House, 31-127 Kraków, ul. Czapskich 5. Tel: (012) 21-94-40/22-64-82. Fax: (012) 21-86-52.

Łódź

Eureka, 90-330 Łódź, Al. Pilsudskiego 12. Tel: (042) 36-37-64.

OXPOL, 90-102 Łódź, ul. Piotrowska 82. Tel: (042) 32-77-24. Fax: (042) 32-87-13.

Pegaz, 90-617 Łódź, ul. Piotrowska 47/49. Tel: (042) 38-12-11.

Poznań

American English Society, 60-611 Poznań, ul. Nad Wierzbakiem 25. Tel: (042) 66-60-61, ext 117.

APPENDICES

Appendix 1. Case histories

Karen Jacobs went to Poland in 1992 and works in a private language school.

On arrival in Poland I had reassuring experiences. I was immediately put in the care of some native speaker teachers, given an advance of pay, a map, some bedding and towels. I moved into a flat organized by the school immediately.

Having lived in Gdańsk for almost two years now, I am still satisfied with the school: its abundance of resources; its policy of teacher cooperation whereby ideas are bounced around and finally stored as photocopiable material for the future; its monthly meetings to discuss any problems and hold mini-training sessions; its assistance with administrative affairs such as organization of work visas, health insurance and payment for rent. In general whatever problem a teacher may have, whether pedagogical, social, financial or personal the school is always ready to help.

Some minus points, common to many private language schools, can't be ignored. In the first place, the fact that the school is attended by 'paying customers', as opposed to simply students, can sometimes interfere with the educational process. For example, even if the student has failed the term's exams or assessment and is too weak to progress to a higher level, if he insists on staying in that group because he has friends there, the school will be unlikely to refuse in order not to lose the student or his money. The problem of mixed ability classes in general partly stems from this situation. To the school's credit, however, it is currently trying to find more satisfactory solutions to this problem.

The second problem is that twice weekly meetings with a group may be unsatisfactory contact time unless students are motivated to study on their own. Progress may be minimal in cases where the student has had no opportunity to get extended exposure abroad, for example. Finally some administrative disorganization has been irritating. This usually occurs on the university premises where the school rents rooms. Too often, rooms which have been allocated for the school's use are occupied with no prior warning given and no change of room arranged. It is the lack of communication between the relevant authorities which is most frustrating and doesn't do anything for the image of the school, regardless of whose fault it may have been.

As a foreign teacher of English in Poland, I have been welcomed and given respect by all members of the community I have had contact with. The status of TEFL teachers seems to be high, corresponding to the great interest in the English language here. More and more Poles need or just want to learn English for business or educational purposes. It is perceived as the language of liberty, allowing them to communicate with outside cultures during business, travel and other exchanges.

Any cultural shock I have experienced comes from the fact that Poland has an essentially homogeneous society in terms of religion, culture and traditions. While the close-knit nature of the community is intriguing and also comforting, it contrasts with Britain's multi-ethnic, cosmopolitan and rather secular society. Any tensions I feel living here probably arise from this difference.

Jennifer Basile is 24 and came to Poland in 1993 as a Peace Corps Volunteer.

You can state a preference for where you would like to be stationed when you join the Peace Corps, and I picked Eastern Europe. I wanted to see the changes for myself. Not just the economic and political changes, but how people's minds are changing.

My first impression of Poland was very positive because I spent three months with a host family. Then I came to my site in Kolo and was separated from all my friends.

I get paid the same salary as the Polish teachers at the high school where I work. The school also pays for my apartment. At first I lived next door to a drunk dorm director who came into the room and made advances. I thought that people here would downplay it or say 'oh she just wants a better apartment', but they were very sympathetic and understanding and dealt with it very quickly.

I teach 18 hours a week. Now and then my students drop by to talk. They are between 15 and 17 years old. I really like the kids. They want to learn and make working fun.

Most people my age are married, so they are busy with their families.

They don't have time to hang out. Most of the other English teachers teach as many hours of private lessons as they teach at the school.

I especially miss the little ones in my family back home. When you don't see them for six months and see how much they have changed, that is when you realize how much time is going by.

In the States we had more drugs than here, and gang warfare over drugs, but as for other problems like alcoholism and dysfunctional families, I think it is the same everywhere you go. I think there is a lot of alcoholism here. It makes me want to help.

I went to a 'Women in Development' conference here organized by the Peace Corps. It was great because we brought all these different women together: very liberal, outspoken women; women in government; women from very small towns; pro-choice women. Poland is changing so much. Their attitude really depended on where they came from.

I'm not the first Peace Corps person in my town, but some of my friends are in towns that have never seen an American.

I have another year to go. I'm a volunteer – I could go home whenever I wanted, but you have a moral commitment. Some of those long, dark winter days, when maybe you don't have heat or hot water, you think 'Oh I just want to go home!' But the better part of me has always wanted to stay. (This article was first published in the *Warsaw Voice*.)

Sebastian Pearce has worked at the British Council Studium in Gdańsk since October 1992, his first teaching position.

A dreary slushy March Saturday? Well, not exactly. Tonight it's off to a party with some of my students; this afternoon I have been watching a rugby international 'live' on BBC TV, and this morning was spent 10 pin bowling. It's neither a recipe nor a recommendation for everyone, but please don't imagine that Poland is simply a drab Eastern European outpost. Emphatically not. Shops and markets are well stocked with fruit and vegetables, the main shopping street in Gdynia is far smarter than most of its British counterparts, and restaurants of all kinds abound.

I was lucky in that my employers provided accommodation and looked after the red tape, and my impressions come from living and working in a major industrial centre. But still, too many people have negative ideas about Poland. However, this is a country whose recent history is visible to all. Many elegant 'old towns' are largely reconstructions, and in Gdańsk we do have a block of flats 1 kilometre long. Generally though, most drab exteriors contain nice flats within, and public transport is substantially more reliable and extensive than in Britain.

When the winter has passed (all five months worth) Poland immediately transforms into the greenest country I have ever been in, and the autumn colours are hugely spectacular too. In Gdańsk this is highlighted by having the sea on one side and a hilly forest on the other.

Polish people are, again for clear historical reasons, often more interested and connected to Britain, France and the USA, than to nearer neighbours, and many people will be delighted to welcome you into their homes as a guest. You are not advised to eat in advance of a visit to a friend as you will be given food whether you want it or not.

You will soon realize that Polish hospitality is second to none and the Poles are good humoured and excellent company.

Learning English for the average Pole is expensive, and in the more established schools being a native speaker is no longer a ticket to instant fame and fortune. People pay too much not to expect something in return, and dissatisfied students will either move classes or cease attending. However since the classroom reflects the world beyond, students are often talkative and full of humour. For instance I learned last week that the Titanic sank because it sailed into an enormous ice-cream!

Having spent 18 months and 2 winters here, I have no plans afoot to move elsewhere. There is no reason for anyone to be too nervous of coming here, unless they are allergic to snow.

Appendix 2. Classroom Polish

Polish pronunciation. Once you have mastered the sounds in Polish, the pronunciation of words does not seem that frightening. Certain letters in Polish combine to form a single sound. The following consonants have sounds that are pronounced as in English: b, d, f, k, l, m, n, p, s, t, and z

a as u in cut	j like y in yes
ą like 'sans' in French	ł like w in wine
c like ts in cuts	n soft n
ć, ci very soft ch as in cheese	ń ny as in onion ni before vowel
ch like h in hot	o like o in got
cz like ch in chip	ó as oo in book
dż like j in jump	r rolled r
dz like 'ds' in weds	rz like s in pleasure
dź like dz but softer	ś, si very soft sh
dzi as above but softer	sz like sh in shop
e like e in red	u shorter than oo in cook
ę like French 'vin' nasal	w like v in vet
g like g in go	y like i in pick
h like h in half	ż like s in pleasure
i like ee in beet but shorter	ź very soft s in pleasure

Although it is generally preferable if classes are taught entirely in English. you may find the following useful.

Noun *rzeczownik*
Verb *czasownik*
Adjective *przymiotnik*
Preposition *przyimek*
Article (there are no articles in Polish)
Pronoun *zaimek*

Tenses *czasy*
Present *teraźniejszy*
Present continuous (there is no present continuous in Polish)

Past *przeszły*
Present perfect (there is no present perfect in Polish)
Future *przyszły*

Question *pytanie*
Answer *odpowiedź*

Singular *liczba pojedyncza*
Plural *liczba mnoga*

Syllable *sylaba*
Consonant *spółgłoska*
Vowel *samogloska*

Polite *uprzejmy*
Impolite *nieuprzejmy*
Stress *akcent*
Intonation *intonacja*
Classroom *klasa*
Homework *zadanie domowe*

Paragraph *paragraf*
Photocopying *ksero*
Register *dziennik*
Staffroom *pokój nauczycielski*
Sentence *zdanie*
Timetable *rozkład zajęć*

Appendix 3. Food and drink glossary

Zupy Soups
Barszcz czerwony Clear beetroot soup
Chlodnik Borscht served chilled
Jarzynowa Vegetable soup
Kapuśniak Cabbage soup
Pomidorowa Tomato soup
Ziemniaczana Potato soup

Ryby Fish
Dorsz Cod
Flądra Plaice
Karp Carp
Ryba smazona Fried fish
Ryba z wody Poached fish

Mięso Meat
Wieprzowina Pork
Bigos Stewed pork, sausage and cabbage
Golonka Hand of pork
Kotlet schabowy Pork chop
Pieczeń Roast pork
Kiełbasa Pork sausage

Wołowina Beef
Brizol Steak
Rumsztyk Rump steak
Zrazy zawijane Beef roles with filling
Cielecina Veal
Pieczeń Roast veal
Sznycel po wiedeńsku Wiener schnitzel
Wątróbka Liver

Kurczak Chicken
Pierś Breast
Kaczka Duck
Indyk Turkey
Dziczyzna Venison

Jarzyny Vegetables

Cebula Onion
Fasola Beans
Groszek Peas
Kalafior Cauliflower
Kapusta Cabbage
Marchew Carrots
Ogórek Cucumber
Pomidor Tomato
Sałata Lettuce
Ziemniaki Potatoes
Szczaw Sorrel
Kapusta kwaszoma Sauerkraut
Ryż Rice

Deser Dessert
Budyń Milk pudding
Kompot Stewed fruit
Lody Ice-cream
Tort Tart

Napoje Drinks
Napoje alkoholowe Alcohol
Piwo Beer
Wódka Vodka
Wino Wine
Białe White
Czerwone Red
Słodkie Sweet
Wytrawne Dry

Bezalkoholowe Non-alcoholic
Czekolada Chocolate
Herbata Tea
Kakao Cocoa
Kawa Coffee
Lemoniada Lemonade
Mleko Milk
Oranżada Orangeade
Sok Juice
Ananasowy Pineapple
Grejpfrutowy Grapefruit
Pomarańczowy Orange

Pomidorowy Tomato
Mineralna Mineral water

Woda sodowa (z sokiem) Soda
water (with fruit juice)

In a restaurant
I'd like a table for two people.
Is this table free?
I'd like to book a table for four.

Stolik dla dwoch osób prosze
Czy ten stolik jest wolny?
Chciałbym zamowić stolik
dla czterech osób

Can I have a menu please?
What do you recommend?
I'm a vegetarian
What vegetarian dishes do you
have?
Can I have the bill please?
We'd like to pay separately.
We'd like to pay together.

Po Proszę menu
Co pan/pani poleca
Jestem wegetarianinem/
Jakie dania wegetariańskie
panstwo macie?
Proszę rachunek
Zapłacimy osobno
Zapłacimy razem

In a bar
I'd like two beers please.
I'd like a glass of red/white wine
please.
What sort of soft drinks do you
have?
I'd like a mineral water please.
Do you sell cigarettes?
Do you serve food?

Dwa piwa proszę
Proszę lampkę bialego/
czerwonego wina
Jakie napoje państwo macie

Prosze wodę mineralną
Czy dostanę papierosy
Czy można zjeść u państwa?

Appendix 4. Useful Polish words and phrases

Numbers

0 *zero*	20 *dwadzieścia*
1 *jeden*	21 *dwadzieścia jeden*
2 *dwa*	30 *trzydzieści*
3 *trzy*	40 *czerdzieści*
4 *cztery*	50 *pięćdziesiąt*
5 *pięć*	60 *sześcdziesiąt*
6 *sześć*	70 *siedemdziesiąt*
7 *siedem*	80 *osiemdziesiąt*
8 *osiem*	90 *dziewięćdziesiąt*
9 *dziewięć*	100 *sto*
10 *dziesięć*	200 *dwieście*
11 *jedenaście*	300 *trzysta*
12 *dwanaście*	400 *czterysta*
13 *trzynaście*	500 *pięćset*
14 *czternaście*	600 *sześćset*
15 *piętnaście*	700 *siedemset*
16 *szesnaście*	800 *osiemset*
17 *siedemnaście*	900 *dziewięćset*
18 *osiemnaście*	1,000 *tysiąc*
19 *dziewiętnaście*	10,000 *dziesięć tysięcy*

Days of the week
Monday *Poniedziałek*
Tuesday *Wtorek*
Wednesday *Środa*
Thursday *Czwartek*
Friday *Piątek*
Saturday *Sobota*
Sunday *Niedziela*

Months
January *Styczeń*
February *Luty*
March *Marzec*
April *Kwiecień*
May *Maj*
June *Czerwiec*
July *Lipiec*
August *Sierpień*
September *Wrzesień*
October *Październik*
November *Listopad*
December *Grudzień*

Hello *Cześć*
Goodbye *Do widzenia*
Good morning *Dzień dobry*
Good day *as above*
Good afternoon *as above*
Good evening *Dobry wieczór*
Please *Proszę*
Thank you (very much) *Dziękuję bardzo*
I'm sorry/pardon *Przepraszam*
Excuse me *Przepraszam* (also *panią/pana*)
Yes *Tak*
No *Nie*

Small talk
Do you speak English? — *Czy pan/pani mowi po angielsku?*
I'm sorry I don't speak Polish — *Nie mówię po polsku*
I don't understand — *Nie rozumiem*
Could you write it down please? — *Proszę to napisać*
What do you do? — *Co pan/pani robi?*
I'm a student — *Jestem studentem*
I'm an English teacher — *Jestem nauczycielem angielskiego*
I work at . . . — *Pracuję w . . .*
I'm from . . . — *Pochodzę z . . .*

Shopping
Where can I buy . . .? — *Gdzie dostanę . . .?*
How much does it cost? — *Ile to kosztuje?*
Do you have a . . . — *Czy macie państwo?*
Can I have a bag please? — *Czy mogę prosić torbę?*
Where is the . . .? — *Gdzie jest . . .?*

Times and dates
Today *dzisiaj*
Tonight *dziś wieczór*
Yesterday *wczoraj*
Tomorrow *jutro*
Next week *w przyszłym tygodniu*
What time is it please? *która (jest) godzina?*

Open *otwarty*
Closed *zamknięty*
When? *kiedy*
Where? *gdzie*

Appendix 5. Festivals and public holidays

Poland's strong commitment to the Catholic faith means all the feast days on the Church calendar are celebrated. In the mountain areas of the south you may also see communities decked out in traditional costumes on such occasions.

On public holidays, in small places especially, everything closes, including restaurants, so don't be caught out.

1 January	New Year's Day. New Year's Eve (*Sylwester*) is celebrated with parties and balls throughout the country.
March/April	Easter Monday. This is marked by boys and men sprinkling or in some cases pouring water on the girls and women (which is also common at Easter fairs).
3 May	Constitution day.
May/June	Corpus Christi (variable holiday during May or June but always on a Thursday)
1 November	All Saints' Day is a day of remembrance when people will visit the tombstones of relatives to lay flowers and wreaths and light candles.
11 November	Independence Day.
25–26 December	Christmas Eve is the traditional time when families gather for the Christmas feast of 12 courses, and one place is always left for whoever might come by. One of the dishes will normally be carp. Following the meal presents are exchanged around the tree and everyone goes to church for midnight mass. Christmas day is spent quietly at home with the family.

Appendix 6. Embassies and consulates

Selected Polish embassies and consulates abroad
Australia: 7 Turrana Street, Yarralumba, Canberra, ACT 2600. Tel: (06) 731 208/11/31. 10 Trelawny Street, Wollahara, Sydney, NSW 2025. Tel: (02) 363 9816.
Canada: 443 Daly Street, Ottawa 2, Ontario, Canada K1N 6H3. Tel: (613) 236 0468. 1150 Pine Avenue West, Montreal, Quebec H3G 184. Tel: (514) 937 9481. 2603 Lakeshore Boulevard West, Toronto, Ontario M8V 1G5. Tel: (416) 252 5471/72.
Ireland: 29–30 Fitzwilliam Square, Dublin 2, Ireland. Tel: (01) 661 4411. Fax: (01) 661 4202.

New Zealand: The Terrace, Wellington. Tel: (04) 712 456.
UK: 19 Weymouth Street, London W1N 3AG. Tel: (0171) 580 0476. 2 Kinnear Rd, Edinburgh EH3 5PE. Tel: (0131) 552 0301.
USA: 2224 Wyoming Avenue NW, Washington, DC 20008. Tel: (202) 234 3800/(202) 234 0626. 233 Madison Avenue, New York, NY 10016. Tel: (212) 889 8360. 1530 North Lake Shore Drive, Chicago, Illinois 60610-1695. Tel: (312) 337 8166.

Selected embassies and consulates in Poland
Australia: ul. Estonska 3/5, 03 903 Warsaw. Tel: (02) 17-60-81/17-60-86.
Canada: ul. Matejki 1/5, 00-481 Warsaw. Tel: (02) 29-80-51. Consular section, Piekna 2/8. Tel: (02) 29-80-51.
Ireland: Lenartowicza 18, Warsaw. Tel: (02) 44-64-40/48-01-40.
UK: Aleje. Roz 1, 00-556 Warsaw. Tel: (02) 28-11-001/(022) 28-10-05/(02) 628 1001/5.
USA: Al. Ujazdowskie 29/31, 00-540 Warsaw. Tel: (02) 28-30-41/28 30 49.

3 | The Czech Republic

Since 1989 and the 'Velvet Revolution', the Czech Republic, and Prague in particular, has been a magnet for hundreds of thousands of visitors, most of whom have been short-term tourists, although several thousand have settled for longer. Prague itself is a major tourist city and has developed quickly over the last few years to try and cater for this influx. The result is that, while it has lost none of its beauty and charm, it is not typical of other towns in the country, and some people are surprised to find how Westernized it is.

Many of the people deciding to stay are from North America and in the main are young people who have either specifically come to teach English or have been attracted to the Czech Republic for other reasons and have found work teaching English as a foreign language to help support themselves. Some, of course, find work outside EFL, perhaps by setting up businesses, or (primarily in Prague) by serving in bars and restaurants.

The ELT market has mushroomed since 1991, but in the private sector standardization is still getting off the ground. An alarming number of private language schools have poor reputations from experienced teachers who have worked elsewhere in the world, whereas the state sector, while short of English teachers after years of teaching mainly Russian, pays poorly.

Many opportunities are open to teach English as a foreign language in the Czech Republic, in both private and state sectors, although jobs are getting harder to come by in Prague, where you can no longer get off the bus and walk into a job, especially without training. More and more qualified teachers are coming to the Czech Republic now than at any time in the past, and schools are choosing teachers with more care. However, jobs are far easier to come by in other towns in the Republic, where you are more likely to get to know the Czech people and culture better, and in many ways have a much more rewarding time.

Both UK- and US-based organizations bring teachers to the Czech Republic, including the Peace Corps, Education for Democracy and EEP. They mainly offer work in state schools and institutes. There are also private language chains such as International House, Bell and Language Link (see organizations pp 9–15).

The Czech Republic is a good place for teachers fresh from completing a course in EFL, as learners are responsive and want to learn English. EFL teachers generally have positive experiences, and apart from those schools which want to follow their own methods, teachers have the freedom to experiment and develop. It is also still a different enough country both culturally and physically to excite those looking for new and refreshing challenges.

To teach English in the Czech Republic it helps if you come with a willingness to learn about the culture and an ability to make friends; you will also need to be able to cope with the frustrations of living in a country going through change, as well as being creative and capable of thinking on your feet.

Although offering little in the way of financial returns, wherever you work, your experience here can be both extremely rewarding and enjoyable. Many people have been known to stay on longer than they had originally planned, and people often come back, either to work at the same place or to take on a new challenge.

PART 1
PREPARING YOUR TRIP
AND FINDING TEACHING JOBS

Before you go

Essentials

The rapid opening up of the country since 1990 has meant that most Western products are obtainable in Prague and the larger cities, but are not as readily available in smaller towns. However, prices for such goods tend to be the same as in the West and the choice not as wide, so you are better off bringing your favourite toiletries; a good pair of shoes or boots; and a warm jacket or coat for the wet snowy winter. Wool products in particular are difficult to find, as is thermal underwear, so bring what you need. Another useful item is an adaptor for three-pin plugs (the sockets are two-pin 220 V 50 cycles).

If you wear contact lenses, pack a supply of cleaning fluid as local versions are not as effective, although still usable. You will also need a copy of your prescription for glasses and contact lenses in case you need to replace them, plus any regular medication you are taking, including a supply of vitamin tablets. Buying things before you come can save you a lot of time and money once you arrive. (See p 18 for further suggestions.)

Teaching materials

The availability of teaching materials is increasing with the number of the major EFL publishers who have representatives in the Czech Republic (see p 137). Private and state schools use recognized course books such as the Cambridge English series (CUP), the Headway Series (OUP) and others, while for children the Project English series (OUP) is popular (see p 138 for other coursebooks). However, it is still advisable to take a selection of reference books for your own use, as well as the other items listed in the introduction (p 19). Czech stationery is easy to get, and cheap, although Blu-Tack is still elusive and Western stationery, where available, is expensive.

If you are going to be working outside Prague, particularly in a small town, the more resources you can take the easier your life will be when it comes to planning lessons and supplementing the course book. Authentic material showing aspects of the way of life in your home country is very useful, and something your students will be interested in. You may also want to arrange with your family or friends for them to send out regularly any magazines or journals you might be able to use in your teaching.

A final suggestion is a chalkboard eraser as these do not appear to be available here. The chalk is of poor quality and using rags is very messy.

Health and insurance

Once you have found full-time employment your employer should pay your social security contributions, which will entitle you to an 'insurance card' and use of the Czech health care system. It is still recommended, however, that you have some health insurance when you come out, at least to cover you until you start work, and fly you home in an emergency. Avoid employers who would like to employ you illegally; if your employers are not paying contributions and you do not have any health insurance, you may end up with a rather high bill should you fall ill (see Health p 114).

The payment of the mandatory health and social insurance contributions represents a significant financial burden for any employer: 49.5% of an employee's gross monthly wages and salaries is paid into the health and social insurance funds (36% paid by the employer and 13.5% by the employee).

Language

Czech is a Slavonic language which is closely related to Slovak. If you possess a knowledge of Polish and Russian this will help you to pick up bits of the language quickly, and should make studying it easier. Note, however, that the speaking of Russian to Czechs, as in other ex-satellite countries of the former USSR, is still not normally to be recommended.

The Czech language is not particularly easy to master, and the apparent lack of vowels and array of consonant clusters can be frightening to a native speaker of English. It also possesses a number of irregularities and inconsistencies, and a case system that can prove a stumbling block to those unfamiliar with the function of cases. However, once you have mastered the alphabet, you can start making yourself understood as the language is basically phonetic (ie each letter or syllable is pronounced as it is written). Take care to remember that the stress always falls on the first syllable of each word. Stressing words incorrectly can often lead to misunderstanding.

The second language of the country is German, which is widely spoken, although a growing number of people, especially in the younger generation, now speak English. If you speak Czech to some degree, you will also be able to make yourself understood in Slovakia.

It is wise to make an effort to study a little before you come, and to have at least a working vocabulary of everyday Czech in order to cope with situations such as buying a ticket, asking for directions and ordering in a restaurant (see Appendix 3). The sooner you start to get to grips with the language the more at home you will feel, and any attempt to speak Czech will be much appreciated by the locals.

Probably the best book to start learning with is *Colloquial Czech* by James Naughton and published by Routledge. There is also a tape which accompanies the book.

Other books include *Teach Yourself Czech, How to Say it in Czech* published by Harrap, and a phrase book, *Travellers' Czech* published by Colletts, although these do not come too highly recommended for the serious learner. These books can be purchased at the major bookshops in the West. *Czech For You* by Milena Kell, is published by Anglictina Expres in Prague and comes with accompanying tapes. Locally printed dictionaries are cheap and easily obtainable once in the country.

A number of schools in Prague offer Czech lessons, and these are often advertised in the English language newspapers, the *Prague Post* and *Prognosis*. In Brno, ILC (see p 98) also runs Czech courses.

Money – expenses and how much to take

How much money to take will depend largely on whether you are coming to a pre-arranged job where accommodation is provided, or whether you are planning on turning up on spec and looking for work. It also depends on whether you plan to live and work in Prague or in the country. While the Czech Republic may still be a lot less expensive than back home, arriving with little money and hoping for the best is a certain recipe for disaster.

If you have a job arranged through an organization with accommodation provided you will not need much money initially, although it is still a good idea to bring a minimum of $500 for emergencies and to tide you over for the first couple of weeks until you find your feet. You will need more if you plan to travel around the region. It is also worth checking with your employer before-hand whether you get a pay advance on your arrival. Salaries are usually paid in cash on a monthly basis.

Unless you are working for an organization where there is a hard currency supplement, then you will probably receive all your salary in Czech Crowns. Technically it is illegal to take these out of the country, although you can change Crowns into hard currency at a bank if you can prove you have exchanged an equivalent amount of hard currency, ie by keeping the receipt.

For teachers turning up without work, you will need enough money to cover living costs and short-term accommodation until you find a job and a more permanent home. Remember that the cost of living is far higher in Prague than in other Czech towns, but wherever you go around $500 should cover living costs for the first few weeks. You may need considerably more to cover long-term accommodation, which will be by far your largest initial outlay, and again keep money in reserve for emergencies, travel, etc.

Landlords usually ask for a month's rent in advance, as well as the final month's rent, and if you have found a flat through an agency they usually demand a month's rent as their fee (see accommodation below). Therefore $1000 is not an excessive amount until you get settled.

When you arrive, change money at a bank rather than one of the many *bureau de change* offices (usually indicated by 'change' or *smenarna*) scattered around the centre of Prague, and other major cities, as the commission will be much lower. Commission can vary from 1–10% so it is worth looking around. Traveller's cheques and Eurocheques are accepted at most banks, although the commission is usually higher than for cash. (NB Scottish banknotes are not normally accepted.)

The unit of currency is the Czech Crown (*koruna*) and will be indicated from now on as Kč. Exchange rates (early 1995):

$	27 Kč
DM	18 Kč
£	43 Kč

Visas

Citizens of the USA, Canada and most West European countries, including the UK and Ireland, do not require a visa to enter the Czech Republic and are entitled to stays of up to three months (90 days) before requiring an extension. However, citizens of Australia, New Zealand and South Africa still require a visa, although in some cases this is not always checked (do not take the risk).

Visas can be obtained from any Czech embassy or consulate abroad and on the border with Germany and Austria (see Appendix 6).

Work permits

It is necessary for all teachers to have residence and work permits in order to be legally employed to teach English in the Czech Republic. A work permit (*pracovní provolení*) is even required for short-term contracts of up to three months and is issued for a maximum period of one year, but can be extended. Schools will usually help with this process, although the ever-changing legislation means that it can take anything from three to eight months before you can receive all the right documentation. You will need your passport, a number of passport photos, the original or a copy of your EFL certificate and/or degree which will need to be officially translated, and a good pen to fill in all the forms!

Work permits are issued at the employment office (*úřad práce*) and it is your employer who will apply for this on your behalf. The employment office in Prague is at Zabrovska 11. The permit usually takes a month to come through.

Residence permits (povoleni k pobytu cizincŭ)

Only when you have a work permit (which indicates you have a contract of employment), can you apply for a residence permit at the *úřad cizinecké a pasové služby*, a department within the police dealing with foreign passport affairs. You will also be asked to show proof that you have somewhere to live. The residence permit takes longer to process than the work permit, but eventually you will receive a laminated plastic card containing your photo and personal details. (From 1994 this has replaced the 'green book'.) In addition you will receive a stamp inside your passport. All of this entitles you to live and work in the Czech Republic up until the end of your contract with the school.

Once you have received your residence permit you will, in theory, be entitled to pay the same rate as Czechs for hotel rooms, train tickets, etc (although this does not work all the time). This can mean substantial savings. Because the residence permit takes so long to process, an official stamped letter from your school stating your position sometimes works in the meantime.

Foreigners who need to obtain a residence permit or extend their residence in Prague should contact:

> **Foreigners' Desk**, Olšanská 2, Žižkov, Prague 3. Tel: (02) 33-54-13-51

A word of warning: the authorities in the Czech Republic are now clamping down on teachers working illegally, and there have been a number of cases of schools being checked. Those found to be employing teachers without the correct documentation have been fined. Consequently schools have become a lot more reluctant to employ teachers illegally and without the necessary qualifications.

Arriving and finding your feet

Travel preparations

Flights from the UK. There are daily flights direct from London to Prague by Czechoslovak Airlines (CSA) and British Airways (BA) with a flying time of just under two hours. The cheapest ticket can be as little as £90 from London one way, although a normal Apex return is around £235. Reservations for Apex flights must be made 14 days in advance. It is normally difficult to find cheap charter flights direct to Prague but it is worth keeping an eye out for bargain deals to cities such as Berlin and Frankfurt and taking the train from there. Flights tend to be more expensive in summer, with the cheapest deals between December and May.

> **Czechoslovak Airlines**, 12a Margaret St, London W1. Tel: (0171) 255 1898.
> **STA Travel**, 86 Old Brompton Road, London SW7. Tel: (0171) 937 9921.
> **Council Travel**, Poland Street, London W1. Tel: (0171) 437 7767.

Flights from the USA and Canada. From the USA there are direct flights from New York to Prague (flying time 10 hours) on CSA, and stopover flights from many other cities on airlines which include British Airways, Lufthansa, Delta and TWA. From Canada there are direct flights from Montreal on CSA. An Apex flight from New York costs around $800 and from Montreal around C$1000. If you are under 26, there are a number of good student deals from Council Travel and STA (STA has offices in Boston, Los Angeles, Philadelphia, San Francisco and Washington DC).

It is definitely worth considering flying to a major European city (Frankfurt is always a good bet, or Munich, Berlin or Vienna) which usually works out much cheaper (around $400 one way) and then travelling overland from there. Check out several agents and look through the papers for the best deals.

> **Council Travel,** Head office, 205 E 42nd Street, New York, NY 10017. Tel: (212) 661 1450.
> **STA,** 48 E 11th Street, Suite 805, New York, NY 10003. Tel: (212) 477 7166.

By train. Trains leave from London's Victoria station daily in the morning, arriving in Prague the following morning, a journey of just over 24 hours. You will have to change trains at least once, depending on which route you take, and it is advisable to reserve a seat and possibly a couchette. Tickets are not much cheaper than flying, unless you are under 26, in which case you may wish to use an Inter-rail pass and see a bit of Europe before coming. Eurotrain offers discount rail fares for those under 26. Campus Travel issue Eurotrain tickets:

> **Campus Travel,** 52 Grosvenor Gardens, London SW1 0AG. Tel: (0171) 730 3402.

By coach. By far the cheapest way to get to the Czech Republic is by coach. Kingscourt Express operates a direct service from London to Prague three times a week from Victoria station. The journey takes approximately 21 hours including short stops on the way. Take some German and Belgian money for coffee, etc, as well as enough food and drink for the journey. Eurolines operate a similar service on Monday and Friday, tickets available from Campus Travel or National Express. Currently both charge around the same for tickets, £50 one way.

> **Kingscourt Express,** 35 Kingscourt Road, London SW16. Tel: (081) 769 9229.
> **National Express,** 164 Buckingham Palace Road, London SW1. Tel: (0171) 730 0202.
> **Campus Travel,** 52 Grosvenor Gardens, London SW1 0AG. Tel: (0171) 730 3402.

By car. If you plan on coming by car then allow yourself a good two days from the UK. The most direct route is via Brussels, Cologne, Frankfurt and Nürnburg, entering the Czech Republic at Waidhaus-Rozvodov. A car is not really necessary in any of the towns, including Prague, as the public transport system is good. Unless you plan on doing a lot of driving around the country, a car can actually be more of an inconvenience and an added expense. If you do decide to bring a car it is worth checking with the AA or RAC in the UK before you set off for any travel tips. Unleaded petrol is widely available.

Remember to bring your car registration papers, car insurance, full driving licence and an international licence if possible.

Renting a car in the Czech Republic is expensive for foreigners, and you may find you have to pay in hard currency, although getting a Czech to rent it for you would be a lot cheaper. Drinking and driving is punished severely in the Czech Republic and can lead to a prison sentence. The rule is, don't drink any alcohol if you intend to drive.

Registering your car in the Czech Republic is not easy, and coupled with the high price of petrol and insurance, you may want to think carefully whether the expense and hassle of bringing one is worth it.

You should be aware that you cannot register your car in the Czech Republic if it is right hand drive, and consequently you will be unable to take out Czech insurance. This means that if you bring a car from the UK you will have to make sure you have adequate insurance cover from the UK for the length of your stay.

For those with left-hand drive cars you must first obtain your residence permit and within the first six months you will need to take the theory part of the Czech driving test. However, the test is in Czech, so this may cause problems! (Rumour has it that you can take a Czech along but this hasn't been confirmed.) You car will also have to undergo an inspection, which is pretty similar to those in the West, but you will need to have a warning triangle and first aid kit. Third party liability insurance must be purchased locally.

Arrival

Transport from the airport. There is one international airport in the Czech Republic, 'Ruzyně', situated 15 kilometres from the centre of Prague. To get directly to the centre of the city take the CSA bus from outside the terminal to náměstí Republiky. Buses run every half hour and tickets can be bought from the driver.

There is also a regular bus service (number 119) from the airport to the metro stop 'Dejvická' on the A line every 15–20 minutes from 4.30am to 11.30pm, after which a night service runs every 40 minutes. Buy a ticket (6 Kč) from a kiosk or the tourist information office in the airport. The journey takes about 20 minutes.

Alternatively there is another bus which runs every 20–30 mins and goes to 'Revoluční'. Whatever you do, stay away from the taxis at the airport as they are likely to be expensive. If you find you have to take one then make sure you agree on a price first (see taxis p 111).

By train. There are two stations in Prague, but you will probably arrive at the main one, 'Praha Hlavni nádraži'. The station is a 10 minute walk from the centre of the city, and you can leave your bags in the 24 hour left luggage situated downstairs. The station is on the red metro line C.

A number of trains that come through Berlin/Warsaw on their way to Vienna/Budapest only stop at the smaller 'Praha Holešovice' station which is at the end of the red metro line C.

By coach. Coaches arrive at the main bus station 'Praha–Florenc' where you can pick up buses to other towns around the country. This is also on the metro lines B and C, station 'Florenc', and only one stop from 'Praha Havní nádraží' where you should head if you need urgent accommodation, information, etc.

Accommodation

Urgent accommodation – Prague

If you arrive by train at either of Prague's two stations you are likely to be approached by various people offering rooms for rent. These are usually the cheapest form of accommodation, 300–500 Kč ($10–$16) a night, and you will probably be shown a photo of the room, along with an indication of where it is in the city. Try to get one near a tram or metro station and check this on a map before taking it. Maps can be bought at the station. (Private accommodation is often available in most parts of the country, as Czechs open up their homes to make what for them can be a substantial amount of money.)

If you wish to avoid these (and some can be a bit dodgy), there are a number of accommodation offices situated in the station itself, offering accommodation ranging from good hotels to hostels. Hotels of any description are pricey, and it is worth remembering that in summer and at Easter Prague gets very busy, and a bed of any sort is hard to get. Nevertheless, you should still be able to find a hostel for around 300 Kč ($10) a night.

If you arrive by plane try AVE Ltd, a travel agency at the airport which helps with accommodation. Other places to try include:

> **CKM Agency**, Žitná 12. Tel: (02) 29-99-41 (Open Monday–Friday 8am–6pm, the agency lists available places to stay in Prague's hostels and cheaper hotels. The CKM office at Jindrišská 28, issues ISIC student IDs and International Youth Hostel Cards.)
> **Top Tour Travel**, Rybná 3, Staré Město. Tel: (02) 232–10-77. (Offers rooms in private accommodation.)

Hello Ltd, Travel Agency, Gorkého náměstí 3 Nové Mesto. Tel: (02) 22-42-83. (Offers hotels, private rooms and apartments.)

Hostels include:

Hostel Braník, Vrbová 1233 (tram 17). Tel: (02) 46-26-42.
Domov- mládeže-Pension (tram 16 to Perunova). Tel: (02) 25-06-88

For urgent accommodation in other cities see 'city by city' (p 119).

Long-term accommodation

Rental accommodation in the Czech Republic usually consists of a small one- or two-room flat in a block (*panelák*) on a housing estate. Most Czech families live in such flats, and it is common for a family of four to have to share two rooms. Although not particularly pleasing to the eye from the outside, they are centrally heated (if anything too warm), and generally adequately furnished. Beds are usually of the fold-out nature, and often there may be only two-ring electric stoves and no oven.

Flats will come supplied with bedding, pots and pans, cutlery, etc but more often than not they will not have a washing machine. Washing tends to get done in the bath or you may be lucky to find someone in your block whom you can pay to do it for you!

In Prague there is a shortage of long-term accommodation and it is not very easy for teachers to find flats at affordable prices. Most teachers live on the outskirts of the city, either alone or in shared flats. Commuting to the city centre can take from 30 to 60 minutes each way. The cost of accommodation varies but on average teachers pay between 4 000 and 6 000 Kč ($135–200) a month for a single flat and 5 000–8 000 Kč ($165–270) to share. It is worth noting that a lot of flats do not have telephones; the current waiting time for a telephone to be installed is two years. In other parts of the country bedsit type accommodation is a lot cheaper, around 2 500–3 500 Kč ($85–120) a month.

Because finding a place to live is difficult, coming to a pre-arranged job where accommodation has been sorted out is a big advantage. If you are not in this situation, one way to start looking for a flat is to check out noticeboards and put notices up yourself (see p 95). If you have access to an answering machine and a Czech friend to help with the language, putting notices on tram and bus stops can produce results.

In Prague you can also check the English language newspapers which advertise accommodation, and visit what was the American Hospitality Centre, but is now an Accommodation Bureau (Malé náměstí 14).

Asking people is probably the best way of finding out the local situation, and getting to know some Czechs will help you enormously. If you have started doing some teaching do not be afraid of asking your students if they know of anywhere or anyone with a place. There is a Czech classified ads paper printed three times a week in Prague called *Annonce* which advertises flats, but again you will need to get a Czech to help you!

A number of accommodation agencies operate in Prague and most of the large cities, but these are expensive, and you will more than likely end up having to pay a month's rent in advance plus the final month's rent. To add to the problem you may be asked to pay in deutschmarks or US dollars. Prices are generally given in deutschmarks or US dollars and then converted into Crowns at the current exchange rate. Landlords and landladies are sometimes prone to putting up rent when they want, so some written agreement is useful as a safeguard. The initial outlay for a flat could be $450 including the agency fee and two months' rent.

As in other parts of Eastern and Central Europe the idea of renting out your flat to foreigners for an extensive period of time is a relatively new one to the Czechs. As a result, landlords and landladies tend to be a little on the fussy side. They may for example come round to visit you regularly and check you haven't rearranged the furniture or got friends staying (people staying overnight can be a problem). It is not uncommon for them to even come round and tidy up! A little understanding and patience is sometimes necessary.

It is possible to rent a room in a family house. This is mainly, but not exclusively, an option in smaller towns around the country. While you will be able to immerse yourself into Czech life and will probably be treated as one of the family, you may find the lack of privacy a problem.

Accommodation provided for teachers working in state schools is usually in a student hostel/dormitory often with a shared bathroom and kitchen.

Bills

On the whole bills (gas, electricity and water) are cheap, are usually included in the rent, and are therefore paid by the landlord or landlady. The rent in such cases will be *inkaso* which means including bills. This of course does not include the telephone bill. Everyone with a telephone is sent a bill (*složenka*) which should be paid at the post office. The same is true for gas bills, etc for tenants whose rent is not *inkaso*.

In some flats there is a common telephone, usually shared with the landlord or landlady. A separate agreement will therefore be needed to divide the costs. Bills usually come once a month.

Arriving without a job

Most people wanting to work in the Czech Republic seem to have a preference for living and working in Prague. This has created a disproportionate number of teachers in the capital compared to the rest of the country. In 1994 there were unofficial estimates that 20 000 American and British citizens were living and working in Prague (with Americans forming by far the largest expatriate community), and a large percentage of these were teaching English to some degree, often without any EFL/ESL qualifications.

Starting points

School term starts at the beginning of September, universities in October; the best time to arrive if you have not got a job is at least a few weeks before then.

For teachers arriving on spec, Prague is where most will start looking for work, and until 1993 such work was very easy to find. However, you can no longer count on walking into a job at the first place you go to, especially if you are unqualified; competition for jobs is now strong. More and more private schools are looking for teachers with EFL/ESL qualifications, although as in a lot of places there are still employers whose desire to make money far exceeds their will to provide quality teaching.

For those looking for work in the private sector, a good starting point is to pick up the Yellow Pages, found in all cities (the directory at the back is in English), from the British Council or Post office, and look under language schools (*jazykové školy*). At present there are around 40 listed in Prague, and a good number in the larger towns like Brno, Ostrava and Plzeň. The British Council may be able to give you some advice on the quality of a number of the schools, and they will at least give you a list, although choosing a good one is something of a lottery.

In Prague there are several places where you can place adverts on noticeboards and meet other ex-pats, such as the British Council (p 103), the American Library (p 115), and The Globe Bookshop and Coffee house (p 115) and Jo's Bar (p 109). Jobs are also advertised on these boards. Jobs can occasionally be found advertised in the *Prague Post* or *Prognosis*, the two English language newspapers. A list of other cities with British Council Resource Centres can be found on p 103.

If you want to work in the state sector, the best thing to do is to visit the schools direct and approach the headmaster or headmistress. A list of addresses can be obtained from the Yellow Pages in any town under *školy*.

The Academic Information Agency (AIA) has a database of primary and secondary schools requiring English teachers. It also recruits for a few major private language schools in Prague. The Ministry of Education is also worth contacting:

> **Academic Information Agency**, Dům zahraničních styků, MSMT CR, Senovážné náměští 26, 111 21 Prague 1. Tel: (02) 26-70-41 (ext 9)/26-70-10. Fax: (02) 26-70-09.
> **Ministry of Education**, Karmelitská 9, 11000 Prague 1. Tel: (02) 51-93-111. Fax: (02) 51-93-790.

City v country

Should you not want to stay in Prague, and not everybody does, you have a better chance of finding work in a state or even private school in other parts of the country. The best way of going about this is to travel around, choose a place you like and then approach schools directly.

Do not always be put off if a town is not especially appealing from an architectural perspective; more often than not it is the people who make a place interesting and fun rather than the place itself. Although salaries will be lower than in Prague, the cost of living is nothing like as high, and you will of course have time to travel around and visit other areas including the capital.

There are of course advantages and disadvantages to working in a small town in the country as opposed to Prague, or even Brno or Ostrava, which, although nothing like the size of Prague, are still quite large cities. First, you may well be the only native English speaker, or one of only a few, in the town. This can give you some sort of celebrity status and you will never be short of people wanting to talk to you, or to invite you round for dinner. You will soon develop a large circle of friends. On the other hand the lack of company of another native English speaker can be hard at times, and a feeling of isolation is not uncommon. You may also start to feel homesick more often. Unless there is a good support system for you, either with the organization you came with (if you came that way), or in the school, small problems can easily grow into large ones and at times seem insurmountable.

If you do not speak Czech well enough, you may feel out of touch with what is going on in the rest of the world. However, access to satellite or cable TV can alleviate this problem.

In the past such factors have caused a number of teachers to leave after a month, creating considerable problems for the school, as replacements have to be found. This also makes some schools wary of employing native English teachers in the future as they are not seen as being reliable.

Nevertheless, if you really want to get to know the country and people, living outside Prague will give you a better insight, and the experience can be much more fulfilling. People will generally have a lot more time for you and your social calendar will more than likely always be full. One of the keys to really getting the most out of living in a small place is to get involved in things going on, both in your school and locally.

Select your town and school carefully and weigh up the situation seriously before committing yourself.

Where to teach English

Places where you can teach English vary enormously, from working in state schools or large companies to simply giving private lessons in a café. Pay also varies depending on where and whom you teach; from the comparatively low salaries offered in the state schools, to the relatively lucrative private one-to-one teaching.

You may be employed at one institution on a full-time contract with accommodation and paid holidays thrown in, or you may find yourself working for at least two private language schools and giving private lessons on top. In addition you may get opportunities outside the classroom, for example proofreading.

Private language schools (Soukromá jazyková škola)

There has been a huge growth in the number of private language schools in the Czech Republic since 1991, with the highest concentration centred on Prague. While there are few new schools now setting up in Prague, more schools are opening in both Brno and Ostrava, as well as in other smaller towns.

Schools vary in size, quality and in terms of conditions under which you are expected to work, so do not necessarily jump at the first place that offers you a job. If there is a British Council Resource Centre in the city (see p 103) they may be able to give you some guidance as to who the credible organizations are. Whichever school you work for make sure you get some sort of contract and that you know what is in it.

The ELT market in the Czech Republic is not as established as it is in Hungary or Poland, for example, and as yet there is no accreditation body to monitor the quality of the schools. There have been numerous horror stories from teachers employed from the UK or the USA, about schools offering low pay, very little or no teacher support, minimum resources and seemingly only intent on making money. A lot of schools will also impose their own methods and materials, and may have given their students false expectations through adverts which offer students 'perfect English in three months'.

Some schools will provide accommodation or at least help to find a place for you. Some even cover the accommodation costs plus bills (except of course the phone bill!).

If you arrive on spec, it is a good idea to look around several schools first before deciding where to work and, wherever possible, try to talk to some of the teachers. Choosing a good school is essential.

Generally teachers work 20–24 teaching hours per week (one teaching hour = 45 minutes) and the teaching is general English to adults or children plus some in-company teaching.

Most courses take place in the morning and evening with classes starting from as early as 7am and usually finishing around 8pm. Class size is usually about 12 students, but may be slightly more and sometimes less for company groups.

It is common to work a four-day week, Monday to Thursday, as Czechs generally like to have their Friday free to go to their country cottages for the weekend. Even if you have classes on a Friday you may find half the students do not show up. Teachers are normally paid by the hour, which ranges from 80–150 Kč.

Below is a selected list of language schools in Brno and Prague.

Brno

ILC Brno, International House, Bosonožská 9, Brno. Tel: (05) 43-21-95-71.

MKM, Cěska 1/3, 602 00 Brno. Tel: (05) 42-21-31-04. Fax: (05) 42-21-11-65.

Travel 20002, Dominikánske Náměstí 6-7, Brno. Tel: (05) 21-01-02.

Travel 20002, Kroftova 45, Brno. Tel: (05) 41-21-12-83.

State Language School (Státni jazyková škola), Vranovská 65, 614 00 Brno. Tel: (05) 45-21-16-82.

Prague

Anglictina Expres, Vodičkova 39, 110 00 Prague 1. Tel: (02) 29-06-19.

The American English School Prague, ul. M. Horákové – Prašna Brána, 160 000, Prague 6, PO Box 181. Tel: (02) 32-01-44.

The Bell School, Nadvěžská 29, 100 00 Prague 10. Tel/Fax (02) 78-15-342/78-22-961.

English Link, Kolodějská 8, Prague 8. Tel: (02) 78-17-625. Fax: (02) 37-42-09.

ILC Praha, International House – Lupacova 1, 130 00 Prague 3. Tel: (02) 27-57-89/27-53-47. Fax: (02) 27-48-40.

London School, Belgická 25, 120 00 Prague 2. Tel: (02) 25-68-59. Fax: (02) 24-70-25.

Pro-English, Hellehova 5, Prague 1, Malá Strana. Tel: (02) 53-45-51/(02) 24-51-06. Fax: (02) 72-47-523.

Praha 8 Language School, Linderova 3, 182 00 Prague. Tel: (02) 82-05-83.

State school sector

Basic/primary schools (základní školy). In basic/primary schools, pupils attend from the age of six to fourteen or fifteen. Western language classes were introduced on the basis of the Ministry of Education Regulation (5 December 1989) and students usually study two foreign languages each for three lessons per week from the fifth year.

Textbooks and other materials from the UK or USA are generally available in these schools as they are now obtainable from special local bookshops, or directly from the publishers' representatives in the Czech Republic.

Nearly all the students are beginners or know very little, and partly for this reason it is not common to have native-speakers teaching in these schools. However, there is a great demand for teachers in such schools, and even unqualified teachers are known to have been employed in them.

Secondary or high schools (Střední a vysoké školy). A secondary school is regarded as a four-year course of study immediately following the primary school and leading to a school leaving certificate (*Maturita*) at the age of 18/19. A number of schools have now also introduced a seven-year programme taking pupils from the age of 11/12 up to 18/19.

Secondary schools are divided into: gymnasia; secondary vocational schools; and specialized secondary schools and conservatories.

Gymnasia. Gymnasia are secondary schools preparing pupils primarily for further education at university or college. In a four-year secondary comprehensive school *gymnazium*, two modern foreign languages are taught as compulsory subjects (usually a combination of English and German, rarely Russian, French or Spanish). This generally takes the form of three 45-minute lessons a week for each language, but can vary from school to school and can even be as many as nine lessons a week for the main foreign languages.

Lessons can start as early as 7am and usually finish at 2.30pm, with an extended form of language training possible wherever pupils are interested and qualified teachers and funds are available. The availability of qualified staff is a crucial determining factor; in 1994 not all foreign language lessons were taught by formally qualified teachers.

The syllabus is laid down by the Ministry of Education, with recommended textbooks, although the final choice of what books to use lies with the school and staff. The syllabus aims to achieve the following objectives: to enable the pupil to communicate in English in everyday situations; to get due knowledge of English-speaking countries, and to be able to give adequate information about the native country.

Priority is now given to speaking and listening comprehension. Teaching materials should also deal with information about British or American life, culture and institutions. English literature is partly taught in the World literature course and partly in the English lessons, mainly in the final two years.

Teachers are required to do a minimum of 21 teaching hours per week but may be asked to do more. It is probably a good idea not to, at least in the first term while you are still finding your feet. It will take you a while to get used to classes as well as the administration, such as filling in the registers (*třídní kniha*), grading, etc. Each class has a register which goes with it to each lesson, and the teacher must fill in what the students have done in blue or black ink, as well as record the attendance.

In nearly all cases, classes will be shared with a Czech teacher, and you will probably have one group for two lessons twice a week. The class size is usually around 20, but there may be more and sometimes less. It is unlikely that you will be given complete beginners and the students will usually have had at least one year of English. You may be given a course book which could for example be the *Cambridge English Course* book 1, 2 or 3, or *Project English* for younger learners. You are almost certain to be asked to do 'conversational classes'. Here you will be left very much up to your own devices as to what you actually do with the students. At the beginning of term you will be given a list of about 25 topics, one or more of which the students will be asked to talk about in their final exam. Apart from that you will generally have no other guidelines, other than to encourage the students to talk.

Resources in state schools are usually limited, but this very much depends on the place. Books normally have to be signed out, and in some cases teachers will find they have to buy their own materials. Photocopying may also be a problem: some places will have a copier, but the number of copies is generally limited and you may even be asked to pay for them. Again, some schools are equipped with video and audio facilities, others are not.

While there tends to be limited teacher support, Czech teachers are usually very helpful and appreciate the opportunity to practise their English, although it is very rare to have the opportunity to observe your colleagues or to be observed yourself. This is not yet common practice in schools, and you may find it difficult to arrange unless you approach your colleagues directly and encourage some sort of 'peer observation', inviting them to come and observe you first.

One problem you may well come across in your school is information flow. There is a saying that 'information is power', and although power is often not the reason for withholding information, you will at times be frustrated to discover things very late in the day, or not at all. Sometimes it is simply a case of nobody taking responsibility for informing you whether your lesson has been cancelled, or whether there is a school trip; at other times the information has been put on the noticeboard, but of course if it is in Czech you are not likely to understand it. It is necessary therefore to constantly question your students and colleagues.

Pay is poor, around 4 000–5 000 Kč ($135–180) a month but the cost of living in the countryside is significantly lower than in Prague. You will also get holiday pay. The school may or may not provide accommodation, and if it does it may well be in a student hostel.

Secondary vocational schools (Střední odborná škola). Apart from the *gymnazia*, there is a widely established type of four-year secondary school (age 14/15 to 18/19), that provides pupils with training in technical subjects, economics (business academies), nursing (schools for nurses), arts (conservatoires) and hotel and tourism management (hotel schools).

Teaching of foreign languages varies between the school types, with greater demand for language competence in business and tourism for example, than in technical schools where only one foreign language is compulsory and where language learning occupies only two lessons a week.

English at these schools also provides the learners with some basic ESP knowledge. Since the primary school leavers who are accepted to secondary do not have an adequate command of common English the first two years are devoted predominantly to this language area.

Specialized secondary schools and conservatoires. There are a number of specialized schools both in Prague and throughout the country which prepare secondary-level specialists such as nurses, tourist guides, etc. These are similar to the secondary vocational schools.

Recruitment to secondary schools. Recruitment for qualified teachers in secondary schools is carried out by individual schools or by the Ministry of Education (see p 104). AIA recruits for primary and secondary schools, Pedagogický Ústav Prahy recruits for the Prague area:

AIA (Academic Information Agency), Senovážné Náměstí 26, 111 21 Prague.
Pedagogický Ústav Prahy (PUP), Na Poříčí 4, 11000 Prague 1.

Universities and colleges (Univesity a koleja)

Opportunities to work in tertiary education are generally limited to those with the required qualifications and experience. However, apart from teacher training positions or teaching British and American studies courses, there is sometimes a need for teachers for general English courses. Teachers normally teach around 14 hours a week, and the students' level of English is normally high. Coursebooks are usually provided or there is at least some sort of syllabus outlining what needs to be covered. As a rule university study is organised into two semesters within one school year. Each semester lasts 15 weeks and is followed by a four-week exam period and a week-long holiday. Exams are marked on a three-grade scale, although some universities have a credit system.

Most courses are five years although since 1990 a number of three-year courses have been introduced, especially in teacher training colleges with so called 'fast track programmes'.

Recruitment for universities and colleges is carried out by the Ministry of Education or alternatively write to the university direct. Addresses can be obtained from the British Council (p 103), USIS (p 115) or the Ministry of Education (p 104).

Companies

Since 1992 an enormous growth in the teaching of English in companies has come about as more Western firms establish joint ventures with Czech companies, and the country builds up more business ties with the West. While there is a demand for ESP, a lot of the teaching is still general English with a business/ESP slant. You may well get some company teaching if you are employed by a private language school, although it is not so common for companies to hire teachers as individuals; they usually like to work with a school. Having said that, it is still worth approaching companies offering your services, as several teachers have found work this way. Computing and marketing firms especially are looking for English language teachers, and of course some knowledge in these particular fields would also be very useful. Contracts can be as short as three weeks or as long as a year and pay is generally good (see 'Teaching business people' p 264).

Teaching privately

A lot of people take on students for private tuition either to supplement their income or to keep them going until they find a full-time job. Generally private students are easy to find, and the rate per hour can be anything from 100 Kč to 150 Kč for a 60 minute lesson, usually depending on the means of the learner and the type of lesson. For example, you can charge a lot more for teaching ESP to a businessman than having a 'conversational' hour with a university student. The rate tends to be lower outside Prague. University noticeboards, the British Council or simply word of mouth can be used to advertise your services. It helps if you have a telephone so people can contact you, either to arrange lessons or to cancel them.

You may be offered Czech-for-English exchange lessons if you show a willingness to learn the language, but care in such cases should be taken. Unless your 'teacher' has some idea of how to teach it is more than likely that lessons will simply turn into conversation classes. This can be fine if your Czech is already at a conversational level, otherwise you may find most of the conversation will be in English, doing little to enhance your Czech!

Summer schools

Summer courses are organized by many language schools, often in the countryside at residential camps. Ask around the language schools or keep your eye open for advertisements. Pay is often poor, but accommodation and food are provided free.

Useful organizations and addresses

Association of Teachers of English (ATE). This is an active organization associated with IATEFL which publishes a newsletter and organizes conferences.

> **Vydava AUA**, c/o the Bell School, Nedveska 29, 100 00 Prague 10.

British Council English Teaching Resource Centres. In 1994 there were eight of these centres around the country, with membership open to practising English language teachers and teacher trainers:

> **British Council Prague**, Národní 10, 125 01 Prague 1. Tel: (02) 24 91 21 79. Fax: (02) 24 91 38 39.
> **British Council**, Olomouc, Křížkovsheko 14 (PO Box 100), 771 00. Tel: (068) 52 23 203. Fax: (068) 52 22 578.
> **British Council**, Cěske Budejovice, Krajinská 2, 370 01. Tel: (038) 327 37. Fax: (038) 329 31.

British Council, Pardubice, Pernštynské nám 54 (PO Box A-31), 531 08. Tel: (040) 51 52 67. Fax: (040) 51 85 57.
British Council, Ústi nad Labem, Vladimírská 1368/4, 400 00. Tel: (047) 25 190. Fax: (047) 25 431.

Ministry of Education, Youth and Physical Training (Ministerstvo školství, mládeže a tělovýchovy). The ministry is responsible for basic and secondary schools, as well as universities.

Ministerstvo školství, mládeže a tělorýchovy, Karmelitská 7 and 8, 118 12 Prague 1. Tel: (02) 519 31 11. Fax: (02) 519 37 90.

Moravian and Silesian Association of Teachers of English (MSSUA). This organization can be contacted at:

CDVU – Pellicova, Brno. Tel: (05) 43-21-24-83.

PART 2
LIVING IN THE CZECH REPUBLIC

How expensive is the Czech Republic?

The Czech Republic is a lot cheaper than Western Europe and even cheaper than Poland and Hungary, although in turn salaries are considerably lower (see p 105). The capital Prague is much more expensive than other towns in the country, especially when it comes to accommodation and everyday living. However, even in Prague, teachers working in the private sector find they can live quite reasonably on their salaries, as long as they don't frequent the many tourist bars, restaurants and ex-pat hangouts on a regular basis.

Living costs

Teachers may find that once they have got used to their accommodation, which may not be as big or comfortable as back home, and have found they can get around cheaply on the excellent public transport, they begin to appreciate their rather privileged lifestyle compared to that of the average Czech citizen.

Eating, drinking and nightlife

On the whole eating and drinking can be relatively cheap. There are a number of good low-priced restaurants, both in Prague and in other towns, although eating out is not so easy for vegetarians. Buying food from local markets and cooking at home is very cheap. With regard to drinking, the Czech Republic is reputed to consume more beer per head than any other country in the world, and pubs and beer halls (*pivnice*) are inexpensive places in which to eat and drink.

Cafés and restaurants. Apart from the tourist places which can be mainly found in Prague, cafés are cheap. Restaurants range from the expensive to the basic and in Prague and other large cities there is a growing number of international restaurants.

Discos and clubs. New bars are opening all the time, although outside Prague they are not so pervasive. Generally there is a small cover charge, and drinks are invariably more expensive than in the local *pivnice*.

Taxes. Under current Czech law everyone must pay income tax. This varies from 15% to 47% depending on your annual income. If they are working full-time most teachers pay around 20–25% of their gross income.

How far does money go?

The cost of living in Prague is higher than anywhere else in the country. On the whole salaries in the private sector are relatively good compared to the average salaries of the locals; however Czechs do not have the same outlays as the foreign English teacher and have better support systems. Nor do they have to pay the rents that foreigners do.

Currently an average salary for a teacher working 25 hours a week is around 7 000–8 000 Kč ($235–265) net a month in the private sector. The hourly rate is between 70 and 90 Kč.

Out of this a teacher's biggest outlay will be on accommodation, and after this has been paid you should be looking to have around 5 000 Kč ($165) a month net to be able to have a reasonable lifestyle.

Generally salaries are sufficient to eat out a couple of times a week and enjoy a good social life, but still require budgeting. Some teachers manage to get by without taking on private students, others find themselves dipping into reserves from home. If you have to buy anything substantial, such as a coat, or make a trip abroad, this can have a marked effect on your salary for that month.

In the state sector teachers are paid considerably less, 5 000 Kč ($165) month, making living in Prague very difficult, if not impossible. You can only really do this if accommodation is provided by the school. Working for a state school in other parts of the country where the cost of living is lower helps, but again there is not a lot of room for rash spending or much saving.

At present the Czech Crown is not fully convertible, although there are plans to make it so in the near future. Officially inflation in 1994 was over 20% pa following the break up with Slovakia, but the government hopes to reduce it substantially.

A guide to costs

Large loaf of bread	9 Kč	Glass of wine in a pub	
Litre of milk	10–12 Kč	(2 dl)	15–20 Kč
Litre and a half of		Month travel pass	
mineral water	12 Kč	(Prague)	150–300 Kč
Jar of coffee 100gms	12 Kč	Packet of cigarettes	
Packet of tea	15–30 Kč	(Western)	45 Kč
Half litre bottle of beer		Packet of cigarettes	
(in a supermarket)	10–20 Kč	(Czech)	25 Kč
Litre of wine	30 Kč	Cinema	30 Kč
Meal in a restaurant	35–100 Kč	Cover charge for a club	20–50 Kč
Beer in a pub	8–30 Kč	Opera/concert ticket	40–100 Kč

These prices were generally correct at the time of printing, but should be treated with caution. They are intended as a guide only.

Tipping

Tipping as a rule means rounding the bill up, as service charge in restaurants is not normally included. Do not leave tips on the table. On average people tip between 5% and 10%, but do not give more as Czechs will either think you are stupid or that you want to show how rich you are. You are expected to pay a few Crowns for leaving your coat and going to the toilet, although tipping taxi drivers is not common.

Everyday living

Eating

The Czech diet is often referred to as simply pork, dumplings and sauerkraut (*vepřo, knedle, zelo*), and while this is a little bit of an exaggeration, eating is largely based around meat and has a certain German influence. Nevertheless, at times the food in the Czech Republic can still be rich and tasty. Because Czechs get up early they rarely have much for breakfast and the main meal of the day is at lunchtime between 11am and 1pm. In the evening they tend to have a lighter meal which may include cold meats.

Traditional home cuisine can be delicious (although rather heavy), and far exceeds what can normally be found in a restaurant. If you teach in a state school you will have access to the school canteen. However, the food here is basic and not particularly appetizing.

Czech specialities. Many of the specialities of Czech traditional food are cooked only at home, although you will come across the following in restaurants: deep fried cheese in breadcrumbs (*Smažený sýr*); scrambled eggs with dumplings (*Knedlíky s vejci*); Czech fruit dumplings (*Ovocné knedlíky*); Prague ham (*Pražská šunka*); Potato soup with vegetables and mushrooms (*Bramboračka*); and pork cutlet in gravy with potatoes (*Vepřovy řízek přírodní, brambory*). For dessert try Buchty buns with soft cheese stuffing (*Buchty s tvarohem*).

Restaurants. A lot of restaurants have now been privatized, and with this the quality of food and service has slightly improved. It is sometimes necessary to book at the more popular restaurants, and most places tend to close early, around 9pm or 10pm. You may be asked to hang your coat up when you go into a restaurant or to leave it with the attendant in the cloakroom for a small sum.

Meals usually start with soup, which is usually very good, and the main course is inevitably a meat dish, usually pork or beef, with a generous helping of gravy. Main dishes are served with *knedlíky* (doughy dumplings) or potatoes. Fish, generally carp or trout, is also popular and is the traditional main meal at Christmas. Both meat and fish are served by weight.

Sauerkraut or gherkins are usually served as side dishes, and salads, although improving, are still the usual bland lettuce or tomato. For desserts it is difficult to get anything other than pancakes or ice-cream.

In Prague a number of ethnic restaurants have opened, these include Greek, Chinese and Indian and are advertised in the English language newspapers.

> **Indická (Indian)**, Štěpánská 61, Prague 1. Tel: 236-9922.
> **Kalypso (Greek)**, Slezská 134, Prague 3. Tel: 733-194.

Eating out cheaply. The cheapest places to eat are the many self-service (*samoobsluha*) restaurants. These are normally stand-up places selling anything from open sandwiches to hot meals. They open early at 6am and are usually very busy between 11am and 2pm.

Beer halls (*Pivnice* or *Hostinec*), as well as being excellent places to sample the local brews, provide cheap meals, although they do not normally provide a very extensive menu and may not serve food at all in the evenings.

There are a growing number of salad bars where salads, mostly mayonnaise based, are sold by weight.

Takeaways and fast food. The traditional Czech takeaway from a street stall is the hot dog which comes with a bread roll and mustard. Larger than the average English sausage, they are more akin to the German frankfurter. Other specialities include potato pancakes (*bramborák*) with bits of salami or bacon in them, and fried cheese covered with breadcrumbs served with a roll. If you are vegetarian be careful as these usually contain bits of ham. Chips are available and are usually served with tartare sauce. In autumn hot corn-on-the-cob is often sold in the streets.

A growing number of Western style fast food places are appearing, especially pizzerias and hamburger stalls. Large chains such as Macdonalds have already moved into the larger cities.

Vegetarian. For the vegetarian the Czech Republic is not the easiest of places to get a balanced diet. Restaurants do not really cater for non-meat eaters. While you may often find non-meat dishes on the menu (there is usually a *bez masa* section, meaning without meat), unfortunately these are not always guaranteed to be free of meat! Vegetarianism is still rather alien to the Czechs and you won't always be met with a great deal of understanding. If you are a vegan eating out is almost impossible.

Eating at home for the vegetarian is much less of a problem as there is a wide variety of vegetables available, although these can be more expensive in winter and the variety is not as wide as in the West. However, for a teacher who is working full-time with a lot of the teaching in the evening and possibly an hour's journey to get home, eating in is not always convenient. You might want to consider bringing you own spices, etc for cooking, as these are not readily available in the Czech Republic.

Cafés, coffee and cakes. The Czechs drink a type of Turkish coffee which is essentially hot water poured over ground coffee in a cup, but espresso coffee is becoming more popular, as is cappuccino in the more up-market places. Coffee is far more popular than tea, and if you are served tea in a cafe it will consist of a teabag and a glass of hot water. If you want lemon you have to ask for it; milk is never offered. For cakes, the place to go is the cake shop (*Cukrárna*). These places often serve ice-cream as well, for which the Czechs have a passion.

Drinking and nightlife. The Czech Republic is one of the finest, and cheapest, places in the world for beer (*pivo*). It produces such famous beers as Budvar and Pilsner Urquell, and there are other beers which, although not as famous, are highly regarded. Try *Braník*, *Velké Popovice* and *Krušovice*. Most of the beer is light, but dark beer is available and tastes like a sweet ale.

Beer comes in different strengths, measured by the specific gravity of the brew and not by the percentage of alcohol. Most beers come in 12° and 10° strengths. The 10° beer is about 3% alcohol.

The Czech Republic also produces some good red and white wines, many of which come from the vineyards of South Moravia. Try *Ryzlink rýnský* and *Silvan* (whites) and *Frankovka* and *Vavřinecké* (reds). Local spirits include plum brandy (*Slivovice*), a gin-like drink made from Juniper berries (*Borovička*) and herbal liquors (*Fernet* and *Becherovka*), which, although an acquired taste, are definitely worth trying. Czechs will tell you they all have medicinal qualities!

Where to drink. The most popular drinking hole is in a beer cellar (*pivnice* or *hostinec*) which generally closes around 10pm or 11pm. These are usually busy establishments which generate a pleasant atmosphere. Patrons are seated at long wooden tables and sharing a table is common; simply ask *Je tu volno?* – Is this place free? You will be served by a waiter who will mark a tab up for the number of drinks you have. When you wish to leave simply say *Platit*. Round the bill up for the tip. Most pubs serve only two kinds of beer. *Svetlé* is light, *černé* dark. If you want half and half say *Řezané*. *Vinárna* are sort of wine bars cum restaurants and are preferred by women (the *pivnice* and *hostinec* being mainly male drinking establishments). A *vinárna* will generally stay open late to around midnight (later if it is a nightclub as well).

Jo's Bar in Prague is a popular ex-pat bar and restaurant and serves Mexican food (open 10am–2am). Some of the best and most famous dark beer in Europe can be drunk at budget prices in U Fleku while soaking up the great atmosphere at this popular bar.

Jo's Bar, Malostranské nám, Prague 1.
U Fleku, Křemencova 11, Prague 1. Tel: 292 436.

Nightlife. In the smaller towns in the country, once the pubs close at around 10pm there is very often little on offer in the way of entertainment. A number of towns have a local disco once or twice a week and that is about it. New bars, clubs, etc are opening up all the time so you have to keep an ear out for the places to go. Your students are always a good source of information.

Although it is not quite on a par yet with Western capitals regarding nightlife, there are several clubs in Prague where you can dance the night away or listen to live music. Most have a small cover charge and beer is a lot more expensive than in the *pivnice*. New places are springing up all the time (and just as many are closing) but for an up-to-date picture of what is happening get hold of a copy of the *Prague Post* or *Prognosis*.

Here are a few nightspots in Prague:

> **Bunker Lodecká 2**, Prague 1. (Every day 6pm–5am. Cover charge. Plays good alternative music with plenty of drinking and jumping around. Live local and overseas bands perform on a regular basis. If you want to cool down and mellow out try the café upstairs.)
>
> **Repre nám**, Republiky r, Prague 1. (In the basement of the wonderful building where Czechoslovakia was signed into existence in 1918. Good atmosphere, live bands and mixed crowd. Cover charge.)
>
> **Radost FX**, Lodecká 2, Prague 1. (Quite an up-market place with café/restaurant upstairs selling vegetarian food.)

Transport

The public transport system throughout the country is clean, cheap and efficient. You can buy tickets (*jízdenky*) at tobacconists (*tabák*), news-stands or from the yellow machines for 6 Kč which can be used on the metro bus or trams. Alternatively you can buy a seven-day, one-month, or three-month pass. You need some form of ID and a passport-sized photo. Failure to show a validated ticket or pass to an inspector will result in an on-the-spot fine. Getting around the country by bus or train is relatively straightforward and cheap.

Trains. Trains operated by the state railways (CD) cover almost every part of the country, and are a pleasant and comfortable way to travel. Since state subsidies have decreased, the price of tickets has gone up, but they still don't cost much. There are basically two types of train: the fast (*rychlík*) trains which stop only at the main towns, and the local (*osobní vlak*) trains which stop at every station and are very slow. In addition, international express trains go to Budapest, Vienna, Berlin, etc. These trains are marked with an R and it is advisable to reserve a seat on these. Tickets can be purchased 48 hours in advance and if you are travelling at the weekend you should make a seat reservation. Getting train information is not always easy and it might be worth investing a few Crowns in a timetable.

One of the advantages of living in the Czech Republic is its location in the centre of Europe, making a number of other countries easily accessible, although travelling to another country can work out expensive on a local salary.

Direct trains operate to the following cities from Prague: Bratislava (4½ hours); Berlin (8½ hours); Budapest (8½ hours); Kraków (14 hours); and Vienna (5 hours).

Buses. Buses are the cheapest way to get around the Czech Republic, and they cover nearly every corner of the country. In some cases it is quicker to take a bus than a train. The state bus company (ČSAD) still operates most of the routes although there are private companies now running, for example CEBUS. Buses between towns start running from as early as 6am when people start to go to work and if you do plan on travelling at this time of day it is a good idea to buy your ticket in advance.

The same applies if you are travelling at the weekend. Tickets can be bought in advance, but for local journeys you can pay the driver when you get on the bus. For luggage that has to be put in the boot you will probably have to pay a few Crowns.

Timetables are posted at the bus stops but are rather difficult to work out. You are better off writing down where you want to go and getting information at the bus station.

Public transport within Prague. In all towns the buses and trams run regularly, and in Prague and Brno there are night buses and trams which run every 40 minutes. Buses and trams operate from 4.30am to 11.30pm daily. Tickets are sold at news-stands, tobacconist's (*tabák*) or metro stations. The tickets must be punched on board and one ticket is valid for one journey. Plain clothed inspectors occasionally come round to check tickets and will show a badge and ask to see your cancelled ticket. Failure to show one will result in a fine. Night buses in Prague have blue numbers in a white box. It is expected that the younger generation, and especially men, will offer their seat for anyone elderly, pregnant, etc.

The metro in Prague with its 'space-age' decor has three lines (A-green, B-yellow, and C-red) and covers the main central areas. It starts running from 5am and stops at midnight. Trains run regularly every 90 seconds at peak times and every three to six minutes off peak.

Tickets must be purchased before travelling at tobacconists, news-stands or from machines at the metro stations and cost 6 Kč. These entitle you to travel for up to 90 minutes on any line and should be punched in the machines at the top of the escalators. You don't need to punch another ticket if you change lines. The same tickets are also used on the buses and trams. Important words to know are *výstup* which means exit, and *přestup* which means connection.

Taxis. There is an abundance of taxis in all towns, especially Prague. They are clearly marked and can be hailed on the street or ordered by phone. Taxis should have a price list displayed on the dashboard and a meter which drivers should switch on at the start of the trip. Make sure they do! Most of the taxis are privately run and are not particularly cheap. Competition between different taxi companies is fierce. If you call a taxi you will be charged from the place where the taxi received the request. It is a good idea to get an estimate of the cost of the journey before you get in and if you have problems ask for a receipt (*účet*) which drivers are obliged to give you. Taxi numbers in Prague include the following:

Profi Taxi. Tel: (02) 61-04-55-55/61-04-55-50
AAA Radio. Taxi: (02) 31-22–112/32-24-44

Shopping

The hours for shops vary but on the whole they open between 6am and 9am and close at 6pm, with small shops sometimes closing for lunch. On Saturdays, most places close at noon, although department stores stay open till 4pm. Everything is closed on Sundays. As yet there are no 24 hour shops and buying anything after 6pm is a problem. Important words you will soon get to know are open (*otevřeno*), closed (*zavřeno*), push (*tam*), and pull (*sem*).

Supermarkets are relatively well stocked and it is possible to buy most types of foodstuffs. In Prague a number of new supermarkets have sprung up selling Western brand names, but at much higher prices than the Czech equivalents. There is not the range of vegetables you would expect back home and the quality is variable. If you shop at one of the open markets, however, you can usually find what you want. Czechs also pickle a lot of food for the winter.

Here are some of the types of shops you may need:

- Barber/Hairdresser's (*Holič/kadeřník*). Very cheap (max 40 Kč). Usually not necessary to book, although some unisex places have special times for men.
- Bookshop (*Knihkupectvi*). Some bookshops have a small section of books in English. Ask *Máte hějake Anglické knihy?* (Do you sell English books?).
- Butcher's (*Maso/Uzeniny*). The price of meat is going up although ham is cheap. You must first order your meat, pay at the cash till and then go back to the counter to collect it.
- Chemist's (*Lékárna*). More and more Western drugs are now stocked, both over-the-counter drugs such as aspirin and prescription drugs. Pharmacies can usually fill foreign prescriptions, but may have to make substitutions. There is always a chemist open 24 hours in most towns.
- Fruit and vegetable shops (*Ovoce and zelenina*). These can be found scattered around each neighbourhood, it is worth locating several as they vary.

- Market (*Trh*). This is the place to go to buy cheap fresh fruit and vegetables. Remember that out of season imported fruit and vegetables are expensive. Markets open around 7am and stay open until all the produce is sold.
- Stationery shops (*Papírnictví*). These shops sell general office supplies, including pens, pencils, paper, posters and exercise books, all at very reasonable prices.
- Supermarkets (*Potraviny*). Most are now privatized and trade under their own names. On the whole they are well stocked, but do not stock much fruit and vegetables. 'K Mart' in Prague and Brno is a good place for toiletries, key cutting, clothes, etc.

Banks and financial matters

Coins come in denominations of 10 h (*hellers*), 20 h, 50 h, 1 Kč (*Koruna*), 2 Kč, 5 Kč, 10 Kč, 20 Kč, 50 Kč; notes are 50 Kč, 100 Kč, 200 Kč, 500 Kč and 1000 Kč.

Few teachers living in the Czech Republic bother to open a bank account although this is possible and relatively easy. You must take a letter in Czech from your employer, proving employment and a regular monthly salary, and your passport for identification. You may want to ask a Czech speaker to go along with you in case there are any language problems (the process sometimes depends on the goodwill of the particular bank clerk you have to deal with). In Prague the Česká Spořitelna bank opens bank accounts for foreigners.

It is also possible to open a hard currency account at a Czech bank with a minimum deposit of around $1000, although this varies from place to place. One bank which does open hard currency accounts is the 'Československá Obchodní Banka, A' which can be found in most cities. A bank account is obviously useful for getting money transferred to the Czech Republic as otherwise this can be difficult and time-consuming. It is often easier to have funds sent to a bank in Germany or Austria and to collect the money from there. Having some Eurocheques is therefore very useful. Major credit cards are becoming more widely accepted in the larger cities, although not as yet in smaller towns. The Czech Republic is still very much a cash society.

Centrally located banks in Prague can be found on Václavské náměstí 42 and Na příkopé 5, 14, 20, 28 and 42. Most are open Monday–Friday 8am to 5pm but close for an hour at lunchtime, usually at mid-day. Komercni banka at 42 is open until 7pm and from 9am to 2pm on Saturdays

American Express, Václavské náměstí 56. Tel: (02) 22-94-87. Fax: (02) 26-15-06.

Health

Western drugs and medicines are becoming more common, although you should bring a supply of any medication you take regularly, including over-the-counter items, and basic first-aid supplies. Tampons are available, as are condoms, but you might be advised to bring your own supply nonetheless.

The health care system is adequate, if still a little outdated. When you need to see a doctor find out where your local clinic is and register. Ideally you should do this as soon as you are settled in long-term accommodation. Take your residence permit along, or some proof that you are legally employed, and your insurance card. If you need to see a doctor before you have received your insurance card, take a letter from the school.

The doctors do not generally speak English, although they may speak some German. You may find it easier to take a Czech along to interpret. Private health care is relatively inexpensive.

In Prague there is a special hospital which is used by foreign personnel at Na Homolce. It caters for outpatients as well as emergencies, and also carries out dental treatment. Before a check-up you need to pay a 1 000 Kč deposit, part of which will be returned depending on the treatment given. Emergency treatment is given free of charge.

> **Clinic for Foreigners**, Na Homolce 724, Motol Prague 5. Tel: 5292-2146 (daytime)/5292-1111 (emergencies).

Launderettes and dry cleaners

Launderettes (*Čistírna*) are few and far between in all cities and towns in the Czech Republic. If you do manage to find one it will usually offer dry cleaning as well which can take anything from three days to three weeks. In Prague there are a couple of launderettes where you can do your own washing, but these are rather expensive.

> **Laundryland**, Londýnská Prague 2. Tel: (02) 25-11-24. (Open seven days 8am–10pm.)
> **Laundry Kings**, Dejvicka 16 (at Hradčanská Metro stop). (Coin operated washer and dryer, open seven days 8am–10pm.)

Libraries and bookshops

All towns which have a university and English department have libraries containing English books, otherwise the British Council and the USIS are your best bet.

The British Council library in Prague on Narodni 10 near the National Theatre is open Monday–Friday, (Monday, Wednesday,

Friday, 9am–12pm; and Monday, Tuesday, Thursday, 1pm–4pm) and has a wide range of books. The library also has a reading room, newspapers, TV and a resource centre with a good selection of EFL materials.

The British Council has resource centres in other parts of the country which not only contain a wide selection of ELT books, cassettes, videotapes, newspapers and magazines, but organize a regular programme of seminars given by British Council and guest lecturers. They also provide a regular meeting place for English teachers (see p 103).

United States Information Service (USIS) in Prague operates a lending library at Volek House, Vlašská 17, close to the US Embassy. It has a large collection of books, magazines and videotapes and is open Monday–Thursday 10am–5pm and Friday 10am–3pm. Unfortunately only Czechs are allowed to withdraw books.

Usually one or two shops can be found in the large cities selling English books, both for ELT purposes and general reading, but with a very limited range. Bring a few books with you as you will always find someone to swap with. English bookshops in Prague include the following:

Bohemian Venture Bookstores, Filosofická Fakulta, Charles University, Nam. Jana Palacha 2, Prague 1. Tel: (02) 231 9516. (Ground floor to the left.)

The Globe Bookstore and Coffeehouse, Janovského 14 Prague 7. (This is a popular second hand bookshop and coffee shop near Vltavská metro run by six Americans. Many people come to buy and browse through a range of quality second hand and a number of new English-language books. You can also purchase English language newspapers here and sit and enjoy a good cappuccino. This is an excellent place to meet people who have been in Prague a while.)

Post

Post offices generally open from 8am to 7pm during the week. The main post office in Prague is open 24 hours and is located at Jindřišska 14, Prague 1. As the post does not always get through, it is not advisable to send money, and packages sent through the post should be registered (*doporučene*). Letters to the USA take 10 days to two weeks and to the UK a few days. You may want mail to be sent to the Poste Restante found in most towns. This can often be safer and quicker than having it sent to your flat. Take some ID (preferably your passport) along to collect mail.

Addresses and telephone numbers

Czech addresses always start with the street name followed by the number. Some terms which will become familiar and their abbreviations are: ulice/ul. (street); náměstí/nám (square); třída/tr (avenue); and nábřeží/nabr (embankment). ul. is often left out of addresses.

The correct way to address an envelope is:

Name	Paul Thomas
Street name followed by number	Zborovska 23
Post/zip code, town, post district	11000 Prague, 1
Country	Czech Republic

Telephone numbers indicated in this book do not include the country code (+42).

Public telephones

The telephone system, like most of those in Eastern and Central Europe, is not very reliable. It is not easy to make local calls from phone boxes, let alone international ones, but things are improving. You are better making international calls from the post office or large hotels where you can also call collect or use a phone credit card. If you are lucky enough to have a phone in your flat be careful as international calls are expensive. It is a lot cheaper to phone the Czech Republic than phone from it.

Most public telephones in Prague are now card-operated and these are rapidly appearing in other cities. Phonecards can be bought from post offices, *tabak* shops or at one of the many news-stands or shops displaying the yellow and blue sign. Coin-operated telephones are still widely used in the country.

It is important to note that over the next few years telephone numbers will be changing throughout the country as it switches to a digital system.

Helplines are as follows: police (158); fire (150); ambulance (155); airport (36-77-40); train information (23-53-836); taxi 24 hour service (20-29-51/20-39-41); Emergency Medical Aid (in English) (29-93-81); Foreigners' Medical Clinic (Na Homolce) (52-92-21-46/52-92-21-91 after hours); lost Visa, Diner's Club card (23-66-688); lost Mastercard (23-92-21-35); lost American Express card (23-524-68); and Central Customs Authority (23-22-270).

International dialing codes are as follows: Canada (00 42 000 151); UK (00 42 004 401); US AT&T (00 42 000 101;) and US MCI (00 42 000 112).

Swimming pools

There are several public indoor and outdoor swimming pools in Prague as well as those at the larger hotels. The largest complex is Podolí, with a large indoor area and an outdoor pool heated for swimming in winter.

Podolí Complex, Plavecký Stadion Podolí. Tel: 43 91 52.

Media, culture and sport

Television and radio. Czech TV has three channels, none of which is particularly exciting, and nearly all foreign films and series are dubbed. In addition there is satellite and cable TV, including CNN and MTV which is becoming increasingly popular. In the south of the Czech Republic you can also pick up Austrian channels.

A number of FM stations play European and American pop music and the BBC World Service (101.1 MHz) is easy to pick up in the major cities. Radio Metropolis in Prague (106.2 FM) broadcasts in both Czech and English, as does Radio Hady in Brno (88.3 FM). A full programme for the World Service can be picked up free in the British Council resource centres. Central Europe Today is a regional news programme in English, available only in Prague.

Newspapers. A wide variety of international publications are available in Prague, including the main British and American dailies, although they are expensive. They can be purchased from hotels as well as at some news-stands. International newspapers are difficult to get in other parts of the country, but it is possible to find them in larger cities such as Brno and Ostrava.

In addition to the foreign publications, there are two locally printed English-language papers, the *Prague Post* and *Prognosis*. The *Prague Post* comes out once a week on Friday and provides general local news as well as listings. *Prognosis*, whose format is similar, comes out fortnightly, also on a Friday. Both can be purchased at many of Prague's news-stands, but are difficult to find outside the capital.

Music

Classical. A number of renowned composers come from the Czech Republic including Dvořák, Smetana and Janáček, and in the major towns there are numerous classical concerts throughout the year. Major music festivals are held throughout the year in the big cities, the largest being the international music festival held in Prague each May.

When possible buy tickets at the box office rather than through agencies, which tend to charge more.

Folk music and jazz. The Czech Republic has a great tradition of folk music and it is still widely popular especially in the country. You are unlikely to see people dressed in traditional costumes though, except at one of the many festivals of song and dance held in various parts of the country. Jazz is making a comeback, especially in Prague, although it is very limited elsewhere. In October the capital plays host to one of the best jazz festivals in Europe.

Rock and pop. There are not many good original bands playing in the Czech Republic, and most of the best musicians tend to play mainly in Prague. Heavy metal is popular among young people and mainstream pop music is played in the clubs and discos. Prague usually attracts several big name bands at some point during the year. Pink Floyd, for example, performed in 1994.

Cinema and theatre. Cinemas can be found throughout the country, with a large proportion showing films in English. In the Czech Republic Western films tend to be subtitled rather than dubbed, although box-office Hollywood movies are dubbed. Going to the cinema is cheap and popular, so go early to get a ticket.

Although cinemas can be a little uncomfortable, there is a relaxed atmosphere about them, and people often take their own food along to eat during the film.

Theatre likewise is popular and inexpensive, but you will rarely find anything in English. Four amateur groups occasionally put on plays in Prague. However, most cities and towns have a permanent theatre which is worth visiting, even if you do not understand everything that is going on. The puppet theatres are especially worth seeing.

In Prague a full list of what is on and where can be found in the *Prague Post* or *Prognosis*. There is also a Czech paper called the *Program* which has comprehensive listings and comes out once a week. For films look out for *české titulky* which means Czech subtitles.

Sport

There are plenty of opportunities both to participate in and to watch sport in the Czech Republic.

The national sport is football, followed very closely by ice-hockey, which is played throughout the winter. Probably the most famous football team is Sparta Prague, which usually supplies a number of players to the national side each year, although crowds usually average less than 10 000. Games are played on Sunday afternoons, are cheap and tickets can be bought at the gate.

Ice-hockey is very popular and games are well supported. Sparta Prague are usually the team everyone is trying to beat. Games are played on Tuesday and Friday around 6pm although there are also games on Sundays.

The Czech Republic is famous for producing such tennis players as Martina Navratilova and Ivan Lendl (both now US citizens whose careers are now over), and the game is widely popular.

In winter many people take to the ski slopes, although the best resorts are in Slovakia. There are, however, resorts in Bohemia and Moravia. Skiing is cheap, but the facilities are generally not very good and there are long waits for lifts.

If you like walking or rock climbing then there are plenty of opportunities for both.

City by city

Brno. The capital of the ancient land of Moravia, now a region of the Czech Republic, is Brno (pronouned Burno with a trilled 'r'). It is situated 100 mile south-east of Prague and just 75 miles north of Vienna. It is also within easy reach of Slovakia, Hungary and Poland. There are regular trains and buses from Prague.

Brno has a population nearing 500 000. It is primarily an industrial city, particularly for the machine industry, although it does not suffer from some of the more obvious problems usually associated with the presence of heavy industry. This is partly due to its relatively open position and spacious layout, and to the fact that it has few traffic problems. Brno is also an important university town.

The architecture of the centre is typical of the Austro-Hungarian era, and there are several beautiful and peaceful areas in the old city, particularly near the cathedral.

There are numerous theatres, cinemas, art galleries and concert halls. Brno has its own opera house and philharmonic orchestra, as well as a number of traditional and experimental theatre companies. There are also over 12 cinemas, a number showing films in English.

The pace of life is slow and at weekends the city can seem quite deserted as people head off to the countryside. As in most towns in the Czech Republic Brno tends to shut down at 10pm during the week, although there are now a considerable variety of pubs, restaurants and clubs, some of which stay open to 5am. Brno is also home to one of the largest discos in Europe at the Bobby Centre. This huge complex has a hotel, squash courts and roller-skating and is popular although it is expensive by Czech standards. Throughout the year Brno plays host to several international trade fairs as well as to a music and theatre festival in October.

There are a number of private language schools in Brno and over 20 schools are listed in the Yellow Pages, although there are others. Of these there are very few who insist on employing only qualified native speakers. The larger schools are ILC, Travel 2002, the State Language School and MKM (see p 98).

Urgent accommodation can be arranged by the Accommodation Service:

> **Accommodation Service**, 2nd floor, nám. Svobody, 10 (Main square opposite McDonalds, private rooms from 250 Kč ($8) a night.)

The Čedok office on Divadelní can also arrange private rooms.

The main information office keeps a list of all language schools in Brno which it sells for a few crowns. The information office is situated in the same building as the British Council at Radnická 8.

> **British Council Resource Centre**, Radnická 8, PO Box 726, 663 26 Brno. Tel: (05) 42-21-27-74. Fax: (05) 42-21-29-38.

Places to go in the evening include:

> **Áčko (The Architects Club)** Starobrněská 16. (Through the court-yard and upstairs. Small laid back bar and coffee house popular with an arty crowd and ex-pats. Serves food and stays open late.)
>
> **Bolka Polívka** (Theatre bar of theatre of same name just off Jakubska. Open all night.)
>
> **Memphis** (Alternative bar opposite new town hall on Dominikanske Námesti.)
>
> **Pegas**, Jakubska 8 (Off Censka near the main square. Beer hall which brews the beer on the premises. Popular drinking hole with some great beer.)

Ostrava. Ostrava, the centre of Silesia, is primarily a coal and steel town and suffers from serious air pollution as a result. With a population of over 330 000 it is the third largest city in the Czech Republic. It is on the border with Poland and a large part of the population is Polish. It has several cinemas and theatres. It only takes half an hour to get from the city to the countryside.

Demand for English is high, and there are several private language schools in Ostrava, details of which can be found in the Yellow Pages. You should also visit the British Council resource centre which may also be able to give you some advice.

Urgent accommodation can be arranged at the Čedok office:

> **Čedok**, Nádražní 9. (Can arrange private rooms and has a list of hotels.)

The British Council Resource Centre is at:

British Council, Masarykovo nám 21 (POB 45) 701 45 Ostrava. Tel: (069) 23 19 20. Fax: (069) 23 17 19.

Plzeň. Plzeň (Pilsen in German) with a population of 175 000 is the second largest city in West Bohemia after Prague. It is home to arguably the best beer in the world, but wins no prizes for beauty, being a major industrial city.

In 1994 there were about 150–200 native speakers of English teaching here. There are no particular pubs where you can meet native speaker teachers, although the British Council resource centre is a popular meeting point.

From Prague it is about one and a half hours by train to Plzeň. The two cities are also connected by bus. Both stations are close to the centre.

Urgent accommodation can be arranged at the Čedok office:

Čedok, Prešovská 10. (Can arrange private rooms and gives advice on hotels.)

The British Council Resource Centre is at:

British Council, nám. Republiky 12 301 13 Plzeň. Tel: (019) 337 76. Fax: (019) 371 41.

The country and the people

The Czech Republic has existed since January 1993 and before that shared only 74 years with Slovakia as one country, Czechoslovakia. Currently the population stands at 10.3 million with the capital Prague by far the largest city with 1.26 million inhabitants. Other sizeable towns are Brno, Ostrava and Plzeň. It is an industrialized country in transition from a centrally-planned system to a market economy.

With a long tradition in general engineering and some consumer-orientated industries, such as Bohemian glass, the country is presently in need of western capital and managerial skills.

Prague, the country's heart and cultural centre, is widely recognized as one of the most beautiful cities in the world with its wealth of unique historical monuments and medieval, byzantine and baroque buildings. Everyone who visits it is overwhelmed by its splendour. Other towns and cities, while not comparable to Prague, nonetheless have their own beauty, and many still retain the old squares and historical buildings untouched for centuries. Hundreds of castles and chateaux stretch across the country, many restored and open to the public.

History

BC	The Celtic Boii tribes inhabit the area and name it Bohemia.
AD	
4th century	Germanic tribes conquer Celts.
6th century	West Slavs settle in area of what is now the Czech Republic.
9th century	Czechs secede from the Great Moravian Empire and form an independent state.
929	The first of the Přemysl's princes, Václav, is murdered by his brother. He becomes the patron saint of the Czechs and is the King Wenceslas in the well-known carol.
13th century	The Czech state becomes a kingdom and reaches its peak under Přemysl Otakar II from 1253 to 1278.
1310–1346	John of Luxembourg gains the Bohemian throne through marriage to Eliška Přemyslovna and annexes the kingdom to the German Empire.
1415	Jan Hus, a clergyman who tried to reform the church and society, also seen as the first protestant, is burnt at the stake in Constance on 6 July 1415.
1419–34	The Hussite Wars.
1490	Vladislav Jagellovský merges the Bohemian and Hungarian states.
1526–1918	Following the battle of Mohacs, the Austrian Habsburg dynasty ascends to the thrones of Hungary and Bohemia and begins 400 years of Habsburg rule.
1618	Thirty Years' War begins in Prague.
1740–1780	Reign of Maria Theresa.
1781–1850	National revival movement in the Czech lands.
1848	First Austrian Parliament.
1866	War between Austria and Prussia is fought on Czech lands. The Czechs fight alongside the Austrians.
1914–1918	First World War.
1918	Formation of the Czechoslovakian Republic as an independent state.
1938–1945	Germans occupy Second Republic.
1945	Uprising in Prague. The Red Army moves in and liberates country.
1948	Communist coup, an estimated 2 million Czechs and Slovaks flee.
1960	Czechoslovakia is proclaimed a socialist state.
1967	Liberalization process begins.
1968	Novotný succeeded by Alexander Dubček as party secretary. Start of what became known as 'The Prague Spring'. Socialism with a human face. Censorship was removed. In August nearly half a million troops from the Soviet Union, Poland and Hungary invaded the country. The Soviet Army withdrew from the country only in 1991.
1969	Jan Palach, a student, burns himself to death in Prague in

	protest against the occupation by Soviet troops and the acquiescence of the Czechoslovak leadership towards the Soviets.
1977	Charter 77 dissident movement founded.

1989 The Velvet Revolution

By late 1989 Czechoslovakia, Albania and Romania were the only countries in Eastern Europe left believing in the old ideals, and in November, the first of several peaceful mass demonstrations ended violently. The economy of this time was deteriorating rapidly and there were splits in the KSČ leadership. Václav Havel brought opposition groups together, and Civil Forum was formed, demanding the resignation of the leadership.

Following an address by Alexander Dubček, the ousted 1968 leader, to a crowd of over 250 000 people in Prague, the government resigned. A national strike and further demonstrations followed before a provisional 'Government of National Understanding' was formed and multi-party elections were planned for June 1990.

On 29 December 1989, Václav Havel a playwright and one of the prime instigators of the 'Velvet Revolution' was elected President by a unanimous vote.

In the spring of 1990 laws on private enterpreneurship were adopted, and in June representatives of the anti-communist civic movements won free parliamentary elections. Pro-market reforms introduced in 1991 had a negative impact on the living standards of part of population, and unemployment became a problem in Slovakia.

In 1993 Czechoslovakia split into the Czech Republic and Slovakia, the so-called Velvet Divorce. Following the elections in June 1992 when the left-wing Movement for a Democratic Slovakia (HZDS) won a majority in Slovakia and the right-wing ODS won a majority in the Czech Republic, it was always going to be an uphill struggle to keep the Federation together.

The Slovaks, who had always resented being ruled from Prague, were fully behind the HZDS leader Vladimir Mečiar, who had promised to declare sovereignty should he gain power. Mečiar was also keen to cushion the move towards a free market economy, whereas the ODS was committed to privatization at a faster pace. The two sides failed to reach agreement and sovereignty was declared. The HZDS also blocked Havel's re-election. The two countries became independent on 1 January 1993. While a lot of Czechs were initially disappointed with the split, they have now become resigned to it, and arguably it is the Slovaks who are having second thoughts as to its merits.

Geography

The Czech Republic is a land-locked country covering 78 864 square kilometres and is located in the geographical centre of Europe with borders onto Germany, Poland, Slovakia and Austria. It comprises three historical lands: Bohemia, Moravia and Silesia.

Although there are large areas of arable land, with lowlands located mainly in the centre of the country, it has two distinct mountain ranges and large areas of forests. The highest Czech peak, Sněžka (1 602 metres), is in the Krkonoše Mountains. The longest river is the Vltava (433 kilometres); the other main river being the Labe ('Elbe').

Climate

The climate is mild with four distinct seasons. The summers tend to be warm and sunny with average temperatures around 20°C and the winters are cool and humid with temperatures averaging −5°C. However, winters can get very cold with temperatures falling well below freezing, down to −20°C in the mountains. In January and February, expect snow, which usually covers the whole country.

The environment

Like many parts of the former 'Eastern bloc' countries, the Czech Republic suffers from over 40 years of neglect of the environment. Air pollution is quite bad in many of the main towns and cities, especially in winter when smog is common. If you do suffer from asthma or other respiratory problems, you should check out the place where you intend to work first.

It is also worth noting that the Czechs smoke a lot, and if anything smoking is on the increase with the promotion of cigarettes from Western manufacturers. It is rare, for instance, to find restaurants with non-smoking sections and in fact many public places are not smoke free.

While the crime rate is very low by Western standards, it is on the increase. One can still feel safe walking the streets alone at night, although care should nevertheless be taken. One thing to watch out for, especially in Prague, is pickpockets, who make a good living from foreigners.

Politics and religion

Politics. Václav Havel is the current President of the Czech Republic, although he is not a member of any political party. He is still widely popular and influential, but less so now than a few years ago.

Parliamentary elections are held every four years with the next ones scheduled for 1996. The electoral system is one of proportional representation. Citizens must be 18 years old to vote and most people do exercise their vote. In the elections in June 1990, 99% of those eligible to vote did so.

In 1994 the coalition government was made up of the following parties: the Civil Democratic Party; the Civil Democratic Alliance; and two Christian Democratic parties.

The Civil Democratic Party led by the Czech Prime Minister Václav Klaus promotes pro-market reforms and is supported by over 30% of the population.

Religion. The Czech Republic is predominantly Roman Catholic although 40 years of communist rule weakened the power of the church. Believers who openly practised their faith were discriminated against by the state, and were not only banned from joining the party, but were not allowed to work in educational establishments.

The Communists closed down many churches and turned them over to other uses. It is only since 1989 that the church has claimed back some of its land and property, although it is still difficult to get in to see a church unless there is a service on.

The once thriving Jewish population has all but disappeared, and there are only around 2 000 Jews left in the country. Other religious orders include Protestants, Moravian Bretheran, Hussites and Lutherans.

The people

The Czechs are often referred to as quiet, reserved people and this may in part have been due to 40 years of communist rule; 'instead of applying force we had to apply with it', as any Czech will tell you. There was a sense of resignation after the events of 1968, and people tended to keep very much to themselves and their own immediate family and friends. In fact this was encouraged by the government in order to keep people form interfering in matters of state.

Nevertheless, Czechs are hospitable people who will happily welcome you into their home and ply you with drink and food. Their hospitality will also extend to invitations to excursions and skiing trips. It is not unusual for Czechs to stop and offer help should you look lost.

Topics of conversation today often revolve around football and ice-hockey, at least among the men, but do not worry if you know nothing about either subject, as they will have lots of questions ready for you. These will range from the standard 'Why did you come here?' to questions about your home country. Czechs find it difficult to talk about politics, religion or their dreams; yet are quite willing to talk about intimate matters such as family problems. Czechs find it strange that a single woman should come to their country on her own.

Men in general are very adaptable, and can usually turn their hand to most things, from fixing a car to building a house. They are not particularly argumentative people and whenever there are two Czechs having an argument there is always a third one who will be calming it. They have a love hate relationship with authority and problems are often blamed on others. Gypsies and 'foreigners', for example, tend to be scapegoats, demonstrating a slightly racial element to the Czech character.

Habits and customs. If invited to a Czech home for dinner, it is customary to take along some flowers, and perhaps something to drink. You should be prepared to get drunk, even if this is not your intention, as you will be offered excessive amounts of alcohol! You will find that even your polite refusals are interpreted as yes or at best ignored.

You should also note that if you pop in to see someone for an hour, you could well end up staying for six.

When you enter a Czech home it is customary to take your shoes off, unless it is a formal dinner or your host or hostess indicates otherwise. You may be given some 'slippers' to wear or you may be left standing in your socks, so make sure they are clean!

Entering a pub or a restaurant, it it customary for the man to enter first.

When friends greet each other they will generally just say *ahoj* which is the equivalent of the English or American saying hi, or *dobrý den* meaning good day. Handshaking is the usual form of greeting for the first time, although it is not common to see Czechs shaking hands with their friends every time they meet each other, as in some countries. Certain traditions are attached to shaking hands, for example, it is the woman who usually offers her hand to be shaken first, and if two men greet each other, the older will offer his hand first. Of course these traditions are not always adhered to, but it is important at least to be aware of them. Czechs very rarely kiss each other as a form of greeting. Before starting the meal Czechs usually say *dobrou chuť* (bon appetit).

Name days (*svátky* or *jmeniny*) are at least as important as birthdays and are celebrated as such. Women usually receive flowers and a kiss, while the men especially like to get drunk on such occasions.

Typical lives. Before 1989 it was easier to make generalizations on what a typical life was for a Czech than it is now. The changes since 1990 have in some form or other affected everybody's lives, some for the better some for the worse. On the whole though, the standard of living in the Czech Republic is considered to be relatively high in comparison with other post-communist countries. As can be seen from the number of big Western cars around Prague, some people have reaped the rewards of capitalism, yet at the other end of the scale others have lost their jobs, and sometimes their homes, and live on what little resources they have.

It is common for a Czech couple to have two children, although it is becoming popular for a lot of parents today to have only one due to the current economic climate. From the age of three they will attend kindergarten, and then from five or six primary school. Children work hard at school and spend their evenings doing homework.

Couples generally marry young, especially in the country where it is common for girls to marry in their early twenties. There is a trend away from this now as people realise more and more they have to concentrate on getting a job first and earning some money. In a lot of ways since 1989 life has become harder for young people as they do not have the support systems that were there previously. Once married, a couple will probably live in a small flat which is either rented from the state or collectively owned. Almost half of the Czech Republic's population live in family-owned homes, one-fifth live in co-operative flats and the rest live in private, municipal and state flats. It is difficult for young couples to own their flats and the construction of new flats has slowed down. Rent is low by Western standards but can still be a lot for a couple with children on an average Czech salary of 6 000 Kč ($200) a month.

A lot of new housing blocks built over the last few years are very unsightly and have quickly fallen into disrepair. Couples wanting to move out of such areas often try to build their own houses, which can take years. Because Czechs live in fairly cramped conditions, they are sometimes surprised when they see a teacher living alone in a two-room flat.

Czechs are traditionally family-centred although the divorce rate is also high, and the woman will in nearly all cases have custody of the children and home, and receive maintenance. Women are also entitled to maternity leave. By law women are equal to men, however feminism doesn't really exist and the Czech Republic is very much organized along gender roles. There are no real indications to show women are ready to fight to bring about changes in men's attitudes and sexism is common. Men are still obliged to do 18 months military service, although conscientious objectors do 27 months in the Civil Service.

Husband and wife both normally work, with a usual working week being 42 hours. The minimum annual holiday is three weeks. Work starts early and trams and buses get busy from 6am. Consequently Czechs go to bed early so be careful not to phone after 9.30pm. The working week is Monday to Friday. A lot of people living in the city have cottages (*chalupa*) in the country which they escape to at the weekend or whenever they can, to do their gardening. Apart from allotments and gardens Czechs may spend their evenings watching TV and their weekends walking in the hills. They also enjoy theatre and cinema and the men especially like to enjoy a drink after work.

PART 3
TEACHING ENGLISH

English today is one of the two most important, as well as one of the most widely spoken, foreign languages in the Czech Republic; the other is German. More and more people are starting to learn English which is the main language for commercial and scientific contacts with other countries and for Czech organizations and institutions dealing with foreign visitors and tourists. As a means of instruction, English is used only in university English Departments. However, there are secondary and tertiary schools where individual subjects are taught in English.

The Czech education system

- Kindergarten (*mateřská škola*), 3–6 years;
- Primary school (*základní škola*), 6 years plus;
- Secondary school (*gymnasia*), 11–18 years or 14–18 years;
- Specialized secondary schools, 14/15–18 years;
- Secondary vocational schools, 14/15–18 years; and
- University/college, 18/19 years.

The beginnings of education in what is now the Czech Republic were connected with the church schools in the 9th and 10th century monastries. The first lay schools were recorded as early as the 13th century.

An important stimulus to the development of education was the founding in 1348 of Prague university by Czech King and Roman Emperor Charles IV. The university, which was the most ancient institution of higher learning in Central Europe and became a centre of both church and lay education, greatly influenced the development of education and, later, the process of national self-awareness. The most ancient university providing technical instruction is Prague's Czech Technical University (CVUT).

After the rise of the independent Czechoslovak state in 1918, schools underwent a marked development. A network of common schools was completed, the number of secondary schools increased, and new universities came into existence. Existing side by side with Czech and Slovak schools of every type was a network of schools and universities for ethnic minorities.

In the period following the Communist putsch of February 1948, several reforms of the school system were carried out. Their characteristic mark was an attempt to fashion a uniform school system subordinated to Communist ideology and central control. Those reforms changed not only the content, methods, and forms of instruction but also traditional school names, the length of classes, and the length of compulsory attendance.

With a system of central, directed control and heavy ideological bias of the curriculum, combined with suppression of any criticism, any positive change was impossible.

Since 1989, as in other countries in Eastern and Central Europe, the education system, including the provision of English teaching in schools, has been undergoing changes. Uniform state education was dismantled, opening the way for the creation of private and church schools and multiple-grade *gymnasia*. Education today is free at all levels, and compulsory between the ages of six to sixteen.

There have already been a number of reforms since 1989 which have seen Russian almost all but disappear from the classroom to be replaced mainly by English. This has led to a huge re-training of Russian teachers to teach other subjects, including English. This has had its problems, with some teachers only a couple of lessons ahead of their students in terms of their own level of English.

Children attend kindergarten (*mateřská škola*) from the age of three, and a growing number of kindergartens are now offering English. At this age though teaching English is simply through songs, games and rhymes. Children then move onto the basic/primary school (*Základní škola*) which is divided into two levels. In the first level they are taught by a single teacher but from the second level (11–15) each subject is taught by a different teacher. Talented students are taken care of in basic schools with an extended curriculum of languages and maths, in sporting schools, etc.

Pupils have their knowledge tested in oral and written examinations, where they are graded on a 1–5 scale (see grading p 131).

In recent years, basic school education has undergone a number of changes. Schoolteachers' powers have been greatly enhanced. Classes are taught from adjusted curricula giving teachers greater freedom of instruction and a choice of textbooks. Curricula have been adjusted and are no longer a binding norm. Gradual transformation of the basic school system has sought to change the overall school atmosphere. Pupils can once again attend religion classes.

During a transition period, high-scoring pupils can leave basic school after eighth grade and enroll in a medium-level school. Private and church schools are established at basic school level, a number of which are using alternative forms of instruction.

Students are then enrolled in secondary schools on the basis of their basic school results and the results of admission exams. Since 1991 adjusted curricula and scheduling in schools has meant that they are now acquiring an individuality that is expected to replace their former uniform cast.

Methods used in the classroom

Traditional methods of instruction such as grammar translation and rote learning are still evident in the classroom, although so-called 'communicative methodology' is being adopted and practised more and more. This shift has been helped by the introduction of new coursebooks, and the influx of qualified native English teachers and trainers. Naturally it is hard to change the way Czech teachers have been teaching English; changes are not going to happen overnight, but new methodologies are gradually being adopted. At the same time Czech teachers still use traditional methods they feel comfortable with. Teachers will, for example, use texts for analysis and then teach vocabulary, usually through translation. For all the criticism teachers receive they have produced excellent results and a high academic standard. In recent years there has been a lot of teacher training to English teachers, which is now bearing fruit.

Interestingly, the changes which are happening in the field of English language teaching are bringing about conflict with other departments, which is exacerbated by the fact that many schools do not have a staffroom as such, so teachers do not have the opportunity to meet and exchange ideas.

The kind of language needed

The majority of students studying English in private language schools attend general English courses rather than an ESP course.

A large proportion of these use English at work (especially in the tourist industry) or for travelling. The level of students ranges from beginner to advanced; however the number of genuine beginners is decreasing and it is still rare to find a proficiency student. There is a growing demand for business English which will increase as the general level of fluency goes up and as foreign trade connections increase. The demand for younger learner classes is growing fast as parents recognize the value of modern languages. Related to this is the widespread popularity of exam courses (especially FCE) because a pass can help students' careers or increase the chance of a university place. Cambridge exam courses are being offered in secondary schools and there is a growing interest in the US TOEFL exam. Students with past learning experience in English generally have a firm base in grammar, but need to improve their speaking and writing skills.

In the *gymnazium* especially, students need to improve their spoken skills which they will have had little chance to practise. This job is invariably thrust upon the native speaker with the Czech teacher dealing with the grammar. When teaching 'conversational classes' the more authentic the material you use, the more interested your students will be. Interesting articles from newspapers and teenage magazines usually prove successful. Learners like acquiring vocabulary and learning dialogues, while on the other hand they dislike anything which makes them think on the spot, or where they have to use their imagination. By giving them advance warning of topics you are going to be dealing with, they will have time to prepare and the results will be much better.

Of course students need to develop all the four skills and your role should be to help them do this as well as making them aware that the language learning process takes a lot of time and effort. In school, however, their primary goal if English is their chosen foreign language is to pass the English exam in the *Maturita*, and your role should be to facilitate this.

Grading

In state schools grades are given on a scale of 1 to 5 with 1 being the highest and 5 the lowest. Grades are given for all subjects and a record must be kept by the teacher. Normally you will be asked to discuss grades with your Czech colleague for classes you share, but do not be surprised if your opinion is sometimes disregarded. This can be very frustrating, but there is generally very little you can do about it.

Exams

As a rule, 'exams' are seen by students as something where they will be asked to write a lot, and 'tests' are multiple choice answers only. The state English exam (*státni zkouška*) can only be taken at one of the state language schools (*státni jazyková škola*), found in nearly every town, and it is held at two levels, elementary (comparable to the Cambridge Preliminary English Test) and intermediate (roughly equivalent to the Cambridge First Certificate). It takes the form of a written paper, listening and oral, and includes topics on British or American life and institutions. There is no translation. This exam is recognized only within the Czech Republic, and therefore other exams such as the Cambridge Exams administered by the British Council, and the US TOEFL exam are becoming increasingly popular.

Before leaving the *gymnazium*, every student must sit the *Maturita*, their final exam. This is made up of four subjects, of which Czech and a foreign language are compulsory. Two others can be chosen from a range of subjects such as history, biology, chemistry, geography. Some pupils may opt to do two foreign languages in their *Maturita*. Before gaining a place at university students must also sit an entrance exam. Essentially, admission is based on successfully passing this, plus a successful record of secondary school attendance and final exams. Competition for university and college places to study English is fierce, even though more places are now being offered. A student who is unsuccessful can reapply the following year, which many people do, usually after further study at a private language school.

Czech students

Czech students attending English courses at a private language school are probably there for one of the following reasons. They may be there for social reasons, although this is becoming less frequent; they may need English for their work, either now or in the future; or they may simply want to use the language to travel or study in an English-speaking country.

Czech students attending courses in private language schools are on the whole hard working and motivated to learn. Generally they have to pay a lot of money, and are therefore sacrificing other things in order to gain knowledge of a language which they see as essential.

Because of the high fees, a fairly high percentage of learners come from the better-off families. Students are very appreciative of having a native speaker of English as their teacher, and will respect such a teacher as long as they see that he or she is trained and competent. There is less tolerance now of the untrained teacher who clearly has no idea about teaching and students are now beginning to protest about such teachers. Most students have been used to the traditional grammar translation method of teaching and, although they may sometimes like to cling on to the traditional approach, they are open to and respond to a more communicative approach as long as they can see the value and methodology behind it. Ease them in slowly, making sure you explain the rationale behind what you are doing.

Students expect the teacher to make them work hard and to give them homework, which on the whole they will do, and they are especially keen on correction. You will find your students in the main friendly, and fairly lively once they get to know you.

In a state school students can vary from highly motivated to uninterested and bored. Those that fall into the latter category are usually the ones that are not taking English in their final *Maturita* exam, and therefore do not see an immediate need to learn it.

However, if the teacher can find topics that stimulate and motivate the students they will show interest. Students at first may appear shy and unwilling to speak in class. This is partly due to the fear of making mistakes and being marked down. Students also find it difficult to formulate arguments in English and discuss.

Students will stand when the teacher walks into the classroom, and this respect is usually sincere. On the whole students have definite ideas on what a teacher should be and initially it will take a little time for them to get to know you and vice versa. For some you may be the first native teacher they have met, let alone had as their teacher. Again, this will add to their inhibitions, yet at the same time arouse their curiosity and interest. Students call teachers by their first name, and once they know you better you will receive invites to the school dances, excursions, etc. All in all Czech students are quite teacher-friendly.

Cheating

Be prepared for your students to try and cheat in tests and exams, especially if marks are being given and recorded. This can take the form of whispering answers or swapping papers and in many cases is quite blatant. Students caught cheating may be surprised if you give them a low grade, as 'helping a friend' is not seen as such a terrible thing. This does not mean you should let it go, and Czech teachers do not generally approve of cheating, punishing students who are caught and in some cases informing their parents.

Make sure that the students are clear about the consequences of cheating and what your opinion on it is; this could take the form of some sort of short class discussion early on in the course.

Discipline

In private language schools you will have very few discipline problems as a large majority of the students will be adults. You may however have a few problems with younger learners, but again these are usually insignificant. There will obviously be some students who would rather be elsewhere than in a classroom learning English, especially after they have been at school for most of the day and these are generally the ones who may be disruptive.

In state schools discipline is generally good compared to their Western counterparts and the type of problems you will encounter will be minor. These include students not paying attention, speaking to each other in Czech or even bringing in and doing work related to subjects other than English. Any discipline problems which you are not able to resolve should be referred to the class tutor who will deal with them accordingly.

Business people and ESP

Czech businessmen need English more and more for their work and there is an increasing demand for company employees to study. Apart from the language itself, students are keen to know how business is conducted in the West and the mechanics of it. For a teacher with little business experience this can prove difficult, and unless you have knowledge in a particular field it is better to concentrate on the language. Learners are usually in their late twenties or early thirties although you may get some who are a lot older (see 'Teaching business people' pp 264–273).

Specific Czech problems

While Czech learners of English share similar problems with a lot of other different nationalities, and none of the problems here is unique to Czech students, the particular issues discussed here do pose difficulties for the students and it is useful to be aware of them.

Grammar

Articles. In English we have the definite article 'the' and indefinite 'a/an'. Czech, however, has no articles and therefore students find it a problem deciding not only when to use the definite or indefinite but whether to omit the article altogether. There is also sometimes a tendency to use 'that' instead of 'the'.

Past tense. Czech has two ways of expressing past: (1) single completed action, and (2) continuing or repeated action. There are no substitutes for present perfect simple or continuous and this is a big problem area for Czech students.

Present perfect exists but it is used only in literary Czech and even then very rarely. This is a problem for learners as they do not understand the concept and are afraid of using it. Students prefer to use either the present simple or past simple where we would use the present perfect.

How long are you here? (x)

Present tense. Present simple *v* continuous is not found in Czech and adverbs (eg now, today, etc) are adopted to indicate the time. 'I am sitting' will therefore appear as:

I sit now. (x)

Future tense. There are two main future tenses in Czech, they convey similar ideas to the two ways of expressing past described above. Plans, arrangements, quick decisions, predictions are not recognized when speaking about the future. Therefore 'will' *v* 'going to' *v* present continuous is a big problem area. If anything learners overuse 'will'.

Conditionals. Czech has three basic conditionals. The second uses a past verb but can refer to the present or future as in English. All three roughly correspond to English but the third is used far less in Czech, which tends to use the second.

Form of conditionals. The first conditional in Czech uses future in both halves. Therefore students tend to make mistakes by direct translation.

If I will have time, I will go. (x)

The third conditional is as difficult to form as in English and auxiliaries are used to put the sentence further in the past.

There are clear differences in English between 'if' and 'when', however this is not the case in Czech. Students tend to see the two as interchangeable.

Word order. Word order in Czech is a lot more free than in English and hence causes difficulties for Czech learners. For example, the subject can come after the verb in Czech.

Yesterday called me my father. (x)

The use of auxiliaries leads to problems and they are often omitted with the question being indicated by intonation.

Who you know? (x)
Go I to the station? (x)

Indirect questions. It is impossible to have a preposition at the end of a sentence in Czech and therefore learners often avoid putting them there in English. Thus the more natural 'Who do you live with?' becomes:

With whom do you live? *(x)*

A similar error arises with asking the time:

Do you know what is the time? (x)

Negative questions. To make a question more polite in Czech you make it negative.

Don't you mind . . .? *(x)*

Don't you have time? *(x)*

Even when students are made aware of the differences they are still reluctant to stop using negative questions.

Relative pronouns. There is no distinction between 'who' and 'which' in Czech, so students tend to overuse 'which'. In Czech, relative pronouns cannot be omitted, therefore students are unwilling to do so in English.

He's the one which did it. (x)

Must. Must is used a lot more in Czech, but can sound impolite in English. We would often prefer 'should' or 'why don't you . . .?'. The negative of must in Czech corresponds to our 'don't have to'. Giving directions can therefore result in:

You must go to the left. *(x)*

Countables/uncountables. These are not difficult for students to group. But the distinction does not matter so much in Czech. There is no 'a few, a little, much, many', rather there is one word in Czech, *mnoho*. There are a few differences, bread, for example, is countable in Czech.

Reported speech. In Czech the tense in reported speech remains the same as in direct speech, whereas in English the tense shifts back one in the past. Thus instead of 'she said she liked jazz' Czech students will often say:

She said she likes jazz. *(x)*

Double negatives. These lead to common mistakes.

Nobody didn't say nothing. (x)

Passives. These are similar in Czech, but are misused in certain cases, for example:

I learn myself. (x)

Make v do: In Czech there is one word *delat* for 'make' and 'do' and learners may often confuse the two English words.

Say/tell/speak. These three words often cause difficulties for Czech learners as the same verb is used for say and tell in Czech.

Phonology

Pronunciation. There are certain differences in pronunciation of consonants between English and Czech. /r/ tends to be over-rolled and /θ/ /ð/ /w/ / ŋ / are not present in Czech. Some final consonants that are voiced in English tend to be unvoiced in Czech, especially buzz (instead of bus) and docks (instead of dogs).

With regard to vowels /ɜ:/ /ɔ:/ tend to get confused (work/walk); /ʊə / gets confused with 'ou' in Czech; and /e/ /æ/ /ʌ/ are difficult for Czechs to make – listen out for 'Your fax has arrived'.

There are no weak forms in Czech therefore this is a big problem area, particularly the schwa / ə /.

Word stress. In Czech the stress tends to be on the first syllable and students transfer this when speaking English. Unlike in English, linking words up in connected speech is considered lazy and is therefore resisted.

Writing

There are far fewer capital letters in Czech (eg nationalities, months are spelt with small letters). This is often transferred when writing in English. There are far more commas in Czech than in English. Czech always uses a comma after 'that' (eg I didn't know that, he was coming).

The letter writing format is completely different, so needs to be taught from scratch.

Published EFL material available

The Cambridge English Course is widely used in both state and private sectors. This was one of the first Western course books to be introduced and is currently printed in the Czech Republic, therefore it costs a lot less than imported books. The Czech version is, however, the old series. Other books include the

Headway series which is becoming more common, again in both state and private sectors. A number of books for Cambridge First Certificate are also appearing now.

Books used in state and private schools include: BBC English; Cambridge English Course (CUP); Headway series (OUP); Project (OUP); Streamline; and Grapevine.

Addresses of publisher's representatives
Cambridge University Press (CUP), Eva Přibilová, The Bell School a.s., Nedvěžská 29, Prague 10. Tel/Fax: (02) 78-22-961.
Heinemann, ing. Richard David, Reed International Books, Obecní Dum – PKS, Náměstí Republiky, Prague 1. Tel: (02) 23-14-127.
Longman, ing. Helena Zanklová, Bohemian Ventures, Dělnická 13, Prague 7. Tel: (02) 87-78-37.
Macmillan, Moravské nam 2, 623 00 Brno. Tel: (05) 27-654/(05) 42-21-48-78. Fax: (05) 53-82-978.
Oxford University Press, ing. Sistek, Orbis Pictus, Soběslavska 40, Prague 3. Tel: (02) 74-89-08.

APPENDICES

Appendix 1. Case histories

Petra Harries came to Prague in 1993 after having completed the RSA Diploma at ILC Hastings in the UK.

I hadn't really planned to come to Prague, but having been offered the job with ILC it saved the hassle of looking for work in January.

Hackneyed as it sounds, Prague worked its magic and this is my second year here. I teach classes of all ages, their jobs varying from penpushers to a brain surgeon. The majority are highly motivated and happy to go along with the more communicative activities once the rationale has been explained.

I frequently go to concerts, the opera, clubs and pubs. Just walking around the place is a treat for the eyes.

Prague is not the healthiest of cities and doesn't look its best when blanketed in smog. Some days you feel the statues on the Charles Bridge are coughing. But I am sure I will never find such a beautiful place to work in and after Prague everywhere else will be somewhat disappointing; like buying a chocolate eclair and finding it filled with custard and not cream . . .

Kevin James Fenton, 22, came to the Czech Republic in 1993 after taking the RSA/UCLES certificate course at IH London.

After completing the four-week course I was eager to find work straight away and put my new skills to the test, but I knew October wasn't the best time to be looking for jobs and there was no work in England. I was told there were opportunities in Eastern Europe and after responding to an advert in the *Times Educational Supplement* found myself three weeks later heading off to Prague.

I was employed by a chain of language schools, initially to work in a small town, but at the last minute this got changed to Prague. The school paid for the coach fare out and on arrival I was put in a flat with two other teachers, which was rather sparsely furnished and without either a phone or washing machine. To add to that it was over an hour to get to the city centre and involved four changes. After six months I started asking my students if they knew of anywhere, and managed to find a room in a family house close to the centre for very little rent.

Initially I was teaching only 12 hours a week although I was contracted for up to 30 hours. As this was a company course which involved a lot of travelling it was enough though, and gave me a chance to find my feet. Generally I teach in the morning and evening which can be tiring, but the students are on the whole great and very motivated although some are reluctant to talk and do speak Czech during lessons. Attendance of students in companies is also poor. I have heard horror stories about some schools with no books, large classes of mixed levels, etc so feel I have been lucky.

Pay works out at around 6 000 Kč ($200) a month after tax and while ths is fine in the districts you can't save anything. I was also lucky in that the school paid towards accommodation. There is lots to do in Prague, such as opera, concerts, football, etc and you can never get bored. Of course on the downside Prague is always full of tourists and pollution is a bit of a problem, especially in winter. For some people the cold was also a new experience and it was funny to hear some Americans say it was the first time they had seen snow! Being British or American is no longer any big deal in Prague although it still is in smaller places where you can be somewhat of a celebrity.

Czechs are easy people to make friends with and I have found knowing some of the language is a great help. Presently I am taking Czech lessons twice a week. I have enjoyed my stay so far and am remaining for at least another year. Prague seems to throw up the unexpected, for example seeing President Havel strolling across Charles Bridge or hearing President Clinton speak here, and things like this make you realize you are in a special place!

Derek DeWitt, a 27-year-old American, came to the Czech Republic in May 1993.

I had been wanting to get out of the USA and travel for a while, and after hearing about Prague from a friend, and reading up on the history, etc I decided to pack up and leave.

I came over with no real expectations or plans, although in the back of my mind I wanted to continue my writing. It wasn't long before I realized everyone in Prague seemed to be teaching English to some degree, and although I was interested, I had neither qualifications nor experience, and felt reticent about being a fraud in front of a group of paying students. I lived for a while on savings but soon realized I needed to get out of Prague which was working out to be expensive and see more of the Czech Republic.

I ended up in a small mining town called Kunta Hora and found accommodation in a pension overlooking the cathedral. Everything was less expensive than Prague and I was soon getting to learn some Czech. We were the only Americans in town and it wasn't long before everyone seemed to know who we were. People were very nice towards us, inviting us to their home for Christmas dinner and generally making us feel welcome. I was now contemplating having a go at teaching although I had no idea how to go about looking for work and anyway we had to leave our flat so we decided to move to Brno. We had been there previously and liked the place and I felt there was more chance of work there. We found a flat through an agency using Czech and sign language and it was great until we were told we had to move out for two weeks because the landlord's mother-in-law was visiting.

I found work fairly easily with a private language school, and the director (who spoke no English) didn't seem to be interested whether I had qualifications or not. I told her I had done some teaching before and that was it. I was absolutely terrified walking into my first class, and to make matters worse there was a wide range of levels within the group. It didn't take the students long to figure out I wasn't qualified and half the students in my first class didn't come back the following week. I started using the British Council Resource Centre and talking to other teachers to pick up ideas which helped a lot, but I really needed to have some formal training. I found some work in a secondary school for a few months which was fun and I have also done a summer camp with students from 14–20 years old which was hard work but enjoyable.

The people in Brno are very friendly and because it is a university town there are lots of young people around. I felt Prague was too big whereas Brno, while being a sizable place, still has the feel of a provincial town. Knowing some Czech is also a big advantage, and I have found students more attentive if they know you can speak the language.

On the whole my time here has been thoroughly rewarding although I feel I would have benefited much more if I had had some training. Jobs are more difficult to find now without specific EFL qualifications and then there is the problem of work permits.

Appendix 2. Classroom Czech

Pronunciation. Czech has short and long vowels, with accents making them longer. Consonants not listed here are pronounced as in English. A letter is softened by an accent; ř, š.

Vowels	*Diphthongs*	*Consonants*
a as in u in but	au as in towel	c like the ts in hats
á as in rather	ie like the ye in yet	č like the ch in child
e as in vet	ia like the ya in yak	ch as in Scottish loch
é as in hair	iu like the u in mute	d as in duplicate
e as in yet	ou like the ew in sew	g as in get

Vowels
i or y as in hit
í or y as in meat
o as in hot
ó as in for
u as in cook
ú or u as in tool

Consonants
h help
j like the y in year
kd pronounced gd
l as in late
me pronounced mnye
n like n in new
p as in paper
r as in rap but rolled
ř – r and ž together
s like sh in ship
t like t in tune
ž like s in measure

Although it is generally preferable if all classes are taught entirely in English, you may find the following useful, especially for beginners.

Noun *Podstatné jméno*
Verb *Sloveso*
Adjective *Přídavné jméno*
Preposition *Předložka*

Article *Člen*
Pronoun *Zájmeno*

Tenses
Present *Čas přítomný*
Present continuous *Průběhový*
Past *Čas minulý*
Present perfect *Předpřítomný*
Future *Budoucí*

Other
Question *Otázka*
Answer *Odpověd*

Singular *Jednotné číslo*
Plural *Množné číslo*

Syllable *Slabika*
Consonant *Souhláska*
Vowel *Samohláska*

Polite *Zdvořilosti*
Impolite *Neslušnost*
Stress *Přízvuk*
Intonation *Intonace, melodie*

Book *Kniha*
Classroom *Třída/místnost*
Clue *Nápověda*
Homework *Domáci úkol*
Paper *Papír*
Paragraph *Odstavec*
Photocopy *Fotokopie*
Register *Třídní kniha*
Sentence *Věta*
Staffroom *Sborovna*

Appendix 3. Food and drink glossary

Jidelní lístek Menu

Polévky Soups

Brambory Potatoes
Zeleninová Vegetables

Hlavní jídla Main dishes
Pečene husa, knedlíky, zelí Roast goose, dumplings, sauerkraut
Pečene kuře s nádivkou, brambory Roast chicken, stuffing and potatoes

Hovézí Beef
Vídeňský guláš Viennese goulash
Uzená plec Smoked pork

Dušený Stewed/steamed
Smažený Fried
Vařený Boiled
Pečený Roasted/baked
Opékaný Grilled

Bezmasá jídla Vegetarian dishes
Špenát s vejcem, hranolky Spinach, egg, chips

Knedlíky s vejci Dumplings with eggs
Smaženy sýr, brambory, tatarská omáčka Fried cheese, potatoes, tartar sauce
Omelta žampióny, bramb, kaše Omelette with mushrooms, creamed potatoes
Jídla na objednávku Dishes to order
Kapr na másle, brambory Carp fried in butter, potatoes
Pstruh na másle, brambory Trout fried in butter, potatoes
Hovězí biftek s oblohou Beefsteak, vegetables

Saláty Salads
Hlávkový salát Lettuce salad
Okurkový salát Cucumber salad
Zelný salát Cabbage salad

Zelí Sauerkraut
Dezert Dessert
Zmrzlinový pohár Ice-cream sundae

Alkoholické nápoje Alcoholic drinks
Pivo Beer
Víno Wine
Víno bílé White
Víno červené Red
Suché Dry
Sladké Sweet

Nealkoholické nápoje Non-alcoholic drinks
Káva Coffee
Čaj Tea
Mléko Milk
Štávy/Džus Juice
Pomeranč Orange

In a restaurant
I'd like a table for two people.
Is this table free?
I'd like to book a table for four people.
Can I have the menu please?

What do you recommend?
I'm a vegetarian.
What vegetarian dishes do you have?
Can I have the bill please?
We'd like to pay separately.
We'd like to pay together.

In a bar
I'd like two beers please.
I'd like a glass of red/white wine please.
What soft drinks do you have?
I'd like a mineral water please.
Do you sell cigarettes?
Do you serve food?
Thank you
Please

Chtěl bych stúl pro dva.
Je ten stúl volny?
Rad bych si zamluvil stúl pro dva.

Múžete mi dat jídelny listek, prosim?
Co byste mi doporučil?
Jsem vegetarian.
Jaká máte jídla pro vegetariany?
Zaplatím prosím/účet prosim?
Zaplatíme každý zvlašt.
Zaplatíme dohromady.

Dvě piva, prosím.
Dvě deci cervenjho/bíleho, prosím.
Jake mate nealkoholické napoje?
Chtěl bych minerálku, prosím.
Prodavate cigarety?
Máte něco jidluz?
Děkuji.
Prosim.

Appendix 4. Useful Czech words and phrases

Numbers

1	*jeden*	21	*dvacetjedna*
2	*dva*	30	*třicet*
3	*tři*	40	*čtyřicet*
4	*čtyři*	50	*padesát*
5	*pět*	60	*šedesát*
6	*šest*	70	*sedmdesát*
7	*sedm*	80	*osmdesát*
8	*osm*	90	*devadesát*
9	*devět*	100	*sto*
10	*deset*	200	*dvě stě*
11	*jedenáct*	300	*tři sta*
12	*dvanáct*	400	*čtyři sta*
13	*třináct*	500	*pět set*
14	*čtrnáct*	600	*šest set*
15	*patnáct*	700	*sedm set*
16	*šestnáct*	800	*osm set*
17	*sedmnáct*	900	*devét set*
18	*osmnáct*	1 000	*tisíc*
19	*devatenáct*	10 000	*deset tisíc*
20	*dvacet*		

Days of the week
Monday *pondělí*
Tuesday *uterý*
Wednesday *středa*
Thursday *čtvrtek*
Friday *pátek*
Saturday *sobota*
Sunday *neděle*

Months
January *leden*
February *únor*
March *březen*
April *duben*
May *květen*
June *červen*
July *červenec*
August *srpen*
September *září*
October *říjen*
November *listopad*
December *prosinec*

Greetings
Hello/goodbye (informal) *ahoj*
Goodbye (formal) *na shledanou*
Good morning *dobré ráno*
Good day *dobrý den*
Good afternoon *dobré odpoledne*
Good evening *dobrý večer*
Excuse me *Prosim*
Yes *Ano*
No *Ne*

Small talk
Do you speak English? *Mluvíte anglicky?*
I don't speak Czech *Nemluvím česky*

I don't understand.	*Nerozumím*
Could you write it down?	*Mužete mi to napsat?*
What do you do?	*Jakou praci děláte?*
I'm a student.	*Jsem student*
I'm an English teacher.	*Jsem učitel angličtiny*
I work at . . .	*Pracuji v . . .*
I am English/American	*Jsem Anglican/Američan*

Shopping

Where can I buy . . .?	*Kde si mohu koupit . . .?*
How much does it cost?	*Kolik to stoji?*
Do you have . . .?	*Máte . . .?*

Time and dates

Today	*Dnes*
Tonight	*Dnes večer*
Yesterday	*Včera*
Tomorrow	*Zítra*
Next week	*Příští týden*
What time is it please?	*Kolik je hodin?*
Open	*Otvřeno*
Closed	*Zavřeno*
When?	*Kdy?*

Appendix 5. Festivals and public holidays

Principal national holidays.

1 January	Following parties on New Year's Eve (*silvestr*) New Year's Day is spent visiting grandparents and god-parents to present gifts.
Easter Monday	See below.
1 May	See below.
8 May	End of Second World War. Liberation.
5 July	Introduction of Christianity.
6 July	Death of Jan Hus.
28 October	Foundation of the Republic (1918).
24 December	*Štědrý Večer* (generous evening) is the traditional time when the family comes together to feast and give and receive presents. The traditional dish is carp.
25 December	Christmas Day.
26 December	Families visit relatives.

Other national occasions and festivals

Easter. A number of festivals take place around Easter, especially in the villages, which are either pagan customs or Catholic traditions. Easter eggs, which started as a pagan custom, took on a new meaning with the advent of Christianity. Today eggs are decorated with beeswax designs and dyed in the traditional manner. You may also be served coloured hard boiled eggs as desserts at Easter.

Another pagan custom symbolizing the chasing away of winter and the welcoming of spring is carried on today by Czech boys chasing girls with braided sticks decorated with streamers (*pomlazka*). The girls in return offer eggs to 'save themselves' from such an attack. You will see these sticks and eggs being sold in markets in the run-up to Easter.

May Day. Celebrations including song and dance welcome the Spring, with decorated trees and May poles.

4 December (St Barbara's Day). Cherry tree branches are sold and brought inside to force and predict a good husband for the girl whose branches blossom by Christmas.

6 December (St Nicholas Day). Children's holiday. Good Bishop accompanied by an 'angel' and 'devil' tours various neighbourhoods, handing out presents to the children.

Folk festivals. There are summer folk festivals all over the country, the largest being at Strážnice.

Harvest festivals. These festivals are celebrated in villages of the Hana region in Moravia. The best place to see *Hanácke Dožínky*, as the festival is called, is in Namest-na-Hane.

Appendix 6. Embassies and consulates

Selected Czech embassies and consulates abroad
Australia: 38 Culgoa Circuit, O'Malley, Canberra, ACT 2606. Tel: (06) 290 1386. Fax: (06) 290 0006. 169 Military Road, Dover Heights, Sydney NSW 2030. Tel: (02) 371 8878.
Canada: 1305 Avenue des Pins Ouest, Montreal, Quebec, H39 1B2. Tel: (514) 849 4495. 50 Rideau Terrace, Ottawa, Ontario K1M 2A1.
UK: 26 Kensington Palace Gardens, London W8 4QY. Tel: (0171) 727 4918. Fax: (0171) 727 9654.
USA: 3900 Spring of Freedom Street NW, Washington, DC 20008. Tel: (202) 363 6315. Fax: (202) 966 8540.

Selected embassies in Prague
Canada: Mickiewiczova 6, Hradčany, Prague 6 125 33. Tel: 24 31 11 08. Fax: 24 31 02 94.
UK: Thunovská 14, Malá Strana 125 50 Prague 1. Tel: 24 51 04 39. Fax: 24 51 13 14. (The British embassy also deals with New Zealanders and Australians).
USA: Tržiště 15, Mala Strana 125 48, Prague 1. Tel: 24 51 08 47. Fax: 24 51 10 01.

4 | Slovakia

Slovakia only became an independent country on 1 January 1993, following the break-up of the Federation of Czechoslovakia, and generally speaking it is less known around the world than its larger neighbour and former partner, the Czech Republic. Nevertheless it is no less interesting or beautiful.

The country is now a parliamentary democracy with a government elected every four years; the next elections are to be held in 1996. The present government espouses a market economy and seeks membership of the European Union, but is keen to see more 'social safety net' measures and a slower rate of privatization than is the ruling ODS party in the Czech Republic. Much has been made of the ethnic issue of the Hungarian minority, but there is very little danger of civil unrest impinging on the lives of foreigners living in Slovakia.

Since 1989 ELT in Slovakia has been developing fast, although as yet there has not been the boom in native English speakers seen in some of the other Eastern and Central European countries. Nevertheless, English has replaced Russian as the main foreign language and is now taught in nursery schools, many primary schools and nearly all secondary schools, as well as in tertiary education. In addition many private language schools have been formed across the country.

The quality of English teaching has likewise been improving; in part due to the introduction of new materials and new approaches which have focused on the more practical use of English.

There is still, however, an acute shortage of trained English language teachers especially in basic (primary) schools, and the gap is being filled in part by retrained Russian teachers, untrained Slovak teachers of English and trained and untrained native English speakers. While trained native speaker teachers of English are welcomed with open arms and are much appreciated for the work they do, there are mixed feelings as to the value of untrained teachers.

The majority of teachers currently working here have come out with one of several organizations sending teachers and trainers to

Slovakia. These include the British Council, East European Partnership (EEP), Education for Democracy, GAP, Language Link, the Peace Corps, USIS and Services for Open Learning (SOL). They work primarily in state schools or institutes of higher education. The British Council also has a Direct Teaching Operation (DTO) in Bratislava (see pp 9–15 for further information on these organizations). Teachers come for periods from four months to a year, although many stay on longer.

Although a general lack of information in everyday life, coupled with the bureaucracy, may at times get you down, the country and people more than make up for it. Slovakia has a lot to offer anyone wishing to take up the challenge of teaching English here and people who have stayed for any length of time have found the experience both enjoyable and rewarding.

PART 1
PREPARING YOUR TRIP
AND FINDING TEACHING JOBS

Before you go

Essentials

Most things can be bought in Slovakia now, although imported goods from the West are expensive. Slovakian equivalents are readily available and much cheaper. Bring along any medication you may be taking. It is also essential to bring a warm coat or jacket for the winter and a good pair of shoes (it gets cold!). You may want to pack your ski boots as opportunities for skiing exist. You will need a two-pin adaptor if you are bringing anything electrical; electricity is 220 V. Note that in the smaller towns and villages the range of goods is considerably more limited than in Bratislava and other large cities (see pp 18–19 for further suggestions).

Teaching materials

Schools use a variety of textbooks these days; they include not only the old locally-produced ones, which leave a lot to be desired, but a variety of UK and US published books. Some of the more widely-used include Hotline, Tip-Top, Strategies, Discoveries, Project English, the Cassell Foundation Series, and the Headway Series (see p 162). One of the problems facing schools, however, is they cannot always afford the books and the financial burden often falls on the students. Another problem is that ordering books through ELT publishers' representatives in Slovakia can still be slow (although distribution is improving).

Not many schools have much in the way of supplementary materials, although most schools have at least some AVA (Audio Visual Aids) provision, such as videos and cassette players. Few have functioning language laboratories. Copying facilities tend to be minimal if they exist at all, at least in the state sector, but most towns have some commercial copying facilities.

In Bratislava, Banská Bystrica, Košice and Prešov, British Council Resource Centres have been established for teachers, containing everything you could wish for in the way of books, cassettes, etc, as well as up-to-date UK journals and newspapers, both EFL publications and a wider variety (see p 162 for addresses). These Resource Centres also serve as a meeting place for teachers of English and making contacts.

Whatever supplementary materials you have in addition to your favourite books should be brought with you (see p 19). Standard stationery such as paper, glue, pens, etc is inexpensive and readily available from the local paper shop (*papiernictvo*). Locally published dictionaries, although of poor quality, can be bought from bookshops.

Health and insurance

Most organizations bringing teachers out will cover your health insurance for the period of your stay in Slovakia, which normally includes repatriation costs should you have to be flown home in an emergency. This should however be checked in advance. UK citizens are covered by a Health Agreement between the two countries entitling them to free emergency treatment, although no such agreement applies to Americans. If for some reason you find you aren't covered, then medical insurance can be taken out in Slovakia.

Local health care is adequate, even if it does appear quite basic due to a lack of funding. Having said that, it is best to ask your colleagues or students to recommend a good English-speaking doctor and hospital. Once you are covered under the local health care system most services are provided free. The larger towns have at least one all night pharmacy (*lekáreň*) selling over-the-counter medicines.

Language

Although it is very similar to Czech, Slovak is a separate language. It is comparable to Polish and Russian in many ways, and a knowledge of these languages will help you initially. Although it is regarded as difficult to master by English speakers, an effort to learn it to some degree will be beneficial, and will help you to understand the people and country better. It will also be greatly appreciated by the locals. German is widely spoken and English is becoming more common, although less so in the rural areas. Very few books are available to help you study Slovak but *Basic Slovak* by Josef Mistrik published and sold in Slovakia is a start. You might also want to try *Slovenčina pre cudzincov* (Slovak for Foreigners). This is entirely in Slovak so a teacher will be necessary to help you work through it. Again, this is available from bookshops in Slovakia.

For those who want to study the language in more depth, four-week intensive summer courses are held at Comenius University in Bratislava. Contact the Faculty of Education:

> Šafárikovo nám. 6818 06 Bratislava. Tel: (42-7) 580 41-49. Fax: (42-7) 598-36.

Money – expenses and how much to take

Slovakia is catching up with the Czech Republic in terms of prices, but can still be considered a cheap country by Western standards. Even if you are going out on an organized programme you are advised to take a minimum of $500 for your initial settling in and to have some more in reserve should you wish to travel, or in case of emergency.

Bring a certain amount of cash in small denominations as well as traveller's cheques or Eurocheques. Credit cards are slowly becoming accepted, though only at the larger hotels and a few places in Bratislava.

For those teachers arriving without work or accommodation you will need to have enough money until you get established. This could mean anything between $500 and $1000 (see 'Banks and financial matters' below).

The unit of currency is the Slovak Crown and will be indicated from now on as Sk. (Note: The Czech and Slovak Republics have separate currencies and Sk cannot be used in the Czech Republic.)

Exchange rates (early 1995):

DM	20 Sk
$	30 Sk
£	48 Sk

Visas

UK, Irish, US and most EU citizens do not require a visa to enter the Slovak Republic and are permitted to stay for up to three months (90 days). To extend you need to go to the local police station or leave the country for a few days, making sure you get a stamp in your passport. Australian, New Zealand and Canadian citizens still need a visa which is valid for 30 days. Visas can be obtained from Slovak embassies and consulates abroad (see p 165).

Work permits

The procedure you have to go through to get work and residence permits is lengthy and tedious, with much form filling and waiting around. However, on the whole schools are helpful in guiding you through this nightmare.

To obtain your work permit (*rozhodnutie*) you first need to fill in a form (*žiadost no povolenie na zamestnanie*) from your local labour office (*úrad práce*). You will be asked to include details about your job, plus the address and signature of your employer. A translated copy of your EFL certificate and/or university degree is also required. After this has been processed you will receive your work permit.

Residence permits

Once you have your work permit you may apply for a residence permit, usually issued for either one or two years. Among other things, you will need to take to the police confirmation of accommodation, a clean bill of health from the Palace of Justice and three photos. You also need a duty stamp (*kolok*) from a PNS stand.

The whole process usually takes a minimum of two months after which you will eventually be presented with your 'green book' (*povlenie na pobyt*). Apart from the fact you will then be legal, this in theory will entitle you to local rates in hotels and on international travel, which can mean substantial savings.

Unfortunately the rules regarding visas, work and residence permits etc have a habit of changing from year to year and even from month to month, which leads to a lot of frustration. For an update on the current situation check with your employers.

Travel preparations

Flights from the UK. Most people fly from the UK to Vienna (Schwechat) airport (there are currently no direct London–Bratislava flights) and travel on to Bratislava by bus or car. There are four buses a day from the airport to Bratislava. Delays can sometimes occur at the Austria/Slovakia border, but normally the Vienna–Bratislava journey takes about 45–60 minutes. Alternatively you could fly to Prague (see p 89) and connect with a flight from there to Bratislava, or simply take a bus or train. The train from Prague to Bratislava takes around five hours.

Flights from the USA and Canada. At the time of writing there were no direct flights to Bratislava from the USA or Canada so you will need to get a cheap flight to a major European destination, ideally Vienna which is the nearest (see above), or another major European city such as Frankfurt.

Arriving without a job

The majority of people who teach English in Slovakia come to a job arranged through an organization or have contacts in the country who help them find work (see pp 9–15). While these are the most common ways of finding work in Slovakia, and probably the best, it is still possible to find work on the spot. In the private sector a number of language schools have opened in Bratislava and other large towns and plenty of opportunities exist in the state sector.

For work in both the private and state sectors the best time to arrive and start looking is towards the end of August. If you wish to apply through an organized scheme you should apply much earlier.

For work in the private sector, the British Council in Bratislava or the other centres around the country may be able to give you some advice on where to start looking regarding private language schools. For work in basic (primary), secondary and tertiary education contact SAIA (see 'Organizations' p 153) who put teachers in touch with basic and secondary schools as well as universities looking for teachers. Alternatively you can approach schools directly yourself.

Where to teach English

Options open to teachers wanting to work in Slovakia vary from state to private schools to higher educational institutes. There are also lots of opportunities to supplement your income by private teaching.

Private language schools (jazyková škola)

Private language schools of varying size and quality can be found in many towns, the largest concentration being in Bratislava. Classes take place mainly in the morning or evening and can involve teaching either children or adults. You may also get the odd company class, although business English teaching as such has yet to take off. Class size varies but you may get up to 18 students in a class ranging from 14 years up for adult classes. Teaching hours are 45 minutes and on a full-time contract teachers will do on average 25 lessons per week. Salaries in private language schools are around 6 000–7 000 Sk ($200–$235) net a month for full-time teachers with accommodation provided.

Below is a selected list of private language schools, city-by-city.

Banska Bystricá
RK Centrum Universa, Skuteckeho 30. Tel: (088) 253-09. Fax: (068) 253-10.
Štátna jazyková škola, Partizánska cesta 9.

Bratislava
British Council, Pánska 17, 01 Bratislava. Tel: (07) 33-10-74/33-11-85. Fax: (07) 33-40-75.
The English Club, Jaskový rad 3, Bratislava. Tel: (07) 37-22-25.
English on Business, Estónska 6, Bratislava. Tel: (07) 24-45-14.
Eurolingua, Drienova 16, Bratislava. Tel: (07) 23-41-89/23-31-37. Fax: 23-41-89.
Language Link, Gorkého 10, 815 17 Bratislava. Tel: (07) 36-75-80. (With 27 schools throughout Slovakia from Bratislava to small villages in the country, Language Link employs a number of qualified EFL teachers each year.)

Košice
The World Co, Alžbetina 47, Košice. Tel: (095) 62-25-420. Fax: (095) 43-76-09.

Prešov
ESO-E, Levočská 2, Prešov. Tel: (091) 25-345.

State school sector

Basic schools (základná škola). Pupils attend from the ages of 6 to 14 and many of them learn English from 10 up. Plenty of opportunities presently exist to work in such schools. Pupils study mainly in the morning.

Secondary schools (stredná škola). From 14 to 18 students go to a variety of schools including *gymnáziá*, commercial academies, technical and other vocational schools, and apprentice schools. English is taught in the more academic of these.

Local salaries are not very high; a typical salary for a state school teacher is around 5 000 Sk ($165) a month after tax, which would apply to a native speaker. However, some teachers work under the aegis of an organization that pays a hard currency subsidy. The schools do, however, usually throw in accommodation, which is a factor worth considering.

Most native English teachers currently work in *gymnáziá* and teach around 20 45-minute periods a week. Classes are normally shared with a Slovak teacher, and although there is likely to be a coursebook this is not always the case. Native English teachers are generally expected to do 'conversational' classes, although they might be asked to do much more.

State language schools (Štátna jazyková škola). These are found in most towns and both children and adults study in such schools in their spare time or on release from their workplace. The schools operate on a fee-paying basis and apart from general English courses help to prepare students for the state language exam.

Universities (Vysoká škola – univerzita)

There are 11 universities in Slovakia, including two technical universities, one in Bratislava and one in Košice. Recruitment is either through the Ministry of Education or through the university itself. Placements are also made through organizations such as the British Council or USIS.

Useful organizations and addresses

Association of Slovak Anglicists (ASA). An organization for teachers working mainly in tertiary education. It organizes an annual conference as well as publishing a journal four times a year.
FFUK Gondovar 2, 81101 Bratislava.

Slovak Association of Teachers of English (SAUA/SATE). Aimed chiefly at teachers working in primary and secondary schools, SAUA/SATE organizes workshops, seminars and conferences as well as publishing a newsletter four times a year.
PO Box 180, 852 99 Bratislava.
Office: Budyšinská 3, 831 03 Bratislava. Tel: (07) 21-26-69 (Tuesday 3–5pm).

Slovak Academy Information Agency (SAIA). The agency has placed well over 1 000 native English speakers in various schools and institutions since 1990 to assist in the teaching of English. Among its activities it offers orientation programmes on arrival and support for teachers during their stay in Slovakia.
Hviezdoslavovo námestie 14, 813 29 Bratislava. Tel: (07) 33-30-10. Fax: (07) 33-58-27.
Košice – Technická univerzita Letná 9, 042 00. Tel/Fax: (95) 348-05.

Slovak Ministry of Education. The following addresses may prove useful:
Slovak Ministry of Education, International Relations Department, Suvororova 12, 80 000 Bratislava.
Slovak Ministry of Education, Hlboká 2, 81330 Bratislava. Tel: (07) 49-18-11 (ext 6).

PART 2
LIVING IN SLOVAKIA

How expensive is Slovakia?

Prices have been rising steadily since 1990 with many imported goods now costing about the same as they would in the West. On the other hand a lot of things are still very cheap by Western standards, eg a beer is less than $1, and you can get a reasonable meal for $3. Public transport is still very cheap, as are certain entertainments (eg sports events, the opera, the cinema, etc). Inflation is high, as is tax, with teachers paying on average around 25%. The cost of living in Bratislava is higher than in other parts of the country.

Accommodation

Urgent accommodation

In Bratislava budget accommodation can be found through ČEDOK on Jesenského 5 which books rooms in hotels and private homes. In summer a number of student hostels open up. Try the Bratislava CKM office at Hviezdoslavovo námestie 19 or BIPS at Pánska 18.

The main information office (Pánska 18, Tel: 33-43-25) also has a selection of accommodation in hostels at 200 Sk ($7) to private rooms 500 Sk ($17) a night.

Long-term accommodation

Finding permanent accommodation on your own can be a problem as a shortage exists throughout the country. However, a lot of schools provide accommodation free, which is a big plus, as it can be ridiculously overpriced, especially in Bratislava.

If you arrange accommodation yourself, it is common for landlords to ask for rent to be paid in hard currency.

The best way of finding accommodation is word of mouth; ask any Slovak and Western contacts you have made. All major cities have flat agencies but these will charge a fee of a month's to a month and a half's rent. You might also want to try putting notices up.

The cost of renting a flat varies, but for a one-room bedsit with separate kitchen and bathroom expect to pay anything from 2 000 Sk ($65) to 6 000 Sk ($200), more if it comes with a phone. (If you do end up with a phone in your flat be careful, international phone calls are expensive!)

Some flats contain a telephone, washing machine, and colour TV, but a lot do not. Most accommodation tends to be in relatively small flats in modern tower blocks, which are generally quite comfortable if nothing to look at from the outside. Furniture is simple but the flats are well-heated.

Some teachers, especially those working in smaller towns (but not exclusively so), live with Slovak families or in student hostels.

Landlords and landladies will probably keep a spare key to the flat and may come in on occasions, even if you are not there. It is a good idea to establish conditions of entry before taking the flat (ie with prior notice or when you are present) and ideally have a clause in the contract to that effect.

As Slovaks go to bed early, noise between 10pm and 6am should be kept to a minimum, which means that parties can often be a problem.

Blocks usually have cleaning duties which are shared among the tenants, so check whether you are expected to do any!

Gas, electricity and water bills are generally included in the rent (telephone bills are not), but if not they can be paid at the post office.

Eating

Slovak cuisine is similar to that of its Czech neighbour, although there is also a Hungarian element. As in the Czech Republic, there is a tendency towards meat dishes. The food can be tasty, although fried food is common.

Eating out is usually reasonable but can vary widely in quality and price. New restaurants are opening (and sometimes closing) rapidly, and standards are constantly improving, although many places still have a very limited menu and service may be indifferent. Reservations are not usually necessary (unless you are with a large group) but remember that restaurants tend to close around 10pm. Tipping is done by rounding the bill up.

Drinking and nightlife

The Slovaks enjoy going drinking and alcohol is reasonably priced. Local wine is excellent as is local beer (try Zlatý Bažank and Topvar). Czech beer is widely available, although prices for some imported beers and spirits can be very high.

Bars range from the very flashy to the monstrously earthy. In Bratislava especially there are a number of nightclubs which stay open until the early hours. There is normally a small cover charge.

Café life is popular (although few compare to the ones in Vienna and Budapest) and cafés which sell coffee and cakes (*Cukráreň*) can be found everywhere. Outdoor cafés spring up in summer.

In the smaller towns and villages nightlife is very limited and places tend to close early.

In Bratislava the British Council (see p 152) has a coffee house and bar which is a good meeting place for teachers. Another popular bar with Westerners and Slovaks alike in Bratislava is Danglars 50 metres from the opera house.

Transport

Public transport is cheap and efficient. In towns and cities, buses, trams and trolleybuses all use the same tickets which are available from coin machines outside major shops. Tickets must be punched on board and are valid for one journey. Monthly passes can also be purchased and a night bus service operates in Bratislava.

Between cities, buses and trains are reasonably priced and reliable. Trains tend to be slower than buses. Note that on Fridays buses tend to be busy so buy your ticket in advance.

Slovakia is well situated for travel to other countries. From Bratislava, for example, it is possible to have day trips to Budapest (3 hours), Prague (5 hours) and Vienna (1 hour) by hydrofoil.

Taxis can be found everywhere and are generally reasonably priced. All taxis are metered so make sure the meters are switched on; rates are displayed on the dashboard and most taxi drivers seem to be honest. It is worth asking for an approximate price first before setting off.

Shopping

Shops are more limited than in the West (or even in Poland and Hungary), but the range of goods is adequate. New shops are opening all the time so keep your eyes open; don't assume you can go back to the same shop and expect it to still be there. There is no shortage of food and drink shops and fashionable clothes, although not wonderful, can be found. When you enter a shop always pick up a basket at the entrance. If you go to the market take a bag along, they are not provided.

Banks and financial matters

Banks are open Monday–Friday at various times and usually close for an hour at lunchtime. Traveller's cheques and Eurocheques can be exchanged at most banks in the larger cities, hotels and exchange bureaus, although a commission is usually charged. Credit cards are only acceptable at a few of the larger hotels. Money can be sent to the main post office in Bratislava at námestie

SNP and it is quite straightforward to open an Sk account at any of the major banks. An American Express office has opened in Bratislava where money can also be sent; alternatively you can send money to a bank in Vienna. It is illegal to change money on the black market and quite honestly not worth the risk.

Libraries and bookshops

A number of bookshops in the larger cities stock a very limited selection of books in English. University libraries have English sections and the British Council has resource centres (see p 162) in a number of cities with a good selection. The American Embassy (see p 165) houses a library and reading room in Bratislava, however lending facilities are for Slovaks only.

Post

Mail can be posted and bills paid at post offices (*pošta*). Letters to the UK take around seven days and to the USA 10–14 days. Receiving packages is straightforward. On receiving a slip just take it to the post office as indicated. Sending a parcel is more complicated and requires wrapping it up in front of a customs official and filling in a declaration form. It is also expensive.

The main post office in Bratislava is located at the corner of námestie SNP 35 and Uršulinská, open 7am–9pm. Others normally open 8am–3pm. The telephone/fax/telegram room is inside námestie SNP 36, open 7am–8.30pm.

Public telephones

The telephone system, while still not without its problems, is currently being revamped. A large number of public telephones are being converted to card phones especially in the cities. Cards can be purchased at the post office or PNS newspaper kiosks.

It is possible to make international calls from phone boxes but they are expensive. It is much cheaper if you call collect or use an international credit card. The country code for Slovakia is the same as for the Czech Republic (42). Numbers listed in this section include the local area code except for numbers in Bratislava. The code for Bratislava is (07).

Useful help numbers include police (158); ambulance (155); fire (150); AT&T: 00 42 000 101; international operator: 0132.

Media, culture and sport

Television and radio. Satellite dishes are appearing on every block of flats and CNN, Sky, MTV and Super Channel can all be picked up. If you do not have a dish you will get two Slovak stations and in some areas Austrian and Hungarian stations.

A good short-wave radio can pick up the BBC World Service in many parts of Slovakia and Blue Danube Radio from Vienna (93.3 FM) has an English/German/French output of news regularly. There are several good local music radio stations.

Newspapers. English language newspapers are essentially sold only in Bratislava from the larger hotels and a few kiosks. The international editions of the *Financial Times* and *Guardian* are available on the day of issue and other UK and US papers are sold the day after issue. Magazines such as *Time, Newsweek* and the *Economist* can also be bought both in Bratislava and the country-side.

Music. There are occasional live rock or pop performances, but lots more in the way of jazz, classical music and opera. All cultural events and entertainment are listed in a monthly magazine available in Bratislava, *KAM*.

Cinema and theatre. Going to the cinema is popular and all of the large towns have their own cinemas. American films are regularly shown, many in the original version.

Sport. Plenty of sports facilities, both for playing and spectating, exist around the country. Popular sports include football, ice hockey, tennis and swimming. The countryside is lovely and quite accessible by public transport, with great opportunities for walking along well-marked paths, climbing, and, in winter, skiing. Both downhill and cross-country skiing are popular, although there are usually long waits for lifts.

Local information

For further information about Slovakia and Bratislava call in at the Bratislava Information and Publicity Service (BIPS) at Pánska 18 in the heart of the old city. Other towns of interest include Košice, Bardejov and Levoča.

The country and the people

Slovakia has a population of just over 5 million people, of whom about 11% are of Hungarian origin. The capital is Bratislava (population 450 000) a historical city going back to Celtic and Roman times. Other major cities are Košice (237 000) and Prešov

(90 000) in East Slovakia, Banská Bystrica (86 000) and Žilina (85 000) in Central Slovakia, Nitra (91 000) and Trnava (72 000) in the west. More than half the population (60%) is Roman Catholic with Protestants, Greek Catholics and Orthodox Christians making up the rest.

The people have a reputation as being hard-working with many skills, balanced with modesty and adaptability resulting from their political history. People today do not seem to be as giving as they were before the changes, and there is a lot of scepticism about the future. Fortunately the younger generation have a lot of go in them and seem determined to make the country work, even though the economic situation is deteriorating and politics like a rollercoaster.

Families play an important role in the lives of Slovaks and the close-knit family circles form the bedrock of society. The people are friendly and calm with a good sense of humour and no bourgeois graces.

Slovaks are renowned for their hospitality, and most people who go there soon make friends among colleagues and students; it is far more common to be invited into a home here than it is in, say, the Czech Republic. Many foreigners often find themselves being bombarded with invitations to visit, have dinner, go to weekend cottages in the mountains, go walking or skiing, and so on.

When you do get invited be sure to take along some flowers or a bottle of wine. Flowers are also given on such occasions as namedays and birthdays.

Life at present is hard for people, especially those living in small towns where unemployment is rising as a lot of the state co-ops close. Slovakia is a very rural country compared to the Czech Republic and people can still be seen working the land with horse and plough. The gap between rich and poor is now very apparent, as is evident from the number of BMWs and Mercedes driving round Bratislava compared to the poverty of the rural farmers.

This small country is trying hard to shake off the bad press it has had in the past and to move forward to play an important role in the region.

Geography

Slovakia is centrally located in the very heart of Europe sharing borders with five countries: the Czech Republic to the west; Poland to the north; Ukraine to the east; Hungary to the south; and Austria to the south-west. The country is famous for its beautiful countryside, from the Tatra mountains in the north to the floodplain forests in the south.

Climate

Slovakia has a continental climate with hot summers and very cold winters, especially in the mountainous regions. You can also expect a lot of snow in these areas. Spring and Autumn are wet but pleasantly warm.

PART 3
TEACHING ENGLISH

The Slovak education system

Like those of its neighbours, the Slovak education system is currently being reviewed and is undergoing changes. Regarding the teaching of English, since 1989 Russian has no longer been compulsory and demand for English has continued to grow.

The education system is structured as follows:

- Nurseries (*Detské Jasle*), 1–3 years;
- Kindergartens (*Materská škola*), 3–6 years;
- Primary/basic schools (*Základná škola*), 6–14/15 years;
- Secondary schools (*Gymnáziá*) 11–18 years or 14–18 years;
- Specialized secondary schools, 14/15–18/19 years;
- Vocational secondary schools, 14/15–18 years; and
- Higher education, 18/19–23 years.

Education is free and compulsory between the ages of six and sixteen. Most children also attend kindergarten from the age of three.

After 10 years of compulsory basic schooling, most children continue their education, either at four-year secondary grammar schools, which prepare for university entrance; or at four-year vocational schools which offer specialized training or prepare students for entrance to higher educational institutes. There are also two- and four-year courses at specialized apprentice training centres and a number of bilingual schools. The establishment of private and religious schools was legalized in 1990. (See the Czech education system for more details pp 128–134).

Methods used in the classroom

While great efforts have been made since 1990 to introduce new methodologies into the classroom, with some success, a lot of the old grammar translation methods are still practised. Lessons still tend to be teacher-centred and students are more readily able to learn facts than to give opinions or to discuss. Former Russian teachers retrained to teach English make up a high percentage of the staff working in basic schools. A syllabus is currently being devised for basic and secondary education, but planning at present mainly revolves around a coursebook.

The kind of language needed

The kind of language needed varies immensely, but there is nothing radically different from the situation in the neighbouring countries. Learners of English need to be exposed to more authentic English after years of outdated language methods and being closed off to a large degree from the English-speaking world.

Learners especially need to improve their aural and oral skills. Communicative methodology focusing on English for everyday life is essential, but it is also important not to throw the baby out with the bathwater and ignore the establishment of a solid grammar foundation.

Slovakian students

A 'typical Slovak student' is like a lot of other 'typical students': the junior kids are very eager, the secondary school ones are standard adolescents, tertiary students vary from the highly motivated, talented and brilliant to the supine like anywhere else, and a lot of students learning privately are very highly motivated. They have generally been exposed to highly traditional pedagogic practices (rote learning, massive regular testing at which they regurgitate the pseudofacts they have half-digested) in the past and therefore may appear rather reticent and 'uncommunicative' at first: they often come across as being rather passive. However once they become acquainted with a more communicative approach they do respond.

Examinations

Examinations in English are at present not standardized. Exams in schools are in the form of written texts and are very much grammar based. They do not indicate the students' ability to communicate and rely heavily on memory. The state exam is popular and widely recognized within Slovakia and can be taken at three levels, elementary, intermediate and advanced, roughly corresponding to the Cambridge exams PET, FCE and Advanced. Exams are taken at the First State Language School (FSLS).

Cambridge examinations are becoming increasingly widespread although the cost prevents many students choosing the Cambridge exam over the state exams. They are administered by the British Council. The American TOEFL exam has also been introduced.

Grading

Students are graded throughout their school years on a scale of 1 (excellent) – 5 (very poor). Grades play an important part in a student's life and for whatever reason it is very rare for students to receive a 4 or 5!

Cheating

It is common to catch students cheating in school tests and exams and to make matters worse this is not always punished or seen as being serious by teachers. Usually the threat of giving anyone caught cheating a 5 is enough to deter students, although vigilance is always necessary.

Specific Slovak problems

The problems for Slovak learners of English are very similar to those of Czech learners. These include articles, prepositions, sequence of tenses, intonation, register. For a more detailed analysis see pp 134–137.

Published EFL material available

Since 1990, quality ELT materials from publishers such as Oxford University Press, Cambridge University Press, Heinemann, Longman, etc have been introduced into schools. The following have been recommended by the Ministry of Education and Science.

- *Primary.* Stepping Stones, Tip Top, Chatterbox, Rainbow, Jacaranda, Project English, Discoveries, WOW, TRIO.
- *Secondary.* Strategies, Starting English, Hot Line, Flying Colours, Connect, Headway, Grapevine.

British Council Resource Centres can be found at the following addresses:

> Banská Bystrica, Lazovňa 3, 974 01. Tel: (088) 72-42-16. Fax: (088) 72-42-17.
> Košice, Jakubov Palác, Mlynská 30, 040 10. Tel: (095) 62-25-153. Fax: (095) 62-25-156.
> Prešov, UPJS, 17 Novembra 1, 080 01.

APPENDICES

Appendix 1. Case histories

Penny Shefton, 31, worked in the theatre before coming to Slovakia with Education for Democracy in 1991.

I had been working in the theatre for a number of years and was already looking for a change when a chance visit to Slovakia in 1989 set my mind thinking. Just over a year later I came out to work with Education for Democracy at different institutes in various parts of the country. The pay was poor, and it was a bit of a struggle to get by although the work was interesting. In 1991 it was a different world. I used to always carry a plastic bag around with me and if I saw something I needed bought it there and then. You never knew when you would see it again. In those days I even saw bartering going on. Since 1993 things have changed dramatically, and this is especially noticeable in Bratislava where you can now purchase anything. When I came here I didn't hear English very much and now it is everywhere.

Teachers at that time could find work without EFL qualifications but now generally speaking teachers must have them. The novelty of having a native English teacher has worn off and students are more concerned now with whether the person can teach or not. The RSA/UCLES course was invaluable and gave me a lot of confidence, but out in the smaller towns and villages where resources are very scarce you also need to be able to think on your feet and improvise. Luckily Slovak students have a good sense of humour and as people they are wonderful.

I have found myself doing things here I would never do at home. For example I was never a country person, but here I just love walking in the beautiful countryside. There are lots of festivals to go to and a rich folk culture. Every region has its own identity and culture.

Bratislava is like a big village and the lifestyle is easy without the stress of a large city. It is now becoming more popular with EFL teachers and there is a growing ex-pat community in Bratislava. This is a lot less so in other parts of the country, but wherever you work in Slovakia it will be an experience you won't forget.

Duncan Clarke, 28, a former journalist, came out in January 1993 (three days after the split with the Czech Republic).

Fortunately, I had been to Slovakia on holiday before and thoroughly enjoyed it, so when I saw an advertisement looking for teachers in Bratislava I jumped at the chance.

My first impressions on my return, however, were of a cold, dull, grim place, although I knew I wasn't exactly seeing it at its best. Initially accommodation was provided in a hostel, but I was soon moved into a flat of my own. I was particularly lucky in that the flat had a washing machine and a telephone, although other items such as a table were lacking, and the hot water sometimes played up. Unlike some places, the school pays for the accommodation; other teachers I know working in state secondary schools generally live in hostels.

This was my first job in TEFL having only recently completed the RSA/UCLES Certificate course, so everything was a new experience for me. I teach around 22½ hours a week and find the students highly motivated, which definitely makes the job a lot easier. They generally want English to get a better job, or possibly to study abroad, although I have had a student whose only desire was to be able to read poetry in English!

Everyone told me it would be cheap in Eastern Europe, and it is by Western standards, but the situation is changing rapidly. I receive around 6 000 Sk net ($200) a month which is enough to have a reasonable lifestyle if you are sensible, but travelling out of the country, especially to Austria is expensive. Vienna is only 60 miles away but you need to have resources other than what you are earning to be able to afford to go there.

There is very little I miss from home, except maybe good bacon and mindless TV, but that is a small price to pay for the opportunity of working and living here.

Appendix 2. Classroom Slovak

Verb *sloveso*

Future *budúci*

Question *otázka*

Answer *odpoved*

Singular *jednotné číslo*

Plural *množné císlo*

Consonant *spoluhláska*

Vowel *samohláska*

Polite *slušný*

Impolite *neslušný*

Stress *prízvuk*

Intonation *intonácia, melódia*

Classroom *trieda*

Homework *domáca úloha*

Paper *papier*

Photocopy *fotokópia*

Register *triedna kniha*

Staffroom *zborovňa*

Appendix 3. Festivals and public holidays

1 January	New Year's Day and the Day of Establishment of the Slovak Republic
6 January	Resurrection Day.
March/April	Easter Sunday. Celebrated since pagan times. You will see boys chasing girls with sticks and sprinkling them with water. Girls in return offer painted eggs!
1 May	May Day is now celebrated with song and dance and marks the arrival of Spring.
5 July	St Cyril and Methodius Day. In 863 AD these two disciples brought Christianity to the Great Moravian Empire.
29 August	Slovak National Uprising against fascism in 1945.
1 September	Day of the Constitution.
15 September	Day of the Virgin Mary.
1 November	All Saints Day.
24 December	Christmas Eve. This is the traditional time when families come together to feast on carp and other meats. Following the meal gifts will be exchanged.

25 December	Christmas Day. Traditionally spent at home with the family.
26 December	St Steven's Day. The first martyr of the Christian Catholic Church is remembered.

Appendix 4. Embassies and consulates

Selected Slovak embassies and consulates abroad
Australia: 47 Culgoa Circuit, O'Malley, Canberra, ACT 2606. Tel: (06) 290 1516. Fax: (06) 290 1755.
Canada: 50 Rideau Terrace, Ottawa, Ontario K1M 2A1. Tel: (613) 749 4442. Fax: (613) 749 4989.
UK: 25 Kensington Palace Gardens, London W8 4QY. Tel: (0171) 243 0803. Fax: (0171) 727 5824.
USA: 2201 Wisconsin Avenue NW, Washington, DC 20007. Tel: (202) 965 5160. Fax: (202) 965 5166.

Embassies in Slovakia
UK: Grosslingova 35, 811 09 Bratislava. Tel: 364 420. Fax: 364 369.
USA: Hviezdoslavovo nam. 4, 811 02 Bratislava. Tel: 330 861. Fax: 335 43.

At the time of printing there was no consulate or embassy in Slovakia from Australia, Canada, Ireland or New Zealand.

5 Hungary

Of all the former East and Central European satellite countries of the former USSR, Hungary has always been one of the more open and economically developed. It made a smooth transition to democracy in 1989, and now has one of the more stable economies in the region.

Since 1989 many Western companies – especially those from the USA, Austria, Germany, Japan and to a lesser extent the UK – have established businesses here as well as bringing with them consultants and experts. This has had an effect on the country as a whole but particularly on Budapest, which is fast becoming a major international city. The city was in fact chosen to host the World Expo in 1996 to coincide with the 1 100th anniversary of the Hungarian State, although it has now been cancelled because of financial problems.

Hungary has a famous cultural heritage and takes great pride in its art, literature and music. To help bridge the communication gap between Hungary and its new Western partners the study of Western languages, English and German in particular, has become a priority. The teaching of English as a foreign language is well established in Hungary and for many years a small number of native speakers of English have been coming to the country to teach, in both private and state institutions. Since 1990 these numbers have multiplied enormously and several thousand native English speakers now reside in Hungary and make a living teaching English as a foreign language. The majority work in Budapest, although a substantial number work in other towns around the country.

Among the many organizations recruiting teachers and teacher trainers for Hungary are the British Council, International House, EEP, Peace Corps, Teach Hungary and Bell (see pp 9–15) for addresses). Until 1994 a lot of people arrived and found work on the spot, but new residence and work permit regulations now make this more difficult.

PART 1
PREPARING YOUR TRIP
AND FINDING TEACHING JOBS

Before you go

Essentials

Going to Hungary no longer means taking anything and everything; most Western brand name products are now readily available although certain items are more expensive than in the West.
You should, however, bring some good footwear, a warm jacket
or coat, and it is worth buying electronic goods, including a
shortwave radio, before you come. If you bring electronic goods,
do not forget to bring an adaptor (sockets take two-pin plugs and
the electricity supply is all 220 V 50 cycles), but note that items
such as PCs, if they are over two years out of date, are heavily
discounted in Hungary. Long-distance phone cards are useful for
calling the US (AT&T, MCI and Sprint are all here). See p 18 for
other suggestions.

Teaching materials

An increasing amount of teaching material is now available in
Hungary. Nevertheless, it is still a good idea to bring anything
authentic such as menus, brochures, photos, tickets, magazines,
etc – anything that will give the students a taste of life in your
home country. Stationery is easily obtainable and relatively cheap.
Nearly all the major EFL publishers are here and printed material
is readily available, although in most cases at prices comparable to
the West (see p 222). Bring along any supplementary materials
you may have as these are not always readily available, especially
in state schools.

It is also worth noting that satellite television is widespread,
and, in Budapest primarily, there is access to English language
newspapers and magazines.

Health and insurance

If you are fully employed in Hungary, national health contributions are paid directly by the employer; partly as a deduction from
your gross salary, and partly as the employer's contributions over
and above your gross income.

In reality, however, this does not always happen. It is therefore
important to check this out with your employer before you start

work. If you are covered you will receive a medical card known as a *TB kártya*, which needs to be shown to the doctor on each visit, and entitles you to use the Hungarian health system. You can take out your own insurance policy if you so wish in Hungary.

It is advisable to bring a supply of any prescribed medicines or over-the-counter medications you may need, and include some aspirin, multi-vitamin tablets and anything for colds and flu. Contact lens products are expensive so it is better to bring a supply. Contraception and tampons are freely available and can be bought in supermarkets as well as at the chemist's. No immunizations or vaccinations are required but a new health test is required (see 'Health' on p 195).

Language

Hungarian is a member of the Finno-Ugric family, and it is thought to be a distant relation of Finnish and Estonian.

It is worth spending some time before coming to Hungary learning a few phrases, numbers etc to give you a bit of confidence when you first arrive. This will also help you get over the frustration of not being able to comprehend anything being said or to understand anything you read (see p 225). There are a number of phrase books, but not many serious books available for learning Hungarian. Probably the best is *Colloquial Hungarian*, with accompanying tapes, by Jerry Payne and published by Routledge. This can be bought at the major bookstores in London and in Budapest at Bestsellers (p 197). Another book worth a look at is *Teach Yourself Hungarian* by Zsuzsa Pontifex, published by Hodder and Stoughton (1993), again with a tape. This book is not as thorough in its treatment of grammar but has some good situational language. You may also come across *Hungarian in Words and Pictures* by Erds et al, published in Hungary. This is rather outdated now but some people have found it useful.

Quite a few private language schools, as well as state institutions, such as the Eötvös Loránd University in Budapest, offer Hungarian courses, and these can usually be found advertised in the English language newspapers in Budapest. Intensive courses are also organized at the universities of Szeged and Debrecen (the latter holds one-month summer courses every year). You will of course also get many offers of Hungarian-for-English exchange classes (see p 183).

Hungarian is by no means easy, but time spent studying it will be rewarded. Learning the language will help you get to know the country better, and you will find Hungarians very appreciative and surprised by your efforts. You will also find that some knowledge of Hungarian is beneficial in your teaching.

Money – expenses and how much to take

As in the other countries covered in this book, it is not advisable to work in Hungary if you are in debt back home. The simple reason being that the Hungarian forint is not yet convertible, and most salaries are paid in local currency. You are unlikely to make enough money to be able to save much, and this money cannot legally be taken out of the country anyway. Hungary is no longer a cheap country and quite a few things are now on a par with Western prices.

It is impossible to say exactly how much money to bring, as it very much depends on whether you are coming to a pre-arranged job or not, and where you will be working. If you are arriving without work, a minimum of $600–1 000 will be necessary to cover settling in and finding your feet, especially if you have to pay an advance on your flat. The single most expensive outlay is accommodation. Some employers help toward the rent and some even pay all of it. However, it is more likely that you will be paying, and a month is usually the minimum that has to be paid in advance.

Most salaries are also paid in arrears, so you will need enough money to cover your living expenses for the first month, that is unless your employer forwards an advance.

It is also advisable to have a certain amount of money with you should you want to travel to neighbouring countries. If you are working for a state institution school, or are full-time in a private school, a letter stating this and that you are paid in forints will allow you to purchase your travel tickets in forints. Otherwise you will be asked to pay in hard currency. It is worth noting here that Budapest is a lot more expensive than the rest of the country.

The unit of currency is the Hungarian forint and will be indicated from now on as HUF.

Exchange rates (early 1995):

DM	76 HUF
$	113 HUF
£	180 HUF

Visas

Visas are no longer required for citizens of most European countries or citizens of the USA and Canada. All you need is a passport which will permit you to stay up to 90 days. For stays of more than 90 days a visa and/or residence and work permits are required. UK passport holders are entitled to stays of up to six months. Citizens of Australia, New Zealand, South Africa and most non-European countries still require a visa.

Visas can be obtained from any Hungarian Consulate abroad with a valid passport and two passport photographs (see Appendix 6). Visas can also be obtained at international road border crossings, and at Ferihegy Airport, Budapest. Visas cannot be obtained on trains or boats. A visa is valid for six months and entitles the holder to stay for 30 days. The cost of a visa varies depending on the nationality and consulate.

Work permits

Should you be recruited for a teaching position before coming to Hungary, your employer is responsible for obtaining your work permit (*munkavállalási engedély*). They will need original copies of your university degree and EFL certificate (sometimes a faxed copy is sufficient), as well as your full name, date and place of birth and mother's maiden name. A certificate showing a clean bill of health is also required. For employers to recruit non-Hungarian nationals for a teaching position they must show that the person is qualified to teach that subject and a degree in an unrelated subject is usually not sufficient. The certificates then need to be officially translated before being presented to the relevant authority. Once you receive the permit from your employer, it can be handed in to the consulate in your home country or the country you were previously employed in, after which you should receive your work permit.

UK citizens can get their work papers sorted out in Hungary; however other nationalities arriving without a pre-arranged job and work visa are required by law to return to their native country or the country they were last employed in to apply for one. In practice people rarely do this and they apply to KEOKH (the foreign national office, Budapest VI, Izabella út 61). It is possible if your case is put convincingly enough to obtain your work permit this way. KEOKH have been known, for example, to let people apply from the consular office in Vienna rather than having to fly back to the USA or Australia. If you do have to go along to Izabella ut. take a good book along to read as you will have to wait a few hours in the queue.

For some teachers coming to Hungary on educational exchanges a work visa is not required. This should be confirmed with the authorities first.

Residence permits

For stays longer than 90 days a residence permit (*tartózkodási engedély*) is required. This can be obtained from KEOKH once you have your work visa. It has to be renewed either after six or twelve months. Residence permits can take anything from four weeks to four months to obtain.

Arriving and finding your feet

Travel preparations

Flights from the UK. Both Malév, the Hungarian airline, and British Airways operate direct flights daily to Budapest from London's Heathrow airport. It is also possible to fly direct to Budapest from most other European cities. The cost of an Apex flight varies depending on the time of year, and what days you can travel. Tickets can be as little as £99 (British Airways April 1994) or over £300. It is also worth checking out cheap flights to Vienna advertised in bucket shops or *Time Out*, and taking the three-and-a-half hour train or bus journey from there to Budapest. (See p 89 for addresses of STA and Council Travel in London.) Reduced fares for students can usually be found, especially in summer. Flights from London direct to Budapest take around two-and-a-half hours.

> **Hungarian Air Tours**, 3 Heddon Street, London W1R 7LE. Tel: (0171) 437 9405
> **Danube Travel**, 6 Conduit Street, London W1R 9TG. Tel: (0171) 493 0263
> **Malév**: 10 Vigo Street, London. Tel: (0171) 439 0577

Flights from the USA and Canada. Malév is among a number of airlines, including Lufthansa and SAS, operating flights from the USA to Budapest via a European city. KLM currently offers some of the best deals to Budapest via Amsterdam. In conjunction with Delta, Malév also operates a daily direct Budapest New York service.

It is, however, usually better to take a cheap flight to a major European destination such as London, Frankfurt or Vienna and from there take a connecting flight, or go overland. There are a number of good deals for students and for those under 26 from agencies such as STA and Council Travel.

Coming from Canada, Lufthansa flies from Toronto and Vancouver via Frankfurt. Alternatively, as with the USA, look for cheap flights to a major European destination such as London or Vienna, and fly on from there or go overland.

Two agencies that specialize in Eastern and Central Europe and normally know the best deals are:

> **Hungaria Travel**, 1603 Second Avenue, New York, NY. Tel: (212) 249 9342.

Sir Bentley, 17280 Newhope Street, Fountain Valley, CA. Tel: (714) 559 6946 or (800) 675 0559.

STA has offices in a number of cities in the USA including Boston, Los Angeles, New York and San Francisco.

STA, 48 E 11th Street, Suite 805, New York, NY 10003. Tel: (212) 477 7166.

Council Travel has offices all over the USA. The head office is:

Council Travel, 205 E 42nd Street, New York, NY 10017. Tel: (212) 661 1450.

By train. Trains leave London's Victoria station for Budapest and connect up with the Ostende–Vienna express. The price of an ordinary train ticket is almost as much as an Apex flight; so unless you are eligible for a student discount, or you are under 26 and wish to purchase an Inter-rail pass, making stopovers on the way, it is more economical to take the coach or fly. The train journey takes about 27 hours. Tickets can be bought from Campus Travel:

Campus Travel, 52 Grosvenor Gardens, London SW1. Tel: (0171) 730 3402.

By coach. There are a number of coach services that run regular trips to Budapest. The cost of a one way ticket is around £80. The coaches are usually full, especially in summer and the journey, a rather long and arduous one, takes about 30 hours. Pack some food and drink, and a few deutschmarks for coffee stops.

Eurolines, Victoria Coach Station, 164 Buckingham Road, London SW1. Tel: (0171) 730 0202. Tickets can be bought from any National Express office.
Attila tours, 36a Kilburn High Road, London NW6 5UA. Tel: (0171) 372 0470.

By car. If you are driving from the UK to Hungary, the best route is the E5 via Ostende, Brussels, Aachen, Köln, Frankfurt, Nürnberg, Linz and Vienna. The total distance is about 1 800 kilometres (1 125 miles). You should allow yourself at least two days for the journey, with an overnight stop (Nürnberg is about half-way). Check with the AA or RAC before you set off for any advice, and don't forget to bring all your car documents, including car registration papers and 'green card' (car insurance). See driving, p 193.

Arrival

Transport from the airport. All Malév flights arrive at the modern Ferihegy Terminal 2 and British Airways and most other airlines at the older Ferihegy Terminal 1. Whichever one you arrive at, the best way of getting to anywhere in the city is to take the airport minibus. This will take you to any location in the city for 600 HUF ($6) from Terminal 1, and 700 HUF ($7) from Terminal 2. Tickets can be purchased in the arrivals hall. The minibus will also pick you up from your door and take you to the airport (Tel: 157-6282; Fax: 157-8993).

There is also a bus service which operates from both terminals, and goes direct to Erzsébet tér in the city centre every 30 minutes for 200 HUF ($2).

Do not take a taxi waiting outside the airport as you are very likely to be charged six times the rate of the minibus, and possibly in hard currency.

The other alternative (although not advisable if you are arriving with lots of luggage) is to take the 93 bus from either terminal to the Kőbánya-Kispest metro station. The metro will then take you into the centre of the city. Tickets can be bought from a machine near the bus stop.

By train. If you are coming by train you will arrive at one of Budapest's three main stations; Keleti pályaudvar (east station), Nyugati (west station), or Déli (south station). If you are coming from the west then you are most likely to arrive at Keleti station. Each station is connected by the metro. Avoid taking a taxi from the station, especially Keleti, where you should also be careful of money changers and an assortment of very shady characters hanging around!

By coach. If you come by coach, where you will arrive will depend on the bus company you use. Most coaches (including Eurolines) arrive at Erzsébet tér which is in the heart of the city and next to the metro station at Deák tér. Attila Tours drop you at the Hotel Wien in Buda from where you can take bus 139 to Déli station and the metro.

Registering your car. If you bring a foreign registered car into the country, by law you are obliged to get local plates within 60 days. A non-Hungarian non-permanent resident is exempt from paying both customs duty and VAT on the vehicle. You first need a letter from your school or company (called a *kezességvállaló nyilatkozat*) that will guarantee payment of all duties if you sell the car illegally. The school or company must be a legal entity. You also need a letter stating the length of your employment (called a *munkáltatói igazolás*) and an official stamp (*illeték bélyeg*) from the post office.

Take your car registration papers, the school/company letter and residence permit to the customs office, section 7 at:

Budapest, Gergely utca 10, Kőbánya (Vámhivatal). Tel: 157-1780. Office hours: Monday (8am–5pm), Tuesday, Wednesday and Thursday (8am–3pm), Friday (8am–12 noon).

If you bring a car into Hungary and pay the tax on it you get different plates to those above and you can legally resell the car to a Hungarian.

The whole procedure can be a bureaucratic nightmare, and if you know you are going to be based in Budapest, with its excellent public transport system, bringing a car can be more trouble and added expense than it is worth.

Accommodation

Urgent accommodation

There is a range of possibilities should you need temporary accommodation in Budapest, from five star hotels to cheap hostels. If you arrive by train you may be approached on the platform by people offering private rooms. These can sometimes work out fine, but can also turn out to be a long way from the centre, and as a rule these should be avoided. Your best bet is to first get yourself a map, ideally the Budapest Atlas, and book through an official agency. There are two agencies at Keleti station, UTAS and Orient, which organize budget accommodation. IBUSZ, the travel agency, has a number of offices where you can book a range of accommodation from private rooms to hotels, the office at V. Petőfi tér 3 is open 24 hours a day. There are also a number of youth hostels which are cheap, although in summer a lot of places fill up and prices increase. A full list of youth hostels can be obtained from Tourinform, which is also the best place for information on Budapest and the rest of the country.

Tourinform, Sütő utca 2, near Deák tér metró. Tel: 117–9800.

Addresses of youth hostels:

More than Ways YH, Budapest XIII, Dózsa Gy. út 152 (entrance from Angyalföldi út). Tel: 140-8585. Fax: 120-8425. ($8 for single room.)

Strawberry Youth Hostel Budapest IX, Ráday u 43–45. Tel: 138-4766/218-4766 and Budapest XI, Kinizsi u 2–6. Tel: 117-3033. (Strawberry Youth Hostels are cheap and both of these are centrally located.)

Long-term accommodation

Long-term living accommodation in Budapest is expensive – from 20 000 HUF ($200) a month for a bedsit – and can be quite difficult to find. There are fewer problems in other towns and rents are also cheaper. If you are coming to a pre-arranged job your employer may have found accommodation for you. It is important to check this out before coming. Make sure you know what the rent will be, and who will be paying. If the school has the contract with the landlady or landlord find out who is responsible for the flat, and whom you should go to if you need anything fixing.

If you have to start looking for a flat yourself word of mouth is probably the best way to start. There is always somebody who knows somebody who is letting a flat, or a room. Do not be afraid of asking any Hungarians you meet, and use any contacts you have.

In Budapest you should also check out the noticeboards at the universities, language schools, music academy, American library and British Council, and leave a notice yourself. At the same time you should have a look in the *Expressz*. This is a Hungarian daily classified paper with a section on flats under *Albérlet*. The best time to get it is in the morning as early as possible because flats go very quickly, better still buy the morning edition the night before on the ground floor of the Uj Magyarország building at Blaha Lujza tér between 4pm and 6pm. Get a Hungarian to help you. Be aware that a lot of the ads are from agencies who sometimes charge a fee simply to look at a flat. You could also put an advert in yourself as it is quite inexpensive. If a flat is rented through an agency it will be more expensive. The price depends mainly on the size (flats are measured in square metres, *négyzet méter* or 'nm') and district, although a telephone and/or washing machine will also raise the price.

Most teachers in Budapest live in one-room flats on the Pest side of the city, as Buda, especially the I, II and XII districts, is generally more expensive.

In other towns around the country teachers usually live fairly close to their place of work, and the excellent public transport system makes getting around easy.

A typical flat will be adequately furnished, and may, in some cases, be overfurnished, with the room or rooms full of the family's antiques. Most flats have wooden parquet floors and beds are usually sofabeds. In general kitchens are small and basic, and contain a gas cooker and fridge. There will be a separate bathroom with constant hot water and a toilet. All Hungarian flats are warm going on hot. If you are unfortunate enough to be on a centrally heated system within the block, you have no control over the heating. All flats have double-glazing and if you live downtown, opening windows to cool down only exposes you to the pollution. Do not expect a washing machine, TV or telephone: these are still considered luxuries. If you are lucky enough to have a flat with a telephone, be aware that calls abroad are expensive. Better to get people to call you!

On the whole landlords and landladies are very nice, but they will probably not be used to renting out to foreigners, and you may find the neighbours a bit unsure of you at first. Teachers have had problems, such as unexpected visits, or complaints about noise, so a little patience and understanding is needed at times. Be aware that houses 'quieten down' by 9pm, so visitors and raucous suppers after then will not be welcome.

Bills

Rent usually includes bills (*rezsi*) ie gas, water, electricity, insurance and upkeep of the building. Check this out, and if you are paying rather than the school find out how much this is on average a month before taking the flat. Also ask the landlord or landlady to show you what the bills look like and how and where you can pay them. Most can be paid at the post office. The telephone bill will be separate and usually comes, like other bills, in the middle of every month, for the previous month.

Arriving without a job

Up until 1994 a lot of people came to Hungary without a pre-arranged job and, although finding work is still not particularly difficult for qualified teachers, it is much harder than it was a few years ago. There is a lot more competition for jobs at the better known private language schools. If you do not want to stay in the only one big city, Budapest, where the market is getting saturated, there are a lot of opportunities in smaller towns and rural areas, especially in the state sector.

Starting points

First of all you need to decide whether you want to work in the private or state sectors, and whether you wish to stay in Budapest or work in another part of the country. If you want to teach in the private sector, you should start by contacting language schools, either by phone or in person (see p 179 for a selected list). Some schools may have work straight away, even if it is only for a few hours a week, or they will take a contact number if you have one. Take a copy of your CV with you to leave behind, should you not get to see the Director or Director of Studies.

The British Council library keeps a list of language schools (although it is not very comprehensive) and gives out an information sheet on working in the state sector; better still check the Yellow Pages telephone directory under *nyelvoktatás*.

The English language weekly newspapers, the *Budapest Week* and *Budapest Sun*, sometimes advertise posts. In March 1992 a number of private language schools got together and formed the Chamber of Language Schools (*Nyelviskolák Kamarája*) to regulate and monitor the standards of the growing number of private language schools, both in Budapest and other parts of the country.

In theory they also run a database for schools looking for teachers and teachers looking for work. They charge a fee of $20 to use this (see below).

If you are interested in working in secondary or tertiary education it is best to contact the places direct. For addresses again look in the telephone directory. For schools look under *iskolák*, which are then separated into *Általános* primary schools and *Gimnázium* for academic secondary schools. You can also contact the Ministry of Culture and Education, Department of Education, who may be able to find a placement for you in a school.

Budapest V, Szalay utca 10–14, 1055. Tel: (361) 153-0600, ext 1454. Fax: (361) 112-8088.

Finally, a lot of jobs are found through personal contacts, whether Hungarians or Westerners. Your chances for work usually increase if you come with a personal recommendation. The important thing to do is to meet as many people as possible and see what comes up. Obviously the longer you stay, the wider your circle of contacts will become and more opportunities will arise.

City v country

While many teachers would like to be based in Budapest, this is not true of everybody. For a number of people, working in other parts of the country is more appealing and challenging. It is also worth noting that teachers sent out with organized programmes are more often than not placed in the smaller towns where the need for qualified teachers and trainers is greater.

The first thing to realize is that culture shock is likely to be higher outside Budapest, although wherever you are it will take some time to adjust to your new situation.

Most towns now have at least a handful of native English speakers working in them, some considerably more. However in other places you may find you are the sole native English speaker. There are a number of advantages to working in such a situation. First you will probably find it quicker and easier to make Hungarian friends as you will be a 'celebrity' of sorts. This will lead to invitations for dinner, trips and numerous other social activities.

You are also more likely to learn the language more quickly as fewer people will speak English.

On the negative side living in a provincial town can sometimes make you feel isolated, and you may miss the company of other native English speakers. It is important to establish early on who to turn to in the school should you have any problems, and be able to communicate your worries to. It is essential to get problems sorted out when they occur rather than letting them fester when they tend to appear much bigger than they really are.

In smaller towns there are often only a handful of places to go in the evening for entertainment and the pace of life is slow. Unless you make an effort to pursue interests you may easily become frustrated and bored. Get involved in as much as you can within the school and out of it, and use your free time to explore the country.

Where to teach English

English teachers, like most Hungarians, often have more than one job. Most have a 'main' place of work where their papers are and somewhere else where they teach a few more hours or give private lessons. Opportunities arise for native English speaker teachers to do other things such as proofreading or voice overs for film or TV.

Private language schools (nyelviskolák)

A large number of native English teachers teach in the many private language schools in Hungary. By far the greatest concentration of these is in Budapest, which has over 150, but there are many others in other towns throughout the country. The size and quality of private schools varies enormously, from very small schools operating out of a flat, to schools employing over 50 teachers.

Among the quality schools are International House, Bell and the British Council who employ only qualified teachers and offer full-time and part-time contracts. Nyelviskolák Kamarája, the organization set up to regulate the quality of schools is a good starting point for finding out more information on reputable schools (see p 184).

In the private sector classes can start from as early as 7am, for students who fit their English in before going to work, and finish as late as 8.30pm or even 9pm for students who come after work, school or university. Afternoons are usually when the teaching of children takes place. Some schools may ask you to teach on Saturday, but most teaching takes place in the morning and evening during the week. Students usually attend classes twice a week, although the length of the lessons and courses differ from place to place. On average people teach 25 contact hours per week (a teaching hour is 45 minutes).

Pay and conditions vary widely from school to school and it is worth checking several schools out first and talking to teachers who have been here a while before committing yourself. Find out what teacher support is provided, whether there are observations, etc.

Most schools offer general English courses, but may also have some work teaching business English in-company. A number of schools now offer preparation classes leading to either the State, Cambridge, Oxford or TOEFL exams.

A lot of private schools will not be able to offer full-time contracts and will pay you only for the hours you teach. It is also rare for them to provide accommodation, although they may give assistance in helping you find somewhere.

Below is a selected list of private language schools which have been officially accredited by the Chamber of Language Schools (*Nyelviskolák Kamarája*).

Atlanta International, Budapest V, Irányi u 3. Tel: 112-8349 and Budapest, Visegrádi u. 9, 1132. Tel: 131-4954

Babilon Nyelvstudió, Budapest, Teréz krt 41, 1067. Tel: 132-4974/ 135-3825. Fax: 132-5326

Bell, Budapest, Tulipán u 8, 1022. Tel: 115-5068. Tel/Fax: 115-6259.

Budapest Nyelviskola Kft, Budapest, Bajza u 1, 1071. Tel: 141-3728/ 141-3412.

Coventry House, Kecskemét, Hetényegyháza, Kossuth u 1/3, 6044.

Élő Nyelvek Szemináriuma, Budapest, Fejér Gy u 8, 1053. Tel: 117-9655. Tel/Fax: 135-6154.

Európai Nyelvek Stúdiója, Budapest, Szentkirályi u 1/B, 1088. Tel/Fax: 138-0730.

Nemzetközi Szabadidőszervező Győr Üzletház, Pf 140 9002.

International House, Budapest, Bimbó út 7, 1022. Tel: 212-4010. Tel/Fax: 135-3787. Postal address: PO Box 95, BP - 1364.

Katedra Nyelviskola, Budapest, Karinthy Frigyes, u 4–6, 1116. Tel: 202 4272.

Lingua School of English, Budapest, Lajos u 142-144, VI em, 1036. Tel: 180 5870. Fax: 133 4742.

Lingvárium, Budapest, Radna u 2, 1026. Tel: 116 2564/133 9618.

Novoschool, Budapest, Üllői út 63, 1091. Tel: 113 5480/113 5489.

Pécs – Baranyai TIT, Pécs, Felsőmalom u 10, 7621.

Szolnok m-i TIT Nyelviskola, Szolnok, Pf 140, 5001.

State school sector

Primary schools (Általános iskolák). English is now taught in more and more primary schools and there are many opportunities to work in such schools. In the lower grades especially, English is usually taught through songs and games and there are no formal exams. Students can study English from the beginning of their schooling, ie first grade, and a large proportion of the students are either beginner or elementary level. Most teaching in primary schools takes place in the morning from 8am–12 noon.

Secondary. There are three types of secondary school in Hungary:

- *Gimnázium*
- *Szakmunkásképző iskola*
- *Szakközépiskola*

Most native English speaker teachers work in a *gimnázium*.

Gimnázium. Gimnázia offer a four-year academic general education to prepare students specifically for university or college. There are many secondary schools and *gimnázia* looking to employ a native speaker of English teacher, although it is rare for there to be more than one native speaker in any one school. Teachers are usually employed on a full-time contract, and although the pay is not good – 25 000 HUF ($250) a month – schools usually provide or pay for accommodation. Meals in some schools are also free or subsidized (school canteens are not known for cordon bleu cooking, and there will probably be only one set meal). You may also be given 'food vouchers' to spend at a local store, and even a 'clothing allowance'.

The average number of classroom hours will be about 18 or 20 (45 minute periods), but there is a certain amount of administration on top of that, plus extra-curriculuar activities. You may for example be asked to organize a school club, and you will be invited on school trips, etc. Administrative tasks will include filling in the register (*napló*) and setting and marking homework. There will be procedures to learn, not all of which may be explained directly so do not be afraid of asking questions!

You are normally asked to take a number of classes for two contact hours a week, sharing all your classes with a Hungarian teacher. Obviously liaising with your colleagues is important, and do not be surprised if there is no syllabus or even a specific coursebook; in a lot of cases this is left up to you and your Hungarian colleagues to decide. Usually native English speakers are expected to do 'conversational classes', whereas your Hungarian colleague will do 'the grammar'.

It is unusual to be given a class of beginners or a group preparing for the school or state exam. Schools often participate in English language competitions which teachers are expected to prepare their students for. Classes vary in size from school to school but around 20 is normal, and in each class it is common to find students of vastly different abilities and levels. The school day starts at 8am and usually finishes at 2pm.

Szakmunkásképző iskola. These are three-year programmes linked to factories or agricultural co-operatives from which students obtain full trade qualifications as skilled workers. If you do happen to teach in one of these schools, you should expect beginner or low level students, with little motivation to learn English in a lot of cases.

Technical/Vocational schools (Szakközépiskolák). There are a large number of technical/vocational schools throughout the country. Students range from 14 to 18 and study engineering, computing, etc. The emphasis is on vocational training with a general education background. The demand for trained English language teachers in these schools is high as learning a second language is now compulsory, and several of the subjects are now being taught in English. If you have had experience of technical training this will be an advantage.

Universities and colleges (Egyetemek es Főiskolák)

A variety of teaching/training posts at the universities and colleges, both in Budapest and around the country, come up each year.

These are usually part-time jobs teaching anything from 4–20 hours a week, although full-time possibilities exist. Full-time can also mean around 12–14 hours a week.

Teaching responsibilities depend on the university or college and your own qualifications. Your responsibility might include teaching literature, methodology, American or British studies or simply language classes. Pay, as in the state sector as a whole, is generally poor.

Outside Budapest there are universities in Debrecen, Miskolc, Pécs, Szeged and Veszprém. Addresses of universities and colleges can be obtained from embassies or consulates abroad, the Ministry of Education or the British Council in Budapest (see p 183).

Dual language schools

A number of dual language schools exist throughout Hungary specializing in foreign languages, including English. Competition for jobs in these schools is fierce and you must be a qualified state school teacher (holding a PGCE or equivalent) as well as an EFL qualification. Recruitment is usually via the UK or US press.

International schools. There are a handful of international schools in Budapest, enrolling children from three years upwards. High schools cover a curriculum similar to that in the USA or the UK. Students are usually children of expatriates working in Hungary for a few years, and come from all over the world, as well as from Hungary. All subjects are taught in English.

The addresses of these schools can be found in the Budapest English language newspapers.

Companies

An increasing number of companies are now investing in language tuition for their employees, as the need for other languages, especially English, grows. Employees usually require general English, along with the language needed for their particular occupation, and if you have a business background this will be an asset. As more and more ESP courses are being requested, whether in banking, law or the hotel industry, a teacher with other specialist skills will obviously be at an advantage. (Make sure you highlight this on your CV.)

One way of getting work in a company is simply to approach the company and offer your services. Alternatively you can approach companies indirectly through contacts. If you do find work with a company, one advantage is that the pay is usually higher, although you will have to do more preparation if you are teaching ESP. A disadvantage is that classes can be as early as 7am before work starts or in the evening after work. You may find yourself with a very split timetable and a lot of travelling. (See 'Teaching business people' pp 264–273.)

Teaching privately

A lot of teachers, whether teaching full-time or by the hour, take on private students as a way of supplementing their income. Private students can be found quite easily through contacts, checking noticeboards in language schools and universities, or putting up notices yourself. You will also find that people will approach you.

The going rate varies, usually according to the person's means. For example a university student would be able to pay no more than 500 HUF an hour, whereas a businessman could pay 1 000–2 000 HUF an hour.

Teaching privately does have its disadvantages. Students cancel more readily and unless you have some prior arrangement about cancellations you will not get paid for cancelled lessons.

Such teaching is not a guaranteed regular income. If you take on a small group you may also have the problem of disparate levels, as the groups are usually friends or colleagues. I recommend waiting and choosing private students who seem reliable, and can fit their lessons around your timetable, rather than taking the first ones that come along and then finding yourself trying to get rid of them. (Do not take a tax inspector on as a private student!)

Exchange lessons

If you undertake to exchange English lessons for Hungarian be clear on the precise arrangement beforehand. If you have an exchange lesson with an untrained teacher, you may find yourself giving free English lessons for little in return!

British Council

Apart from the 'direct teaching operation' (DTO) in Budapest, the British Council runs a number of schemes throughout Hungary. These are mainly teacher training positions in tertiary educational institutes and lower primary projects. Most of these positions are in the provinces, although there are a few posts in Budapest. Applicants should be experienced teachers or teacher trainers and should apply through the:

> **Overseas Appointments Services**, The British Council, Medlock Street, Manchester MI5 47A. Tel: (0161) 957 7383. Fax: (0161) 957 7397.

Useful organizations and addresses

> **British Council**, Budapest, Benczúr utca 26, 1068. Tel: 121-4039. Fax: 142-5728.
>
> **English Speaking Union (ESU)**, Budapest I, Dezső utca 3. Postal address: 1395 Budapest 62, PO Box 113, Hungary. Tel: 175-0857/156 8440. Fax: 156-8499. (The Hungarian branch of the ESU organizes a number of events throughout the year including lectures, meetings, exchange programmes, etc.)
>
> **English Teachers' Association of Hungary**, Budapest, Dózsa György út 104, 1068. Tel: 132-8688. Fax: 131-9376. (Attached to the Ministry of Education they will forward any enquiries to schools or colleges who have expressed interest in employing a native speaker of English.)
>
> **International Association of Teachers of English as a Foreign Language – Hungary (IATEFL – H)**, ELTE, Budapest, Ajtósi Dürer. Sor 19–21, 1146. Tel: 143-4722. Fax: 252-2897. (At present there are over 400 members made up of English teachers from primary schools to university lecturers. IATEFL – H brings out a newsletter four times a year as well as holding an annual

conference to which speakers are invited from the UK and USA as well as from local institutes.)

International House Teacher Training Institute, Budapest, Bimbó út 7, 1022. Tel: 212-4010. Tel/Fax: 135-3787. Postal address: PO Box 95, BP-1364. (Full-time and part-time RSA/UCLES CTEF-LA and RSA Diploma courses are run throughout the year as are a variety of shorter courses on areas such as teaching business English.)

Kecskemét Association of Teachers of English (KATE), Kecskemét, Akadémia krt 20 1/31, 6000. Tel: (76) 347-487. (Local association of teachers which organizes workshops and seminars as well as publishing its own newsletter.)

Nyelviskolák Kamarája – The Chamber of Language Schools, Budapest, Ráth György u 24, 11222. Tel/Fax: 155-4664.

The Budapest Pedagogical Institute (Fővárosi Pedagógiai Intézet), Budapest, Horváth Mihály tér 8. Contact: Ábrahám Erzsébet. Tel: 210-1030. (Occasionally organises seminars for native speakers and Hungarian teachers who work in state schools, and recruits for teachers in Budapest.)

The National Pedagogical Institute, Budapest, Bólyai u 14, 1023. (Sometimes recruits for teachers outside Budapest.)

USIS (United States Information Service), Budapest, Bajza u 31, 1062. Tel: 142-3502/122-8600/142-4160.

PART 2
LIVING IN HUNGARY

How expensive is Hungary?

Compared to the West, Hungary is still relatively cheap (although more expensive than the other countries covered in this book) and tourists who come for short visits find their money can go a long way. However the cost of living is going up every year and if you are paid a local salary, as will most likely be the case, comparing prices to how much things cost back home can be misleading. Some items in Hungary are on a par with prices in the West and sometimes higher.

Living costs

For those teachers who work in the private sector in Budapest it is possible to live in a pleasant one-room flat in a fairly central position. Teachers in the state sector generally live where the school can find accommodation for them, which usually means living in the suburbs. The excellent public transport system in all towns means running a car is both a luxury and inconvenience. The price of petrol is also almost on a par with that in the UK. If you live outside Budapest you are likely to find cheaper and better accommodation and the cost of living will be lower.

Eating and drinking

Eating and drinking at home is not expensive, and you should be able to afford to eat out regularly. If you shop at the local supermarkets and open markets prices are cheap. The growing number of Western products with famous brand names are expensive, but Hungarian equivalents are widely available and cheaper. Wine and beer are popular and relatively cheap.

Cafés and restaurants

Cheap espresso cafés can be found everywhere. Budapest is full of cafés, where you can work, sit around, or simply chat with friends. If you stay away from tourist cafés you will find they are relatively inexpensive.

Restaurants are a lot cheaper outside Budapest, although even in the capital you can find relatively good places where you can eat for a very moderate sum.

Discos, clubs and nightlife

There is a growing, and ever changing number of bars, discos and clubs, both in Budapest and throughout the country; although outside the capital nightlife is still somewhat limited, and tends to revolve around people rather more than places. On the whole discos and clubs are not that expensive, providing you stay away from the large hotels, and the increasing number of 'night clubs' offering topless dancing with evil looking bouncers on the door.

Clubs usually have a cover charge and drinks cost more than in the pubs. Where there is live music there is usually a cover charge.

Taxes

Income tax is high in Hungary and there are three levels depending on your gross income. On average teachers pay around 25%. UK citizens are exempt from paying income tax in Hungary for the first two years provided taxes are paid in the UK. Value added tax (VAT) is levied on most items and is either 10% or 25%.

How far does money go?

A teacher working 25 hours a week should be looking to take home around 50 000 HUF per month net (about $500). Whether this is made up from one job or several will depend on where you are working. The hourly rate varies a lot from place to place but in general it is 600–900 HUF, before tax. After rent, which will be 20 000–25 000 HUF ($200–250) or higher if you have a two-room flat, plus bills, you should have around 30 000 HUF a month to spend. Providing you don't go wild every evening this should give you a comfortable, if not lavish lifestyle. The cost of living in the country is lower, therefore you can obviously live on less, but you may spend more on travelling if you regularly visit Budapest.

Inflation is high compared to rates in the UK and USA (1994, around 23% pa).

A guide to costs

Large loaf of bread ...... 60 HUF	Glass of wine in a pub ... 80 HUF
Litre of milk .... 30 HUF	Monthly travel pass 1 150 HUF
Litre of mineral water ... 30 HUF	Packet of cigarettes
Jar of coffee 100gms .... 250 HUF	(Western) .... 150 HUF
Packet of tea .... 120 HUF	Packet of cigarettes
Bottle of beer	(Hungarian) .... 90 HUF
(supermarket) .... 60 HUF	Cinema .... 180–250 HUF
Bottle of wine	Cover charge for
(supermarket) .... 140 HUF	club .... 150–200 HUF
A meal in a	Opera/concert
restaurant .... 500–800 HUF	ticket .... 200–900 HUF
Beer in a pub .... 120 HUF	

Tipping

Some people rely almost entirely on tips to supplement their very low income. Hence it is the custom in Hungary to tip almost everybody (except teachers!). It is not obligatory but expected in a lot of situations. In restaurants it is usual to give 10–15% tip. Other places where tipping is expected include cloakrooms, petrol stations, bars and hairdressers. You round the bill up to include the tip rather than giving it separately.

Everyday living

Eating

Hungarian cuisine is tasty, although essentially meat-orientated, with pork, beef, veal, chicken or turkey forming the centrepiece of most dishes. The food is not as spicy as people are led to believe, and most of the paprika used in the dishes is not of the hot variety, although this is available on request. Meals are generally very filling, especially home cooking which will invariably include numerous courses.

Hungarians do not tend to have much in the way of breakfast at home, rather they will have something in the office.

The main meal will either be at lunchtime or in the evening. Before tucking into your food always wish those you are eating with *jó étvágyat* (bon appetit).

Hungarian specialities. Gulyás is the country's most famous dish abroad, but goulash served overseas is rarely as tasty as that in Hungary, which is actually a soup rather than a stew or casserole. If you see it as a starter on the menu, be careful, it can be a meal in itself. Stuffed cabbage (*töltött káposzta*) filled with meat and rice is very popular, as is chicken paprika (*paprikás csirke*) served with noodles (*nokedli*), and eaten in many Hungarian households at the weekend. Although Hungary is a landlocked country there are several types of fish to be found in the rivers, and Lake Balaton. Look out for fish soup (*halászlé*) which can be very tasty and filling.

Restaurants. There is now a wide variety of restaurants in Budapest and the range is growing in other parts of the country. Hungarian restaurants vary from small and cheap (*kisvendéglő*) to expensive gourmet restaurants. The growth in private restaurants over the last few years has been prolific, and Budapest in particular has seen quite a number of Chinese restaurants and the usual fast food chains open up.

In a Hungarian restaurant (*étterem*) meals usually start with soup, followed by a main meat course, served with either chips, rice or potatoes, and finally a dessert.

Meat is often fried and served in breadcrumbs. Desserts include pancakes of different varieties and ice-cream. One definitely to try is a *somlói galuska*, a sponge cake covered with chocolate and cream.

There are generally several salads and pickled vegetables to choose from, depending on the time of year, but meals rarely come with any fresh vegetables. Service has improved over the last few years, but it can still be slow, especially when you want to pay! Check your bill as sometimes mysterious extras do get added on.

For a comprehensive list of good restaurants get a copy of Sam Worthington's *Good Living Guide to Budapest*.

Not-so-expensive Hungarian restaurants in Budapest include:

> **Tabáni kakas (The Taban Rooster)**, Buda I, Attila ut 27.
> **Náncsi néni**, Buda II, Ördögárok út 80.
> **Csendes – The Quiet**, Pest V, Múzeum körút 13.
> **Bohémtanya**, VI Paulay Ede, utca 6 (near the opera house).

Eating out cheaply. Small restaurants (*kisvendéglő*) or 'bistro' type places, which are normally self-service, are often the cheapest option. Due to the privatization of many restaurants, finding a good cheap place to eat is becoming harder. However, Hungarians always have their favourite, usually hidden away in a small side-street, so asking a local is the best way to discover where to go.

Vegetarian. As Hungary is predominantly a meat-eating country, there is a distinct lack of vegetarian restaurants, and very few vegetarian dishes appear on the menus. However over the last two years a couple of vegetarian restaurants have opened in Budapest (although sadly one has since closed) as have numerous salad bars and three Indian restaurants.

There is no shortage of fresh fruit and vegetables, even in winter. So, although eating out can cause a few problems for vegetarians, there are plenty of things to cook at home. Two popular dishes which can be found on most menus are deep fried mushrooms (*rántott gomba*) and deep fried cheese (*rántott sajt*) in breadcrumbs. Of course, there are lots of pizzerias and Chinese restaurants where you can get vegetarian food when you get fed up of the mushrooms and cheese.

> **Vegetárium**, Pest V, Cukor utca 3. Tel: 138-3710.
> **Maharaja Indian Restaurant**, Buda III, Bécsi ut 89–91. Tel: 188-6863.

Cafés, coffee and cakes. In Budapest and other cities such as Eger, Pécs and Győr, cafés range from the stand up 'eszpresszó' to the grand coffee houses; the latter being a pleasant venue in which to while away a couple of hours in elegant surroundings. There is also an abundance of cakes which can be bought from *cukrászda*. Hungarians' intake of eszpresszó coffee is almost on a par with the Italians' and it is strong to those not accustomed to drinking it. Many places, however serve cappuccino, or milky coffee (*tejes káve*).

Tea is invariably a teabag put into a cup of hot water, accompanied by lemon, but you may occasionally be lucky enough to be given a choice of several fruit teas.

A few of the grander coffeehouses in Budapest are listed below. These are not particularly cheap by local standards but are definitely worth visiting.

> **Gerbeaud**, Pest V, Vörösmarty tér 7.
> **Lukács**, Pest VI, Andrássy út.
> **Művész**, Pest VI, Andrássy út 29.
> **Ruszwurm**, Buda I, Szentháromság utca 7.
> **Angelica**, Buda I, Batthyány tér 7.

New York, Pest VIII, Erzsébet körut 9–11.
Vienna Coffeehouse, Fórum Hotel.

Drinking

The equivalent of a British pub or American bar, and the most popular place to go and drink is a *söröző* (beer place) which stays open late, sometimes until 2am. Usually you can eat here too. There are many imported beers to go with the local ones, and although beer is in bottles, draught beer is becoming more common. Popular local beers include Dreher and Kőbányai, both light beers (*világos*) similar to lager, though brown beer (*barna*) is also available. Several places now sell Guinness, but at prices that mean most teachers can only afford to drink it on special occasions or at least not in large quantities!

Hungary also produces some of the finest wine in Europe, which can be bought from most supermarkets and 24 hour shops, or directly from the vineyards. Alternatively you can visit winebars (*borozó*) which are no-frills, smoke filled places (nothing like the up-market expensive wine bars in the West) and are usually situated in cellars. Here you can sip away with the really serious wine drinkers of Hungary. *Borozós* are generally open from around 12 noon to 9pm. Avoid the stand up places in the streets which are often full of drunks.

Other drinks which you are sure to come across include fruit brandies, *barackpálinka*, apricot brandy being the most popular, others include *cseresznye* (cherry), *szilva* (plum), and *körte* (pear). *Tokaji*, a fortified wine is worth trying, as is *unicum*, a dark brown liquid, great for colds and indigestion, which is an acquired taste worth attempting to acquire.

Popular pubs in Budapest frequented by both ex-pats and Hungarians include:

> **Chicago**, Pest VII, Blaha Lujza tér. Tel: 269 6753. (Good beer and good food with a friendly staff. Done out like an American diner. Has a 'Happy Hour'.)
>
> **Fehér Gyűrű**, Pest, Balassi Bálint u 27. (Pleasant atmosphere with good mix of people. Book a table as it is often busy.)
>
> **Fregatt**, Pest V, Molnár u 26. (The original English style pub in Budapest and one of the first to sell Guinness. Still popular despite the increasing competition.)
>
> **Irish Cat**, Pest V, Múzeum Körút 27. (Another haunt for those who like Guinness. Good selection of food and live folk music.)

Nightlife

The following is a selection of popular nightspots in Budapest, but for a full run down check the listings in the *Budapest Week* or

Budapest Sun. In other towns around the country there are at least one or two places where you can stay out until the early hours. Ask your students where the best places are. Be careful of places with the sign 'Nightclub'. These are usually bars with a floor show and involve handing over large quantities of money for drinks!

Franklin Trocadero Cafe, Pest VI, Szent István krt 15. Tel: 111-4691. (Probably the most ethnically diverse of all the places in the city with a nice lively atmosphere. Latin music every night including live bands.)

Made Inn Music Club, Pest VI, Andrássy ut 112. Tel: 132-2959. (Popular in summer with its large garden terrace. Live music and disco most nights.)

Morrison's Music Pub, Pest VI, Révay u 25. Tel: 269-4060. (Theme pub popular with ex-pats complete with old red phone box and other assorted memorabilia. Difficult to squeeze past the bar to the sweaty dance floor through the back.)

Picasso Point, Pest VI, Hajós u 31. Tel: 132-4750. (Laid back bar with disco downstairs at the weekends. Pleasant atmosphere and a good place to meet, talk and drink. Popular with ex-pats.)

Tilos Az A, Pest VII, Mikszáth Kálmán tér 2. (Alternative venue for the young arty and alternative crowd. Bands play in the cellar every weekend. Good music in the upstairs bar and cheap beer.)

Véndiák, Pest V, Egyetem tér 5. (Very crowded small night spot in the centre of town. Place to let your hair down and jump about to both new and old favourites.)

Transport

The public transport system in Budapest and throughout the country makes getting around very easy and cheap. Although prices have soared since 1990, buying a one-month pass (*bérlet*) at the beginning of the month will save you a lot. You can purchase these at most metro stations and you will need a passport-size photo. The pass expires on the 5th of the following month.

Tickets can be purchased at metro stations, machines at tram stops or some tobacconists, but not on the buses, trams and trolley-buses. A ticket is valid for any form of transport within the city for one journey. You very rarely have to wait more than 5–10 minutes for anything and some buses and trams run all night. The system basically works on trust, as the only people who check your tickets are the inspectors that come around. (These can only be recognized after they have slipped their red armband on.) If you haven't got a validated ticket or pass you will pay an on-the-spot fine. This applies on the metro, buses, trams and trolley-buses.

Getting around the country

Trains. The Hungarian State railway (MÁV) covers most parts of the country. Domestic trains are either passenger trains (*személy-vonat*) which may be just quicker than walking, or the faster *Express*, for which you usually have to pay a seat reservation (*helyjegy*).

If you work in the state sector you are entitled to a discount card which allows you to purchase domestic rail tickets at 50% of the standard fare. (In theory you are supposed to have worked in the country a year before being entitled to this, but it is worth asking as some schools do somehow manage to get one straight away).

Tickets (*jegyek*) for domestic journeys can be purchased on the day of departure or booked in advance. You can book either a one-way (*egy útra*) or return (*oda vissza*). Tickets for international trains should be booked in advance and include seat reservations. Students with ISIC cards can get up to 50% reductions off international tickets. You may be unable to pay for an international ticket in forints unless you have an official stamped letter from your employer stating you receive a forint salary. Most international trains have some sort of buffet service, although it is advisable to take your own food and drink. A domestic and international timetable (*Nemzeti* or *nemzetközi menetrend*) can be purchased from the MÁV Hungarian Railways office VI, Andrássy ut 34.

Direct trains operate from Budapest to the following cities: Vienna (3½ hours); Bratislava (5 hours); Bucharest (17 hours); Prague (9 hours); Berlin (15 hours); Kraków (12 hours); and Warsaw (17 hours).

Long distance buses. An alternative way of getting around Hungary is on one of the yellow *Volán* buses. These are sometimes a lot quicker than the train, and can be a lot cheaper. Tickets are usually bought on the bus. The two main stations in Budapest are at Erzsébet tér (Deák tér metró) and Népstadion (both on the red metro line).

Public transport within Budapest

Buses. Buses cover all parts of the city. They are blue and numbers are either black or red. A red number with the letter E after it means non-stop. The red numbers indicate express buses which skip stops. Boarding and alighting can be done at any door except on some routes after 8pm when only the first door is opened and the driver checks you have a valid pass or ticket. Tickets have to be punched on the bus.

Trams. Like buses, trams require you to punch your ticket on board. They run frequently, start early in the morning and some run all night. Trams are a distinctive yellow and the most popular route is the 4 and 6 tram which runs day and night in an arc through the city connecting Pest and Buda.

Metro. One of the quickest and most effective ways to get around Budapest is on the city's underground. It has three lines coded yellow, red and blue. These cover most areas of the city and all meet in the centre at Deák tér. They run at regular intervals, just over two minutes in the rush hour and tickets need to be purchased and punched before getting onto the platform. If you change lines you need to punch a new ticket.

Trolley buses. These operate several routes and function like the bus and tram services.

Taxis. Most towns have plenty of taxis and Budapest is full of them. Although costs have gone up a lot the past couple of years they are still affordable. As a rule avoid taxis which do not belong to one of the major companies, as these are more expensive. Make sure that the costs are clearly displayed on the dashboard (eg K/M = 60 FT) and the meter is switched on. A new law in 1994 made it legal for taxis to have eight different settings on their meters to allow them to charge more on public holidays, etc. This also means, however, that they can decide what setting to put it at anytime, even without you knowing. Some taxis may ask you if you want the meter on or off, but unless you know how much the price should be, have it on, and in all cases agree on the price per kilometre and an approximate price of the journey before setting off.

Wear your safetybelt at all times; a ride in a taxi can sometimes be a nerve-racking experience. Avoid taking taxis from the airport, the railway stations and the main hotels, as taxi drivers are always looking to exploit unsuspecting foreigners at these locations. In towns you are not familiar with ask someone what the local situation is. You can order taxis by phone, giving your full name, address and telephone number.

Major taxi companies in Budapest:

Főtaxi: 122-2222. (Recognizable by the chequered pattern on the door.)
Volántaxi: 166-6666.
Yellow Pages: 155-5000.
Budataxi: 120-0200.
Rádió taxi: 127-1271.
Tele 5: 155-5555.
Citytaxi: 153-3633.

Driving

Hungary is not particularly driver-friendly and the recent upsurge in Western cars on the road has made driving more difficult. It is quicker and safer to use the public transport system, and you do not have to spend time looking for a place to park your car. Cars parked illegally are regularly towed away and there is a hefty fine to get them back.

Drivers are generally quite aggressive and it is not long before you receive the obligatory dent or two. A car can, however, be a useful way of getting out and seeing more of Hungary and the surrounding countries. Renting cars is quite expensive for foreigners, and buying a car in Hungary, though possible, should be avoided because of the legal problems (see pp 172–173 for information on bringing cars into the country).

Hitching

Hitching is quite common in Hungary and you always see people thumbing down to Balaton at the weekends. It is also common to see soldiers hitching home on leave. I have never heard of any problems hitching around Hungary, and it is a good way to meet people and practise your Hungarian.

Air

International air travel from Hungary is generally not that cheap, although recently there have been some very good deals coming onto the market. It is worth asking around before buying a ticket to get the best offers on hand. Malév now flies direct to the USA and flights to London can be found for around $270 return. Cheaper flights are often on offer from Vienna, particularly to the USA. A good place to try for low cost tickets is:

> **Vista Travel**, 1075 Budapest, Károly Körút 21 (near Deák tér). Tel: 269-6032. Fax: 269-6031.

Shopping

Up until a few years ago shopping sometimes meant the occasional wait in a long queue or a trek around shops to find a particular item. Nowadays the shelves are full and carry not only Hungarian products but a lot of Western brand names as well. While it is possible to buy most things now in Budapest, the same is not always true for other parts of the country.

Service has improved immensely but do not expect always to be served with a welcoming smile and the assistant's undivided attention. Department stores open Monday–Friday 10am–5pm/ 6pm and Saturday 9am/10am–1pm. Grocery stores open at around 7am. Not all shops open on a Saturday morning and those that do close at 1pm. Most shops stay open until 8pm on Thursdays. Useful words you will soon get to know are *Zárva* (closed), *Nyitva* (open), *Tolni* (push) and *Húzni* (pull). Always pick up a shopping basket on entering a shop.

Here are some of the types of shops you may need.

- *ABC*. These are like supermarkets or mini-markets and you can buy most foodstuffs here. These formerly state-owned super-markets are now becoming privatized and a lot have been bought by Western companies such as Julius Meinl. Take along a bag otherwise you will end up paying for new ones.
- *Barber's/Hairdresser's (fodrász)*. Reasonable prices compared to the West. It is a good idea to book first, and don't forget to tip!
- *Bookshops (könyvesbolt)*. See under libraries and bookshops (p 197).
- *Butcher's (Hús/Hentesáru)*. Meat is very expensive and in most of the larger butcher's you have to take your bill to a separate till to pay before being able to collect it. Lamb and veal are available only from specialist butchers. Remember that cuts are different.
- *Chemist's (Gyógyszertár or Patika)*. Over-the-counter drugs are relatively cheap if you get them on prescription, and you will normally find someone who speaks some English. Find out the nearest chemist to you to have a night service; a notice displayed on all chemist's doors gives the name of the nearest chemist open to dispense prescriptions.
- *Flea markets*. Two flea markets worth a visit in Budapest are Ecseri piac (XIX, Nagykőrösi út 156) open Monday–Saturday and Kelenföld (XI, Kondorosi út) open Sundays. There is also a big market on the first Sunday of every month in Pécs.
- *Fruit and vegetables (Zöldség/Gyümölcs)*. A wide range of fruit and vegetables is available, especially in summer. During certain months depending on what's in season you will find yourself eating large quantities of cherries, melons or peaches. In Budapest you can find fruit and vegetable stalls open 24 hours, just in case you want to pop out and buy some potatoes at 3am!
- *Markets (piac)*. Every town has its open market selling local produce. These are the cheapest places to do your shopping for all your fruit and vegetables. Again, take along a bag or two!
- *Non-stop*. These 24 hour shops mainly sell alcohol, but you can buy milk, cheese and bread as well, usually with a considerable mark-up.

- *Stationery (Ápisz).* These sell paper, pens, files, etc at reasonable prices.
- *Tobacconist's (Dohány, Trafik).* Apart from cigarettes you may also be able to buy bus tickets here.

Banks and financial matters

The unit of currency is the Hungarian forint (HUF) and there are plans to make it convertible by 1996. Coins come in 1, 2, 5, 10, 20, 50, 100 and 200 denominations. Notes come in 50 (brown), 100 (red), 1000 (green) and 5000 (light brown) denominations.

You may also receive fillers in your change although they are practically worthless. New coins were introduced in 1993 and currently both the old and the new coins are in circulation.

Hungary is mainly a cash society, although a growing number of places accept credit cards. Visa cards can be used in most banks to get money out, although this will probably be in forints. You may be better off bringing Euro-cheques.

You will probably receive your salary in cash at the beginning of the month. This will be for the work you have done in the previous month. It is possible to open an account, the easiest is at the OTP (HUF or hard currency accounts) or the Post Office. However you are restricted to the branch your account is held in.

Money can be transferred from abroad to Hungary through the Foreign Trade bank (see below) and more expensively via American Express. If you do have money transferred to a bank make sure you give the correct branch address. (For urgent money transfers it is quicker to have money sent to a bank in Vienna where you can pick it up in one business day.)

Money can be changed at banks, hotels and change bureaus at reasonable rates. Avoid changing money on the streets as this is illegal and there is also a good chance you will be cheated. The rate between the black market and official exchange rate is negligible enough not to take the risk.

Magyar Külkereskedelmi Bank Rt, Budapest, Türr István u 9, 1821. Tel: 266-4206. Fax: 118-5150.

Health

If you are legally employed in Hungary and your employer is paying your social security contributions, you will be entitled to a social security card and use of the public health care system. It is important to check this with your employer as not all schools will pay contributions, which are currently 53% of gross earnings. If you are not covered you will have to pay for any treatment and health care you receive. This could turn out to be quite expensive. If you are a UK citizen under a reciprocal agreement between the two countries you will receive free health care and treatment in emergencies only.

On the whole the health system is good and a number of doctors speak at least some English or German. For information on English-speaking doctors and dentists contact your embassy or other teachers. You may also want to enquire among your students. There is still a practice of 'tipping' doctors and dentists, although this is essentially for Hungarians and not usually expected from foreigners. It does not apply to those working in private practices. Consult a Hungarian to find out the amount to tip depending on the service.

Launderettes and dry cleaners

There are not too many launderettes in Budapest, and even fewer in other parts of the country, but they can be found. The place to look for is a *patyolat* where you can either do your washing yourself or have it done for you. Dry cleaners (*száraztisztitás*) are more common, but you usually have to wait at least 48 hours to get your clothes back. You can get dry cleaning done in a few hours for an extra charge. Laundries in Budapest can be found at:

> Budapest V, József Nádor tér 9. (Open Monday, Wednesday, Friday 7am–7pm.)
> Budapest VI, Liszt Ferenc, tér 9.

Libraries

The British Council Library contains about 13 000 books, including a large EFL section with cassettes to accompany certain material. There is a small fee to join.

> **The British Council**, Budapest VI, Benczúr, utca 26. (Open 10am–5pm Monday–Friday, closed 1pm–2.30pm.)

There are four British Council Resource Centres outside Budapest in Pécs, Győr, Miskolc and Szombathely. There are plans to open one in Veszprém in future.

The US Embassy library also has a wide selection of American books, videos and magazines, and downstairs in the basement, USIS keeps a selection of EFL material, which they will happily lend to teachers working in a state school for free. It is situated just around the corner from the British Council:

> **US Embassy**, Budapest VI, Bajza utca 31. Tel: 142-4122. (Open 11am–7pm Tuesday, other weekdays 11am–5pm, closed Saturday and Sunday.)

Budapest's Foreign Language Library has a large selection of English books, plus a beautiful reading room.

> **Foreign Language Library**, Budapest V, Molnár utca 11. (Open 12 noon–8pm Wednesday, 9am–8pm other weekdays, closed Saturday and Sunday.)

University libraries are worth checking as they usually have English sections.

Bookshops

There are several bookshops in Budapest selling books in English other than EFL material. In other parts of the country books are harder to get hold of. Bestsellers has a wide range of books from the classics to works by central and East European writers, and will order anything for you in forints. It also stocks Western stationery and Blu-Tack!

> **Bestsellers**, Pest V, Október 6 utca 11. Tel: 112-1295. (Open 9am–6.30pm Monday–Saturday.)
> **International Bookshop**, Pest V, Váci ut 19.

Post

Post offices usually open 8am–6pm on weekdays (smaller ones close at 3.30pm) and until noon on Saturdays. There are two post offices in Budapest that are open day and night; one at the Western Railway Station (Nyugati Pályaudvar – VI, Teréz Körút 105) and one at the Eastern Railway Station (Keleti Pályaudvar 72 – VIII, Baross tér 11/c, T– 122-1099). Always use a post/zip code if you want to ensure your mail arrives as soon as possible. Stamps are purchased from the post office or tobacconists.

The post is not always reliable and it can take up to 10 days for a letter to come from the UK and two weeks from the USA, although statistics in 1994 showed that the average time for a letter to or from the USA was six days.

Don't throw away anything you find in your post box or on your door. It may mean money (!) you have to collect at your local post office. If you are unsure about anything ask a Hungarian.

Addresses and telephone numbers

When giving your address to people make sure you ask them to put your surname first as the Hungarians do, and underline it. (To be safe put your name on the post box in both styles, eg John Smith, Smith John.) The post/zip code is essential and should come after the street and number.

The following are common terms: *utca* (street), *ut* (avenue), *tér* (square) and *körút* (boulevard).

Telephone numbers listed in this book only include the town code if the town is outside Budapest. Remember if you are calling another town from Budapest, or Budapest from any other town you must dial 06 first, wait for the tone and then the local code and number. The country code for Hungary is 36 followed by 1 for Budapest. For international calls dial 00 wait for the new dial tone and then the country code etc.

The correct way to address an envelope is:

Surname followed by first name	Booth Richard
City	Budapest
Street name followed by number	Andrássy ut 45
Post code	1064
Country	Hungary

Budapest is divided into districts which are often indicated in Roman numerals on maps, but not when addressing letters (see above).

Public telephones

The telephone system, which for years has been one of the most unreliable in Europe, is now being totally upgraded. This doesn't mean you will always find a phone that works, or always get through to the right number, but things have improved. Public telephones are mainly the push button variety. For local calls the minimum charge is 5 HUF for two minutes between 7am–6pm and for six minutes after 6pm and at weekends. Most countries can be called direct. Telephones take 5 HUF, 10 HUF and 20 HUF coins. One in three telephone booths in Budapest and the other larger towns are now card phones. (Cards can be bought at the post office and newsagents. Avoid hotels as they are more expensive there.) Note that due to the upgrading of the system new telephone numbers are slowly being introduced.

Help lines are as follows: for information in English, German or French (117-2200, weekdays 7am–8pm); police (07 or 118-0800 and 111-8668, they speak most European languages); fire/emergency (05 or 121-6216); ambulance (04, or 111-1666, English or German); and automobile assistance (169-1831 or 169-3714, round the clock emergency breakdown service, English spoken).

Collect calls, fax and telex can be made from the international telephone centre at V. Petőfi Sándor utca 17–19. Collect calls and credit card calls to the USA can be placed directly with the AT&T operator (00, wait for tone and then dial 360-111).

Swimming pools and thermal baths

For a country that won eight swimming medals (including five golds) at the 1992 Olympics in Barcelona, it is surprising that there are not more swimming pools. Swimming is still very popular and thousands of people fill the pools (and Lake Balaton) in summer. In Budapest apart from the expensive hotel pools there are other pools, including two on Margit Island and Csillaghegy (Budapest III, Pusztakúti ut 3) open daily 7am–6pm in summer; Monday–Friday, 7am–6pm, (Saturday 7am–3pm in winter). Pleasant surroundings with some nude sunbathing in a specified area.

Budapest is famous for its thermal baths, and they are well worth a visit. A full list can be obtained from most tourist offices. The best-known spa outside Budapest is the thermal lake at Hévíz.

Media, culture and sport

Television and radio. Three Hungarian TV channels offer a growing number of Western imports such as Dallas and Monty Python. Game shows are also on the up.

A large number of flats now have satellite TV, which includes Sky, Super, Eurosport, CNN and MTV as well as a couple of German channels. What you get depends mainly on your area. Channel 1 shows the BBC World Service news late at night at different times. The *Budapest Sun* carries a full TV programme.

Several radio stations play popular music and Radio Bridge 102.1FM daily broadcasts an evening newscast in English. A morning news programme at 8am ('Central Europe Today') covers news in the region. The BBC World Service can be picked up on shortwave, although with varying degrees of success depending on the time of day. A full weekly programme in *London Calling* is available from the British Council Library.

Newspapers. Foreign newspapers and magazines are available at the major hotels and newsagents in Budapest and in certain towns in the country. These include *The Daily Telegraph* (currently the cheapest), *The Times*, *The International Guardian* and *The New York Times*. Most of these can be bought on the same day of issue at around 1pm. There are two weekly English language newspapers published in Budapest, the *Budapest Week* and *Budapest Sun*, which cover stories on Hungary and the region as well as listings for the cinema, clubs, etc. For a more in-depth view into Hungarian culture and the arts, buy the *Hungarian Quarterly*.

A weekly magazine *Pesti Műsor* gives a full weekly entertainment guide and comes out every Wednesday. Although this is in Hungarian, it is worth buying as it gives a comprehensive guide to what's on. Films in Hungarian or dubbed into Hungarian are indicated by 'mb' (*magyarul beszélő*)

Music

Hungary has a proud music history and composers such as Bartók, Liszt, and Kodály are known throughout the world. The range of music on offer caters for nearly all tastes and ranges from classical and jazz to ethnic Hungarian folk bands.

Classical. Classical music concerts are held regularly at several venues around Budapest, the main hall being the *Zeneakadémia* (Academy of Music) where there is usually something on every night. Budapest is also home to two wonderful opera houses which are worth going to, even if it is only to look. Tickets can be bought at the venue, or at Vörösmarty tér 1 on the ground floor. The county towns have their own concert halls and some even have opera houses.

Budapest hosts an international music and arts festival in March with concerts and performances from Hungarian and international artistes, as well as other music and arts festivals at other times during the year.

Folk music. Hungarian folk music is alive and well and is tied in with the 'Dance Houses' all over the country. These have a unique atmosphere and have little in common with 'folk clubs'. Information on dance house events is available from the *Petőfi Csarnok* (Tel: 142-4327).

Jazz. There has been a revival in jazz music, with new venues springing up to accommodate the large number of excellent musicians. The Merlin Jazz Club regularly hosts some of Hungary's best jazz musicians and international guests; for a more low-key atmosphere try the Jazz Cafe next to the Fehér Gyűrű (see p 189). The town of Debrecen hosts an international jazz festival each year in September.

Pop music. Popular music is currently going through a transition period as the popular bands from the 1960s and 1970s do their final farewell tours and new bands struggle to find good venues. There are a number of good local bands now emerging, the more popular ones usually play at the *Petőfi Csarnok* in the *Városliget* (city park). During the summer months a growing number of top Western acts turn up in Hungary. In 1993 U2, Santana and Depeche Mode all played in Budapest, and in 1994 Michael Jackson made a video in the city.

Cinema and theatre. Going to the cinema is not only popular but very affordable and nearly every town has a cinema where US and UK films are regularly screened, many in their original language with Hungarian subtitles. (At weekends be sure to arrive early to guarantee a seat.) Only a few of the big Hollywood box office hits are dubbed. A full cinema guide can be found in the *Pesti Műsor* and all films shown in English are listed in the *Budapest Week* and *Sun*. There is also a relatively good selection of French, Italian and German films. Art cinemas, which often include some good Hungarian films, are flourishing.

Theatre is popular and affordable with rep companies all over the country. In summer the Merlin Theatre puts on productions in English.

Sport

Whatever sport you may be interested in, you can probably find somewhere to do it in Hungary. The last couple of years have seen the arrival of golf, baseball, squash and even cricket to add to the more traditional Hungarian sports of horse riding, football, hunting, tennis and swimming. Rambling is very popular and at weekends people head off to the hills. For anyone wanting to do aerobics or work out in a gym there are plenty of fitness centres around, including weightlifting clubs.

City by city

Debrecen. Debrecen is the third largest town in Hungary and a major industrial centre. It is also a university town and has a number of private language schools.

Győr. Although Győr is a major industrial town situated in the west of Hungary close to the Austrian border, much of its baroque centre is well preserved. Being so close to Austria it is a popular tourist town. It has a number of private language schools as well as a British Council Resource Centre.

Eger. Lying in the north-east of Hungary this beautiful town is famous for its wine and its castle, much visited from spring to autumn. It is also well situated for exploring the Mátra and Bükk regions. International House opened a school here in 1994.

Miskolc. Hungary's second largest city is nothing to look at architecturally, and the collapse of communism has led to high unemployment. It is a major university town and has a number of private language schools. For local information on EFL try the British Council Resource Centre.

Pécs. Pécs has a population of 150 000 and is located in the south of the country. This city is full of splendid buildings, museums and galleries and includes a number of excellent examples of Islamic architecture. It is a major university town which gives it a youthful feel although there are not too many private language schools. It does, however, have a British Council Resource Centre which provides information.

Veszprém. Another beautiful town close to Balaton, Veszprém is a university town with a number of native EFL teachers. There are plans to open up a British Council Resource Centre in 1995.

The country and the people

Hungary has undergone many changes, especially recently, in its rather turbulent history; but remains a beautiful and interesting country. It offers the visitor the chance to see a country modernizing itself after years of communist rule, yet still maintaining customs and traditions that have been cherished for centuries. The life, energy and beauty of Budapest put it on a par with the major cities in Europe, if not the world. With a population of over 2 million out of a national population of 10 million, Budapest is the country's centre for business, the arts, and many other areas. Only a handful of other towns boast populations of over 100 000, yet local and regional pride give them their own distinct character and liveliness.

History

895–896	The Hungarian tribes (Magyars) whose origin has never quite been established, reach the Carpathian Basin and settle.
955	Magyar raids into Western Europe.
1000	King Stephen crowned. He was to become known as the founder of the country. It was his influence that ended the tribal wars and converted the Magyars to Christianity.
1000–1541	Independent Hungarian kingdom.
1541–1686	In 1526 the Hungarians lose an important battle at Mohács to the Turks; 15 years later the Turks begin an occupation of Hungary that is to last for the next 150 years.
1686–1867	In 1683 the European powers help to drive the Turks from Hungary. The end of Ottoman rule leads to Austrian rule.
1848–49	Lajos Kossuth leads a bid for independence. The Hungarians rise up against the Austrians on 15 March 1848 (now celebrated as a national holiday).

1867–1918	The Austro–Hungarian monarchy.
1914–18	Hungary fights alongside Germany in the first world war.
1918–19	Hungarian Soviet Republic.
1919–46	Miklós Horthy is Regent. By the Treaty of Trianon in 1920 signed as part of the post first world war peace settlement Hungary lost two-thirds of its territory and one third of its Magyar population.
1941	Hungary enters the second world war as Germany's ally hoping to regain some of its lost territory. Thousands of Jews murdered.
1944	Germans totally occupy country after Horthy tries to make a separate peace with the allies.
1946–48	Hungarian Republic (coalition government).
1948	Communist and Social Democratic parties merge to form the Hungarian Workers Party. Establishment of a People's Republic, quickly followed by Stalinist regime.
1956	23 October students demonstrate in Budapest against Soviet occupation. Imre Nagy made Prime Minister and announces that Hungary will leave the Warsaw Pact. Fighting continues throughout the country until 4 November when a full Soviet invasion quashes the uprising. 200 000 people flee to the West. Nagy, along with hundreds of others is executed. After fleeing to Moscow, János Kádár returns to become Prime Minister.
1968	New economic management, abandoning strict central economic planning and paving the way for a limited market economy. This continues throughout the 1970s, while Hungary remains a close Soviet ally.
1988	Kádár deposed and Hungary moves towards democracy.
1988–89	Communists agree to give up monopoly on power.
1990	Return to parliamentary democracy with free elections won by the Hungarian Democratic Forum.
1993	In December József Antall, the Prime Minister, dies of cancer.
1994	Second free multi-party elections return the Socialists (the reformed Communists) to government with an overall majority. One of government's first acts is to cancel the World Expo which was to be held in Budapest in 1996.

Geography

Hungary lies in the heart of the Carpathian Basin right in the centre of Europe. While not a very big country (about the size of Ireland), it offers a rich and varied landscape, from the rather bare Great Plain (*Puszta*) to the majestic beauty of the Danube Bend. The highest peak in Hungary is Kékes (1015 m) in the Mátra Range to the north, but there are few 'mountains' as such. To the south-west of Budapest is Lake Balaton (4598 km^2) where many

Hungarians spend their summers. The lake is shallow around its shore and has an average depth of 3–4 m making it ideal for swimming.

Climate

Hungary has a temperate continental climate and the summers are generally long and hot. Budapest especially can get very stuffy in summer. July and August are the hottest months and temperatures often reach 30°C and above. The winters are cold, with temperatures falling below −5°C. January and February are the coldest months; and the rainiest months are November, May and June. Snow usually falls in January and February.

The environment

Budapest has a major problem with air pollution especially in Pest. Pollution comes mainly from car exhaust fumes filling the air with high levels of lead and carbon monoxide. People complain of respiratory problems such as asthma and bronchitis. Such air pollution is less apparent in other parts of the country.

Hungarians are slowly becoming more environmentally conscious; catalysers on new cars, for example, are now compulsory and bottle banks have been introduced. Due to strong opposition from a large cross-section of society moves to build a dam in the scenic Danube Bend region were thwarted in 1992.

Violent crime is rare in Hungary although burglary and car theft have increased substantially since 1990. While Budapest is basically a safe city, there are certain areas where care should be taken. These include Keleti station and the XI district. In particular watch out for pickpockets around tourist areas such as Váci ut and on trams.

Politics and religion

Politics. March 1990 saw the first free elections in Hungary since 1945; despite voter apathy, the Hungarian Democractic Forum (MDF) won a decisive majority over its rivals, the Alliance of Free Democrats (SZDSZ) and the Federation of Young Democrats (FIDESZ). Prime Minister József Antall formed a coalition government with the Smallholders Party and the Christian Democrats and held power until his death in 1993. Boros Péter stepped in and headed the government until the elections in May 1994.

In these four years the government became increasingly unpopular, mainly due to the economic hardship felt by a large proportion of the electorate. However, at a time of instability in the region political stability was at least maintained. The parliamentary elections in May 1994 saw the return to power of the 'reformed communists'. Although commanding an absolute majority in Parliament, holding 209 of the 386 seats, the Hungarian Socialist Party led by Gyula Horn decided to form a coalition government with the liberal SZDSZ (Alliance of Free Democrats).

Religion. Hungary is predominantly (67%) Catholic although many Hungarians are not practising Catholics or regular church goers. People tend to be more religious in the small towns and villages than in cities like Budapest. Pope John Paul II visited Hungary in 1991 and started a small resurgence in religion, although most Hungarians are rather ambivalent about it.

Other denominations include Calvinists (20%) and Lutherans (5%) with smaller minorities of Greek Orthodox and Jews. Over 600 000 Hungarian Jews were killed during the second world war, and today the only significant Jewish community in Hungary is in Budapest.

Like other parts of Eastern and Central Europe Hungary has recently been attracting a large number of missionaries from different parts of the world, as well as sects such as Hare Krishna and the Church of Scientology.

The people

The first thing one can say about Hungarians is they are survivors. Throughout its history, this now small country has been invaded, occupied and had its borders changed many times. The Turks, the Austrians and more recently the former USSR have left their mark on architecture, food and the people. Yet throughout it all, the Hungarians have always managed to come through more or less intact, and have retained their own traditions and culture.

Hungarians can come across as being a pessimistic people, especially where politics is involved, but beneath this is a deep sense of optimism and pride in their country. Wherever you go in Hungary you will meet warm generous people, who will be genuinely interested in you and your country. Family and friendship are very important and once you are befriended you will have a friend for life. A strong sense of loyalty means that friendships are not superficial.

In company Hungarians are talkative and love to argue, though rarely managing to lose their sense of humour. They can also be temperamental and impulsive. Their hospitality is second to none and they welcome people into their homes openly. Once there you will be wined and dined graciously.

They are hardworking, both at school and at work. They often take on more than one job to support their families and work long hours. At the same time they are competitive, and the recent changes since 1989 have in some ways enhanced this competitiveness.

Hungarians are very open, so don't be surprised to be asked about your love life and how much money you earn, even by people who are not your closest friends. Hungarians will want an explanation for something rather than just accepting it. They believe they are unique in everything, and that any achievement in the world in some way or another has had a Hungarian connection. All in all a wonderful, warm friendly people!

Habits and customs. During your stay in Hungary, you will no doubt find yourself invited to a Hungarian home for dinner. It is customary on such occasions to take a gift of some sort, usually flowers for the lady and a bottle of wine for the man. In many homes you may be asked to take your shoes off. This is simply a form of politeness so you do not traipse dirt around the flat. Your hosts may offer you some slippers (*papucs*) or you may want to take your own.

You will be overwhelmed by the amount of food and drink your hosts will offer you, and it is very difficult to say no. Even polite refusals are often interpreted as simply 'politeness' and you will be given more anyway. It is also important to praise the food, not just at the end of a meal, but all the way through; *finom*, meaning tasty, is a good word to remember.

When drinking during a meal it is customary to say *egészségedre* (to your health), to the company. However, when drinking beer do not clink glasses. This is not customary, as a mark of respect to those killed during the Habsburg era.

Hungarians will always shake hands when they meet each other and part, even daily when they know each other very well. When a man and woman meet it is customary for the woman to offer her hand first. At a certain point in a friendship Hungarians greet each other with a kiss on both cheeks. Take the lead from the Hungarian. This applies to both men and women.

Hungarians like to celebrate, and apart from birthdays (*születésnap*), namedays (*névnap*) are always a good time for a party. Again, in the case of women, flowers are usually given. Wine or champagne may also be brought into work to celebrate.

Typical lives. Children will often go to kindergarten from the age of three. Mothers are allowed up to three years maternity leave and many take it and stay at home with their children up to that time. For many, the school years are spent working towards getting a place at university or college. Young Hungarians tend to be conscientious and to work hard at school. Families are close, and Sunday lunchtimes are occasions when the whole family will get together, which may mean up to four generations. Due to housing and economic problems it is very rare for children to leave home before they are married, and it is not uncommon for a new couple to live with one set of parents until they get a place of their own (the grandparents may also be sharing the same house).

For those who manage to secure a place at university, the next five years (or in some cases three years) are spent enjoying life. It is very hard in some subjects, for example English, to gain a place and many people who fail to get in work for a year and try again. Once accepted, the academic demands are not particularly oner- ous, but five years is a long time. It is at university that a Hungarian is likely to meet his or her future life partner and it is not unusual for students to marry while still at university.

Once married, finding a place to live is not that easy. Usually accommodation is rented, as only a lucky few will have the money to buy a place or have one left to them. Once young Hungarians start work they usually find one job is not enough to live on and it is common for Hungarians to have two, three or even four jobs. It is normal for a working day to be 12 hours long. Women are therefore left with the responsisiblity of bringing up the children plus looking after the house, and in a lot of cases having a job as well.

In a traditional family the woman will tend to do everything around the house. With the new generation these accepted roles of the man and woman are changing very slowly.

The divorce rate is high in Hungary and with the long working days, accommodation problems and the general stress this is perhaps not surprising. The average number of children in each family is two. Divorce can prove expensive for the man as he is unlikely to get custody of the children or the flat. Men generally retire at 65 and women 55. (The legal age is now 60 and 55 respectively, but legislation is being proposed to raise these.)

PART 3
TEACHING ENGLISH

The Hungarian education system is undergoing major reforms at the moment, and a new national curriculum is currently being written. It is difficult to assess its qualities accurately and depend- ing on whom you speak to, you will get different opinions as to its merits.

The foundations of the existing education system were laid down after the second world war when Hungary was transformed into a socialist country.

The Hungarian education system

Education is free, and compulsory for 10 years between the ages of six and sixteen, although most continue their education beyond this. Children attend the basic school (*általános iskola*) from six to fourteen where they study a number of general subjects together with some practical training. There is also provision for talented pupils, especially those with linguistic skills. The grades are divided into groups which stay together throughout their primary education. During the 1960s and 1970s secondary education expanded, mainly due to the growth of vocational schools. Secondary education now comprises the following types of schools.

* the grammar school (*gimnázium*) which offers four-year academic courses, including some vocational training;
* the four-year secondary vocational school (*szakközépiskola*) where emphasis is on practical education, giving pupils a full vocational training with a general education background;
* three-year apprentice training schools (*szakmunkásképző intézetek*), linked to factories or agricultural cooperatives, through which pupils obtain full trade qualifications; and
* two- and three-year vocational schools of other kinds (eg shorthand/typing).

There has also been the introduction of seven- and eight-year programmes with children starting secondary education at 10 or 11 years old.

The level of academic knowledge gained at secondary school is high. After secondary education those that wish to and are successful either go to a university or college. The main difference between a university and a college is that the college degree is not as prestigious. Students who fail their entrance exams to university usually go to a college (or reapply for university the following year).

Methods used in classrooms

The grammar translation method is still evident in some schools, especially in smaller towns in the country. Students are expected to repeat words and phrases around the class with very little real communication taking place. Emphasis is put on memorization of texts and dialogues.

However, all this is rapidly changing as more and more teachers are being exposed to different methodologies, for example communicative methodology, and are experimenting more. Teachers, especially the younger ones, are trying to keep up with the new trends in ELT; in some cases though they are setting them.

The greater availability of Western course books has also helped to modernize teaching. Teachers graduating from teacher training colleges today have far more exposure to the English language than their predecessors and greater opportunity to travel. The influx of native English teachers and trainers has also helped.

Teachers coming to work in Hungary should introduce new methods and ideas slowly to their students; bombarding them with new methods straight away may be counterproductive.

However, there is still the problem of meeting the requirements to pass the school or state exam, and this means a high input of grammar is necessary.

The kind of language needed

In general, Hungarian students still tend to be passive learners of languages and what they need are oral and aural skills. At some schools repetition drills are the only oral practice students get. For the native English speaker the initial problems are less to do with structure and more to do with getting the students to talk.

Often students receive a solid grammar base, but lack the functional language to communicate outside the classroom in real situations.

Grading

From primary school through to the end of university, students are constantly worried about their grades. The scale is 1 to 5, 5 being the top grade, and 1 being a fail. 1 is very rarely given as it could mean a pupil has to repeat the year. Grades are given on assessment, tests and final exams, and in most schools for behaviour and how hard a student works. Grades are recorded in the *ellenörzö könyv* (grade books) which each student carries throughout his or her school life, and which are signed by both the teachers and parents.

Grades are also recorded in the *napló* (register). You will be expected to consult with your Hungarian colleagues when deciding on grades for your students.

Exams

Whatever your feelings may be about them, exams are important in a Hungarian student's life. He or she is required to pass in a variety of subjects to graduate from secondary school and then has to sit a set of rigorous exams to get into university. If students have attained the intermediate or advanced State Language Exams in

English, they are exempt from attending English lessons in school, although they may still attend if they wish.

The state exams in English are better known as the *Rigó utca* exams (named after the street where they are administered). They are held at three different levels; elementary, intermediate and advanced. The intermediate or medium level exam is the most popular, and success at this level can mean exemption from English in school, an increment in pay, extra points for university entrance exams and is a requirement for some jobs. Although by far the most popular exam in terms of the number of people entering, it is not necessarily a true indication of the level of competence of the student. It is roughly equivalent to the Cambridge First Certificate with regard to level, and is divided into parts A and B. The C-type exam is simply parts A and B combined.

Part A comprises grammar, translation and reading, Part B tests oral skills; students have to answer questions from a prescribed list of topics such as holidays or health. There is also a picture description.

Books are available in many bookshops outlining these topics and giving sample questions. For many studying English the medium level exam is a goal. Exams are held three times a year in February, May and October.

The Cambridge exams were introduced in Hungary in 1988 and are slowly developing as competition to the state exams as they become more widely recognized by students and employers. Rigó Street is the current open centre for taking these exams as well. However, the exam fees are far higher than for the state exams and hinder more widespread adoption of the exams. They are held twice a year in December and June.

Other exams available include the Oxford exams, Pitman and TOEFL (the exam for Hungarians wanting to enter the US universities). London Chamber of Commerce exams are also taken at some centres.

Hungarian students

A survey conducted in 1993 showed that the person most likely to be proficient in English would be a young female student, salesperson or professional. Almost half (45%) of the proficient English speakers are under 25, and over half are female. Another interesting statistic was that 71% of those asked agreed that 'to have power and influence in Hungary today, Hungarians need to speak English'.

There is of course no such thing as a 'typical' Hungarian student, although large numbers do have things in common. It is, however, first worth distinguishing students in state schools from those at private language schools.

In an average class in a *gimnázium* you will probably have students of mixed abilities and levels, as well as differences in motivation. There will be those who will be highly motivated and really appreciate the opportunity of having a native English speaker as a teacher; then again there are always students who won't be interested in the subject at all.

Hungarian students are generally highly motivated and keen to learn. They are on the whole well disciplined and have a high respect for the teacher. In class they work conscientiously and are not afraid of speaking. They are not boisterous and have a rather calm, serious approach to learning. In state schools they expect and do a lot of homework.

In the private sector adults will do homework if set, although some with heavy work commitments won't have time. The student who goes to a private language school is either paying for it himself, which for most constitutes a big investment, or else has a company paying, in which case English is probably needed for his or her job. In both cases the students are there to learn rather than treat it as a social occasion, and are therefore usually highly motivated.

If students have studied languages before, at school for example, their previous learning experience may have been of the Prussian 'teacher up at the front and lecturing' style, so a more low-profile teacher role and a more active student role may take a bit of getting used to. Students may also initially be a bit put out that you cannot explain things to them in Hungarian, so be sure that at low levels situationalized presentations are clear, as are your instructions. A few words and phrases in Hungarian will be useful (see pp 225–228). Of course gestural support for instructions is a must at low levels.

Elements of the grammar translation method are still very much favoured with the state language teaching system, exemplified by Rigó utca Intermediate and Advanced State Language Exams. Higher level students may therefore expect to do some overt grammar work as well as working on their fluency. Guided Discovery teaching techniques are recommended in such cases.

Hungarian students who have studied languages before may be used to progressing systematically through a coursebook. If this is not your approach tell your students so, and perhaps also explain the rationale behind your decision. Do not forget though that if students have spent a lot of money on coursebooks they will expect to use them.

Discipline

In Hungarian schools you will not find anything like the discipline problems you may have come across in the UK, the USA or other parts of the world. Problems you are likely to encounter include students not paying attention, speaking to each other in Hungarian, or preparing some other work in class.

Hungarian teachers will give a warning first and finally write a note in the *ellenőrző* (grade book), which has to be signed by the parents, should the 'offence' be repeated. Corporal punishment is illegal.

Cheating

Unfortunately cheating, which can range from whispering answers in class to copying in exams, is common and not really seen as morally wrong. Students feel they are helping friends out and would expect them to do the same in return. This does not mean you have to accept the situation.

Business people and ESP

There are currently several hundred joint ventures in Budapest and the country as a whole, and thousands of new companies have been established since 1989. This has created a need for business English language tuition.

People in business usually start work early and finish late. Their English lessons are therefore either early in the morning at 7am or 7.30am or in the evening after work. In either case workers are usually tired and you may have to be less demanding. Many younger Hungarians have a good standard of English, especially those working for joint venture companies, and such students often need more specialized language for their field of work. Many of the older generation of managers, however, have very limited English (they may speak German), and what is taught is usually general English within their work context whenever possible. This can cause extra anxiety for such managers as they are under increasing pressure to learn. One of the problems of company teaching is the split levels in the classes, which in a lot of cases the companies will do nothing about (see 'Teaching business people', pp 264–273).

In a lot of cases English taught in companies is simply general English. However, there is a growing demand for specialized courses to be run, tailored to clients' needs. A lot of businessmen will know the vocabulary associated with their work, but will need tuition in how to use the language properly in context, to give presentations, to negotiate, etc. They also need training in how business works in the West as this is an area which is new to them. Businessmen have very little time and may often cancel their lesson or turn up late. It is advisable to ask them to phone you if they have to cancel to save you a trip to the company. There are a lot of business materials on the market now, but rather than choosing a particular book to use, it is better to build materials around the students' work.

Teaching children

While children are now starting to learn English from the age of three, it isn't until they are in secondary school that they are really exposed to formal teaching. Very young learners are exposed to English through songs and rhymes. You can encourage them to do actions along with the songs. Hungarian children are very enthusiastic. Children have a much shorter attention span than adults and this means you have to prepare a number of activities and changes of focus. You also need to vary the pace of your lessons, having quiet moments as well as lively ones (see 'Teaching children and adolescents', pp 257–263).

Specific Hungarian problems

Hungarian learners of English have particular problems, and those outlined here are meant to serve as a reference. By being aware of some of the difficulties learners may have, you will be better equipped to anticipate problems and develop strategies for dealing with them.

Grammar

Tenses. Whereas English has six tenses, in Hungarian there are only three. Other concepts are expressed by, for example, adding a prefix or a suffix to the verb.

Present perfect tense. As in a lot of languages, the present perfect, which strictly speaking is an aspect rather than a tense, does not exist in Hungarian. The concept is therefore confusing for students. In Hungarian the same concepts are expressed by using either the simple past or simple present; usually combined with verbal prefixes or time expressions.

The present perfect shows the present situation in relation to past actions.

- *Unfinished past.* An action or state which began in the past and has continued until now (used with for or since), eg I have lived here for two years. In Hungarian this is always expressed by a present tense, therefore you may get sentences like:

I live here for two years (x)

In the negative, Hungarians prefer the past:

I didn't eat out for ages (x)

- *Completed action.* In Hungarian 'She has eaten my sandwich' would be expressed by a past tense:

    She ate my sandwich *(x)*

- *Experience.* Something that has happened at some point in the past but the exact time is not important, eg I have lived in Egypt. In Hungarian this may be expressed by a past tense, plus an adverb of frequency. This often results in learners overusing 'already':

    I was already in Egypt (x)

- *Present result.* Something which happened in the recent past and the results can be seen now, eg I've just arrived. Hungarian learners may use 'just now' plus a past tense. The word order may also be wrong:

    I just now arrived. (x)

For teaching purposes it is not so much the form that is a problem for students; this they will learn relatively quickly. Rather it is the concept that has to be made clear to them.

Present v future tenses. In Hungarian you can use the present simple tense to express a future concept; mostly with a time expression. In English, to express a planned action (ie where the decision has already been made), we would use 'going to' or the present continuous. Thus 'What are you going to do after you finish university?' can appear as:

What do you do after you finish university? (x)

Whereas in English we would use 'will' to express an intention at the moment, eg 'I'll have a beer', in Hungarian this would simply be expressed by the present simple.

I have a beer. (x)

Hungarians find difficulties distinguishing between 'going to' and 'will' and tend to overuse 'will' when talking about the future.

Present continuous tense. The present continuous tense is used to describe actions happening now, 'I'm sitting' (present meaning);

an arranged future, 'I'm flying to London tomorrow' (future meaning); and temporary situations, 'I'm staying here for a week' (present meaning).

There is no 'continuous' form in Hungarian, thus learners will find it difficult to make the distinction between simple and continuous in all tenses.

Since there is only one present tense in Hungarian, learners tend to overuse the simple present tense to express these meanings listed above, and in turn may also miss out the auxiliary.

I sit. (x)
I stay here for a week. (x)

Past continuous tense. The past continuous is used to describe a continuing action at a specific time in the past, eg 'I was watching television when the doorbell rang'. Hungarian learners make mistakes by using two simple past forms:

I watched television when the doorbell rang. (x)

Passive voice. The passive voice exists in Hungarian, although it is mainly used to express states, eg 'the door is locked', and is very different to the passive in English. The structure is far less productive than in English, and where English uses the passive, in most cases Hungarian learners will use the impersonal 'they'. Thus instead of saying 'The bridge was built in 1918' Hungarians will say:

They built the bridge in 1918. *(x)*

Conditionals. Conditionals express the relationship between two actions. There are three basic patterns:

- *The first conditional:* 'If I pass the exam I'll buy a car'. This refers to the present or future where the condition may or may not happen.
- *The second conditional:* 'I'd buy a house if I had the money'. This refers to the future or present where the condition is unlikely or impossible.
- *The third conditional:* 'I'd have gone if I had had the money'. This refers to the past where the condition didn't happen.

The ideas expressed by the English conditionals can in most cases be expressed by Hungarian equivalents. Problems arise not in the concept but in the form.

In Hungarian the same tense is used in both clauses and this may be transferred to English. Thus the first conditional may be expressed as:

If I pass the exam I buy a car. (x)
If I will pass the exam I will buy a car. (x)

The second conditional tends to be constructed as:

I would buy a house if I would have the money (x)

A common error with the third conditional is:

I would have gone if I would have money (x)

When teaching conditionals you should also highlight the contractions (eg I'd and I'll) which students find difficult to hear and are reluctant to produce.

Reported speech. We use reported speech when we are telling someone what somebody else said without using quotation marks. 'She said "I love opera"' is direct speech, using the exact words that were spoken. 'She said (that) she loved opera' is reported speech. The main rule for reported speech is to put all tenses one back into the past.

In Hungarian there is no moving of tenses back as there is in English.

'He said "I promise I will write to you"' would in reported speech be rendered as 'He promised he would write to you'. However, Hungarians may say:

He promised he will write to you. (x)

In spoken English we tend not to use the back shift all the time, and this confuses students even more. Refer to a grammar book for correct usage.

Questions. In indirect or embedded questions a group of words makes the questions longer and more tentative.

- He visited you (uninverted).
- Why did he visit you? (inverted, direct)
- Why do you think he visited you? (uninverted, indirect)

Indirect or embedded questions don't exist in Hungarian and cause learners all sorts of difficulties.

What do you think why did he visit you? (x)

Negatives in polite requests. In Hungarian you can use a negative form to add politeness to a request or suggestion. This is not normally the case in English. A negative sentence usually comes across as being rude. Thus 'Do you know what time it is?' is expressed as:

Don't you know what time it is? *(x)*

Sentence structure. Hungarians have a lot of problems with word order and sentence structure. In Hungarian, word order and sentence structure is more flexible than in English, leading to errors in English. In Hungarian the subject and object are marked by their case endings and not by their position in the sentence. As a result of this in Hungarian the word order can be very flexible. This results in Hungarian students having problems with the English word order and saying sentences like 'There lived a king in the castle' and 'In the field grazed some cows'.

Articles. Hungarian has both definite and indefinite articles just like English. In Hungarian the definite article expresses general things and therefore there is a tendency to overuse it:

The most people (x)
The dog is the man's best friend (x)

Where in English we would also use the indefinite article 'a', in Hungarian this is often left out altogether.

I'd like beer. (x)

Articles are often incorrectly used with geographical and place names:

We went to the Oxford Street. (x)

Relative clauses. The Hungarian word *ami/amit* covers all three relative clauses: 'what', 'which' and 'that'. There is a tendency for learners to overuse 'what' instead of 'that' or 'which'.

He is often late what makes me angry. (x)
Everything what we saw was beautiful. (x)
He showed me the shirt what he bought. (x)

Phrasal verbs. Phrasal verbs are a problem for all language learners and Hungarian learners are no exception. They should be practised in a meaningful context.

Vocabulary

Say/tell. In Hungarian there is only one word to express both 'say' and 'tell', hence learners often get them confused.

He told that he had finished. (x)

When using 'tell' it must be followed by a personal indirect object, ie 'He told me (that) he had finished'.

Hungarian learners will often overuse the phrase: 'I have to say/tell . . . (that) . . .'.

Countable and uncountable nouns. There are quite a number of nouns which are used as countable nouns in Hungarian (ie they are used in the plural or with the definite article) but which cannot be used in this way in English. Here are some of the most common.

He gave me lots of good advices where to go. (x)
What sort of equipments do you need? (x)
How much experiences have you had? (x)
The room was full of very nice furnitures. (x)
We had lots of homeworks. (x)
She gave me informations about the conference. (x)
Passengers may carry two luggages without extra charges. (x)

Prepositions. Difficulties occur mainly with Hungarian interference. Where in English we would use 'in' Hungarians use 'on':

She's on a lesson. (x)
Your brother looks nice on the picture. (x)

Learners often have problems knowing when to use 'until' and 'by'.

I'll get home until 4 o'clock. (x)

'Until' is used to talk about a situation continuing and stopping at a certain moment, whereas 'by' refers to an action which will happen at or before a particular moment in the future.

There is also a problem with 'while' and 'until' as Hungarian has the same word for both. You may get sentences such as:

I'm going to see him a lot until he is in Hungary. (x)

Third person singular. Since there is only one personal pronoun which expresses third person singular in Hungarian, both male and female, learners constantly use 'he' when referring to a woman and vice versa. They have the same problem with possessive pronouns.

Numbers. In Hungarian nouns keep their singular form after numbers. This can be a problem for students at lower levels.

Two boy. (x)

Hungarians put adjectives into the plural, for example:

They are olds. (x)

Much v many. In Hungarian there is one word, *sok*, to express 'many', 'much', 'a lot' and 'plenty'. Therefore learners find it difficult to know which one to use. They tend to use 'much' and 'many' in positive sentences whereas in English we would use 'a lot'. They also use a singular noun after *sok*.

He's got much friend. (x)

Nervous v excited. These two words are often confused with learners often misusing excited:

I was so excited before my exam. *(x)*

Politeness. Hungarians tend to reply to the question 'How are you?' with 'Thanks fine'. This is directly to do with Hungarian interference.

'Please' tends to be underused by Hungarians. They also tend to use it in response to thank you.

Another problem with please is that Hungarians tend to translate it directly from *tessék*, which is very versatile in the number of situations it can be used in.

False friends and interference. False friends are words which are the same or very similar in the learner's language but have a different meaning in English.

Sympathetic – nice or kind: **He's a very sympathetic teacher** *(x)*
Propaganda – publicity: **There was lots of propaganda about the meeting. (x)**
Farmer – jeans
Administrator – secretary
Programme – plans: **What's your programme for the evening? (x)**

Other common mistakes include:

I felt myself very well on the party (x)
We made an excursion to the nature. (x)

Writing

At the lower levels it is necessary to make students aware of when English uses capitals. For example, Hungarians will not use capitals for geographical names used adjectivally:

Paul was a young British boy. (x)

Hungarian students tend to write long and complicated sentences in their own language, and will try to do the same in English. Train them to write short sentences using simple structures until they feel more confident.

In letters the layout is different and therefore must be taught and there is also a habit of being too formal.

A Hungarian *életrajz* is closer to an American resumé than to a British CV – but not that close. Resumé and CV writing is an essential skill.

Pronunciation

While Hungarian learners don't have too many problems with English pronunciation there are certain areas that need special attention.

Stress. Wordstress in Hungarian always falls on the first syllable of a word where in English stress is more flexible. Hungarians may transfer this rule mistakenly to English.

    shampōō → shāmpoo

Intonation. Every syllable in Hungarian is given equal time value. The stresses in sentences often fall regularly, regardless of meaning, since shifting emphasis is conveyed by a shift in word order, not in stress pattern. The Hungarian voice range is generally narrower and the voice is pitched lower than in English.

When some or all of these features are transferred into English the effect may be one of over-emphatic speech, of sing-song monotony, or rather abrupt flatness.

Intonation in Hungarian Yes/No type questions has a ⎯⎯⎯⎯⌃ pattern which Hungarians may transfer to English:

    ⎯⎯⎯⎯⎯⎯⎯⎯⌃

    Did you go to the cinema yesterday?

Sound. There are no weak forms in Hungarian, hence students have problems both producing them and hearing them in English.

The following are certain sounds which Hungarian learners have problems with and suggestions on how to deal with them.

- /TH/ Get students to place their index finger on their lips and as they say the sound their tongue should touch their finger.
- /w/ may be pronounced /v/, eg west – vest. Show students the rounding of the lips.
- /θ/ may be pronounced /s/ or /t/, eg thin – sin/tin.
- /ð/ may be pronounced /d/ or /z/, eg then – den/zen.
- /ŋ/ may be pronounced /ŋg/, eg banger – Bangor
- /p/ is not very aspirated in Hungarian, so initial /p/ may sound like /b/, eg pond – bond.

- /t/ is not very aspirated in Hungarian, so initial /t/ may sound like /d/, eg tin – din

Because Hungarian follows regular sound-spelling equivalence, Hungarians may have a tendency to pronounce words as spelt:

>comfort /kDmfo:rt/
>London /LDndDn/
>Sword /sw ɔ: rd/

/r/ may be trilled and sounded when it is silent in standard British English.

>word /v ɔ:rd/
>car /ka:r/

The 'Schwa' is a weak sound which is written phonetically as ə. It is the most common sound in English and does not exist in Hungarian. Students often have problems both hearing it and producing it, preferring to use strong forms instead.

>It's *for* you /fə/ – /fɔ:r/

Diphthongs. A diphthong is two vowel sounds which run together to make one sound.

>fair /eə/

In Hungarian there are no true diphthongs and each vowel is pronounced on its own. Learners therefore find these difficult. They either try to give the two sounds equal weight, or they reduce diphthongs to an approximate single vowel sound.

>/əʊ / may be pronounced as a single / ɔ:/.

Hungarians may find it difficult to differentiate between

>/D/ / ɔ:/ /əʊ/, eg cot – court – coat
>/æ/ may be pronounced /e/, eg bad – bed.
>/i/ may be pronounced /i:/, eg ship – sheep.

Hungarians may find it difficult to distinguish between

>/æ/ /D/ and /ʌ /, eg cat – cot – cut

A book written for Hungarian students learning English outlining main problem areas is *Problem English* by Susan Doughty and Geoff Thomson. You may find this useful as a reference source.

Headway Pronunciation (OUP) by Bill Bowler and Sarah Cunningham is another excellent supplementary book for pronunciation exercises. Problems which are Hungarian-specific are highlighted.

Published EFL material available

Bookshops
BELT, Budapest II, Bajvívó u 8, 1027. Tel/Fax: 201-0019. (Specializes in ELT books and has a wide selection of books from various publishers.)
Libra Books (Longman), Pest VIII, Kölcsey u 2.

Publishers
Cambridge University Press (CUP), Budapest, Tulipán u 8, 1022. Tel: 115-5068. Fax: 115-6259.
Heinemann, Budapest, Török Flóris u 128/A, 1204. Tel: 147-9226.
Longman, Budapest, Kölcsei u 2, 1085. Tel: 134-2160. Fax: 117-9648.
Magyar Macmillan, Budapest, Móricz Zs. körtér 3/b, 1117. Tel/Fax: 186-8951.
Oxford University Press (OUP), Budapest, Tarcali u 20, 1113. Tel: 166-1557.
Penguin, Budapest, Bank u 6, 1054. Tel: 111-7912.

APPENDICES

Appendix 1. Case histories

Andrew Hebeler, a 24-year-old American, came to Hungary in September 1993. He found work in a private language school in Budapest.

After finishing my college degree in English and Political Science I became interested in the idea of going to Europe to teach. I had already done some teaching in the States which had whetted my appetite, and I was recommended to take the four-week RSA/UCLES CTEFLA course at International House in London before looking for work as this would not only increase my job opportunities but give me essential training. Following the course, Eastern Europe seemed to be a good place to look for work, and after considering the Czech Republic I eventually settled for Hungary as I had heard Prague was already full of Americans and I wanted something other than a mini-America abroad.

Luckily I knew someone teaching in Budapest who was able to put me up for the first couple of weeks. With very little money left, finding work urgently was a necessity. I got hold of a list of private language schools and a map and spent a week trudging round as many schools as I could. All of them asked the same sort of questions but were mainly interested in whether I was qualified or not, and though they all expressed interest, the majority had no vacancies. However, by the end of the week I had been offered work at three language schools with a total of 24 teaching hours. Each of the schools paid by the hour for the lessons taught and thankfully one school gave me an advance on my salary. One of the schools sorted my work papers out but left it to me to get my certificate officially translated, which then cost around 3 000 HUF.

My timetable was made up of general English classes and some company teaching, although this was also basically general English. Some days I would start at 7.30am and finish at 8.30pm which wasn't ideal but that was only a couple of times a week. Although I had to travel around the city I was lucky in that everything was pretty central and the transport system is so good. I did teach at one company though which took an hour to get there and for which I did not receive any extra money for travelling time!

All of the three schools had an adequate supply of teaching materials and were equipped with audio and video aids. One of the schools even provided monthly seminars for the teachers and carried out observations. However, the problem was these observations were also used as a marker for your pay!

Students all had a coursebook which was either *Headway* or *Grapevine* and one of my groups was preparing for the Oxford exams. I was also asked to take a group for conversation, sharing it with a Hungarian teacher who would concentrate on the grammar while I was supposed to 'make them talk'.

My students were friendly, pleasant and motivated to learn. Initially they were interested in me and America, but I was definitely not a novelty for them as they had been taught by a native-speaker before. At times I had difficulty getting the students to talk and stimulating discussion, and found they would prefer to discuss lighter rather than serious topics. The average age of my students was around 18–20 with the company students from 30–50.

Budapest is a very comfortable and easy city to live in and I use my free time to visit museums, etc. The social life is excellent with plenty of things to do and see. It is also very easy to get out of Budapest for some 'fresh air', and to see other parts of the country.

One of my regrets is not being able to speak the language better, but as I am now going to stay for a second year I will make more of an effort. All in all my experience has been a good one so far and pretty much as I expected. I was initially surprised, however, how similar things were to other parts of Europe, as I had thought Hungary would be more different. Now after being here for some time I realize that once you scratch the surface and look deeper you find a very different and unique place.

Robin Schroeder came to Hungary under the EEP programme in 1992 to teach English in an engineering polytechnic.

I arrived in Dunaújváros on a scheme run by the East European Partnership in conjunction with the Hungarian Ministry of Higher Education to teach English at the Miskolci Egyetem Dunaújvárosi Főiskola Kar (an engineering polytechnic).

The decision to come to Hungary as opposed to other job offers outside the scope of EEP was simply the security of a respected and reliable organization. On offer were return airfares, mid-term grants, financial benefits, relocation allowance, medical insurance, professional support, tax-free salary, a fully-furnished all costs inclusive flat plus many other smaller 'perks'.

The debit may be the local salary in forint and the two-year minimum contract (with the option to extend up to five years). The salary per month is sufficient to cover all basic needs from eating, drinking and travel within Hungary. However, it certainly doesn't allow extensive out-of-country travel, something that is easy to do with Hungary's central location.

Dunaújváros is a small provincial city of 60 000 people, 75 kilometres due south of Budapest sited on the banks of the Duna. It was originally developed to service the steelmill. A town like many others in Hungary, not on the tourist map and therefore crying out for native speakers of English. It therefore means unlimited opportunities for additional work, and not solely in the field of education.

With my Ministry contract requiring 15 hours teaching per week there is ample scope to supplement my income with a second job, third job . . .

There are of course disadvantages to being in a provincial town; isolation is one as other native speakers are rare.

The people are warm and friendly and the hospitality exceptional. The standard of living on the whole is very good; the students are excellent and teaching is fun.

Nicola Hawkins came to Hungary with the Central Bureau in 1992 to teach English in a secondary school.

All I knew about Székesfehérvár before I arrived was that it had a population of 120 000. I had envisaged a vast, industrialized city, but found it felt much more like a provincial town, with an ancient and rather beautiful centre, giving way to high-rise blocks and sprawling suburbs. I was also surprised to find myself to be something of a novelty as one of only six native speakers resident there. The town has no university, only a teacher-training college and countless schools, which meant it was quiet, especially at weekends. There was no shortage of entertainment to be found, however, in the form of three cinemas, a theatre, plenty of pubs and restaurants (which seemed to spring up overnight) as well as a swimming pool and other sporting facilities.

József Attila Gimnázium had 800 pupils and is gradually expanding from a four- to an eight-year school. It is also in the process of reverting to a Roman Catholic school, owned by the church once more. The staff numbered about 60, including a large friendly English department. The head decided to spread me fairly, if thinly, between the eight teachers, which meant that I taught 15 different classes for one lesson a week each. Some of the teachers expected me to be a fully qualified English teacher, as a Hungarian arts degree is also a qualification to teach. I had to make it clear that I was unprepared to teach grammar, although some of them still wanted me to use the school textbooks. I was given as much help as I wanted, but it was increasingly left up to me to devise my own tasks and topics for my lessons. I saw myself as most usefully employed in helping the students to speak. They themselves acknowledged their oral skills were weak compared to the vast amount of grammar they have to digest. They also lack any opportunity for travel. Some of my classes were extremely passive and weren't inclined to speak at all, whereas others were confident and eager to speak, sometimes motivated by the prospect of passing the state language exam. My classes ranged from 12 to 16 year olds, and from beginners to advanced, but they generally responded well and I was able to build a good relationship with them over the year.

Hungarians are nothing if not appreciative and I was overwhelmed not only by their gifts, but by their friendship. I was welcomed into so many homes and families. I had problems with both pay and accommodation, but was able to resolve them with the help of the other teachers. Like them I took on several private students to supplement my income. The demand for a native speaker is enormous and I felt at times that people thought I was a kind of magic wand, which I certainly wasn't. I remained in touch with two other British girls who arrived when I did, and like them decided one year wasn't enough and stayed for a second.

Appendix 2. Classroom Hungarian

Pronunciation

Vowels	*Consonants*
a as in hot	g always hard as in go
á as in start	r rolled 'r'
e as in yes	c like the ts in bits
é like a in make	cs like ch in chop
i as in hit	gy like duty
í as in see	ny as in onion
o as in doll	s like in shop
ó as in hall	sz as in sun
u as in put	ty as in tunic
ú as in rule	zs as in measure
ö French peu	j like the y in yes
ő as above but longer	ly like the y in yes
ü as in French tu	
ű as above but longer	

Although it is generally preferable if classes are taught entirely in English, you may find the following useful, especially for beginners.

Parts of speech
Noun *Főnév*
Verb *Ige*
Adjective *Melléknév*
Preposition *Elöljáró*
Article *Névelő*
Pronoun *Névmás*

Tenses *Igeidők*

Present *Jelen*
Present continuous *Folyamatos jelen*
Past *Múlt*

Present perfect *Befejezett jelen*
Future *Jövő*

Other
Question *Kérdés*
Answer *Válasz*
Singular *Egyesszám*
Plural *Többesszám*

Syllable *Szótag*
Consonant *Mássalhangzó*
Vowel *Magánhangzó*

Polite *Udvarias*
Impolite *Udvariatlan*

Book *Könyv*
Classroom *Tanterem*
Clue *Nyom*
Homework *Házifeladat*
Intonation *Intonáció*
Paper *Papír*

Paragraph *Bekezdés*
Photocopy *Fénymásolat*
Sentence *Mondat*
Staffroom *Tanári szoba*
Stress *Hangsúly*

Appendix 3. Food and drink glossary

Levesek Soups
Bableves Bean soup
Gombaleves Mushroom soup
Gulyásleves Goulash soup (meat,
    vegetable and paprika soup)
Meggyleves Cold cherry soup
    (excellent in summer)

Hús Meat
Csirke Chicken
Pulyka Turkey
Marhahús Beef
Sertésborda Pork chop

Pörkölt Stewed slowly
Rántott In breadcrumbs
Roston sütve Roasted
Sült/Sütve Fried

Saláta Salads
Paradicsom Tomato
Uborka Gherkin
Káposzta Cabbage
Fejessaláta Lettuce

Zöldség Vegetables
Bab Beans
Borsó Peas
Burgonya Potatoes
Krumpli Potatoes
Fokhagyma Garlic
Gomba Mushrooms

Hagyma Onions
Káposzta Cabbage
Karfiol Cauliflower
Kukorica Sweet corn
Paprika Peppers
Sárgarépa Carrots
Zöldbab Green beans

Fagylalt Ice-cream
Palacsinta Pancakes
Gyümölcs saláta Fruit salad

Szeszesital Alcoholic drink
Sör Beer
Bor Wine
Fehér White
Vörös Red
Száraz Dry
Édes Sweet

Kávé Coffee
Tea Tea
Csokoládé Chocolate
Kakaó Cocoa
Tej Milk
Üdítő Juice
Narancs Orange
Alma Apple
Gyümölcs Fruit
Ásványvíz Mineral water

In a restaurant
I'd like a table for two people.

Is this table free?
I'd like to book a table for
    four people.
Can I have a menu please?
What do you recommend?
I'm a vegetarian.
What vegetarian dishes do
    you have?

*Szeretnék egy asztalt két
    személyre.*
Szabad ez az asztal?
*Szeretnék egy asztalt foglalni
    négy személyre.*
Kaphatnék egy étlapot?
Mit tudna ajánlani?
Vegetáriánus vagyok.
*Milyen vegetáriánus ételeik
    vannak?*

Can I have the bill please?	*Fizetni szeretnék*
We'd like to pay separately.	*Külön szeretnénk fizetni.*
We'd like to pay together.	*Egybe kérjük a számlát.*

In a bar

I'd like two beers please.	*Két sört kérek*
I'd like a glass of red/white wine please.	*Egy pohár vörös/fehér bort kérek.*
What sort of soft drinks do you have?	*Milyen üditő van?*
I'd like a mineral water please	*Egy ásványvizet kérek.*
Do you sell cigarettes?	*Lehet kapni cigarettát?*

Appendix 4. Useful Hungarian words and phrases

Numbers

1	*egy*	21	*huszenegy*
2	*kettő*	30	*harminc*
3	*három*	40	*negyven*
4	*négy*	50	*ötven*
5	*öt*	60	*hatvan*
6	*hat*	70	*hetven*
7	*hét*	80	*nyolcvan*
8	*nyolc*	90	*kilencven*
9	*kilenc*	100	*száz*
10	*tíz*	200	*kétszáz*
11	*tizenegy*	300	*háromszáz*
12	*tizenkettő*	400	*négyszáz*
13	*tizenhárom*	500	*ötszáz*
14	*tizennégy*	600	*hatszáz*
15	*tizenöt*	700	*hétszáz*
16	*tizenhat*	800	*nyolcszáz*
17	*tizenhét*	900	*kilencszáz*
18	*tizennyolc*	1 000	*ezer*
19	*tizenkilenc*	10 000	*tízezer*
20	*húsz*		

Days of the week

Monday *hétfő*
Tuesday *kedd*
Wednesday *szerda*
Thursday *csütörtök*
Friday *péntek*
Saturday *szombat*
Sunday *vasárnap*

Months

January *január*
February *február*
March *március*
April *április*
May *május*
June *június*
July *július*
August *augusztus*
September *szeptember*
October *október*
November *november*
December *december*

Greetings

Hi/hello/goodbye (informal)	*Szia/Sziasztok* (more than one person)/*Hello*
Goodbye (formal)	*Viszontlátásra*
Good morning	*Jó reggelt*
Good day	*Jó napot*
Good afternoon	*Jó napot*
Good evening	*Jó estét*
Please	*Kérem*
Thank you (very much)	*Köszönöm (szépen)*
I am sorry	*Bocsánat*
Excuse me/sorry	*Elnézést*
Yes	*Igen*
No	*Nem*

Small talk

Do you speak English?	*Beszél angolul?*
I'm sorry I don't speak Hungarian.	*Sajnálom, nem beszélek magyarul.*
I don't understand.	*Nem értem.*
Could you write it down?	*Leírná kérem?*
What do you do?	*Mi a foglalkozása?*
I'm a student.	*Diák vagyok.*
I'm an English teacher.	*Angol tanár vagyok.*
I work at a language school.	*Egy nyelviskolában dolgozom*
I come from London.	*Londoni vagyok.*

Shopping

Where can I buy . . .?	*Hol vehetnék . . .?*
How much does it cost?	*Menyibe kerül?*
Do you have . . .?	*Van . . .?*
Can I have a bag please?	*Kaphatnék egy szatyrot?*
Where is the . . .?	*Hol van a . . .?*

Times and dates

Today	*Ma*
Tonight	*Ma este*
Yesterday	*Tegnap*
Tomorrow	*Holnap*
Next week	*Jövő héten*
What time is it please?	*Hány óra van?*
Open	*Nyitva*
Closed	*Zárva*
When?	*Mikor?*
Where?	*Hol?*

Appendix 5. Festivals and public holidays

Principal national holidays

1 January	New Year's Day
15 March	Commemorates 1848 Revolution and War of Liberty against the Habsburgs.
March/April	Easter Monday
1 May	Labour Day. Now just a public holiday rather than a day of parades.
May/June	Whitsun Monday.
20 August	In honour of King Saint Stephen I, founder of the Hungarian state. Marked by impressive firework display in Budapest and festivals everywhere.
23 October	Commemorates 1956 Revolution.
25 December	Christmas Day. However 24 December is the most important day for close family, with the giving and receiving of presents and the Christmas feast.
26 December	Generally a day when people visit relatives and friends.

Other celebrations

1 March	The Mohács Carnival. March also sees the Spring festival in Budapest. A month of dance, music and art including international and local participants.
First Sunday of May	Mother's Day. Early May also sees the *Ballagás*, which is the high school senior's celebration.
6 December	Mikulás Day when Father Christmas comes and gives chocolates to the children who leave their shoes/boots out for the occasion.
31 December	Szilveszter! Parties and revelling in the streets. It is traditional at midnight wherever you are to sing the national anthem, followed by the swilling of champagne and the ritual kissing of everyone around you.

Appendix 6. Embassies and consulates

Selected Hungarian embassies abroad.

Australia: 79 Hopetown Circuit, Yarralumla, Canberra, ACT 2600. Tel: (06) 282 3226. Unit 6, 351/a Edgecliff Rd, Edgecliff, Sydney, NSW 2027. Tel: (02) 328 7859.

Canada: 7 Delaware Avenue, Ottawa, ON K2P 0Z2. Tel: (613) 232 1549/(613) 232 1711.

Ireland: 2 Fitzwilliam Place, Dublin 2. Tel: 661 2902. Fax: 661 2880.

UK: 35b Eaton Place, London SW1. Tel: (0171) 235 2664. (Open Monday–Friday 10am–12 noon.)

USA: 3910 Shoemaker Street NW, Washington DC 20008. Tel: (202) 362 6730/(202) 362 6795 (visa enquiries). 223 E 52nd Street, New York. Tel: (212) 752 0661.

Selected embassies in Budapest
There are no embassies in Hungary representing either Ireland or New Zealand. The nearest are in Vienna.
Australia: Budapest VI, Délibáb u 30. Tel: 153-4233/153-4577.
Canada: Budapest XII, Budakeszi út 32. Tel: 176-7711/176-7712.
South Africa: Budapest VIII, Rákóczi út 1-3. Tel: 266-2148.
UK: Budapest V, Harmincad u 6. Tel: 266-2046/266-2888. Fax: 266-0907.
 (For emergencies between 10pm and 6am: (06) 601-4542.)
USA: Budapest V, Szabadság tér 12. Tel: 112-6450/119-6000. Fax: 132-8934. (After hours tel: 153-0566.)

6 | Romania

Since the fall of Ceaucescu in December 1989 Romania has been making a slow and painful transition to rid itself of the legacy of the old regime. While the country has opened up more to the West, it still lags behind some of its neighbours both politically and economically, and is not the easiest of places to live and work in.

Regarding ELT, the situation is gradually improving. English is now the most popular foreign language taught in state schools in Romania, followed by French; however, there is still a great shortage of trained teachers to meet the current demand. The private sector is virtually non-existent, and only International House in conjunction with the Soros Foundation has established a private language school of note, in Timisoara (see p 237). Tentative plans have also been made to open schools in Cluj and Ijasi.

Native English teachers working in Romania are few and far between, and those who are there in nearly all cases come attached to one of a number of programmes running in various parts of the country. These include: the British Council, EEP, Soros, Teach Hungary (placements in Transylvania), Peace Corps, Fulbright, USIS, GAP and Teaching Abroad (for more details on these organizations see pp 9–15). Church organizations also send people who combine their missionary work with teaching English.

While some teachers come for short periods of up to three months, others stay for a year and sometimes longer. Several of the posts offered are for teacher trainers, or for people with experience in ESP; although there are of course many opportunities for trained teachers to work in state schools.

Other organizations do offer placements in secondary schools to people without any teaching experience or EFL qualifications. You are usually required to pay a fee for this privilege (which can be over £500), and once you are there you will receive little or no salary and will in effect be supporting yourself. Your salary is usually paid to your host family to cover accommodation and food. If you are tempted by such an organization offering you the 'experience of a lifetime' consider carefully before committing yourself. Without training and adequate support you could end up having the worst experience of a lifetime. Your money may be better spent on getting some training if you seriously want to teach English, or on travelling around Romania if you are simply interested in seeing the country.

Romania is a beautiful place and, although life can be difficult at times, providing you are trained and well prepared you will find your time there a rewarding and stimulating experience.

For more information on Romania contact the national tourist office in the USA or the UK.

> **Romanian National Tourist Office**, 573 Third Avenue, New York City, NY 100016. Tel: (212) 697 6971.
> **Romanian National Tourist Office**, 17 Nottingham Place, London W1M 3FF. Tel: (0171) 224 3692.

PART 1
PREPARING YOUR TRIP
AND FINDING TEACHING JOBS

Before you go

Essentials

Although there are no serious shortages and you can in theory get hold of most necessities, do not expect them to be always easily obtainable or of the same quality as in the West. A few comforts from home are recommended when going to Romania. Teabags and spices, for example, can be difficult to find.

It is important to take a medical kit with you, which should include some syringes, painkillers, multi-vitamins, diarrhoea tablets and a supply of any medication you are taking. Condoms, tampons, etc can be obtained, but again you might want to take a supply with you to be on the safe side. Contact lens wearers should pack a few bottles of cleaning fluid, as well as your glasses. If possible bring a good tape-recorder, as this may not always be available where you work. Oddly enough tin-openers are often difficult to find, as are good corkscrews and sharp knives. You will also find a torch very useful as some entrances to buildings are unlit, and you may have the odd power cut. If you are going for a long period, and you have room, take along a water filter, as the tap water is not always too healthy. For this reason too, you will find a half-litre water bottle is handy for long train journeys. You won't find water on the train, and the bottled water you can buy comes with flip-off caps which can't be replaced once opened.

Mosquitoes can be a problem, especially in summer, so pack a coil or spray. Electricity is 220 volts, and you will need a two-pin adaptor if you are bringing anything electrical.

In general, while it is true that Western goods are creeping into the shops, on a Romanian salary they are very expensive.

Teaching materials

The quality and quantity of teaching materials varies. For example, some of the bi-lingual schools are very well equipped with tape-recorders, videos, etc and will be using Western books, whereas most normal schools will have access only to the Romanian school textbook (currently being re-written). None of the major ELT publishers is in Romania at the moment, but it will only be a matter of time before they come.

Discoveries is the only Western book printed locally and you will come across it in schools. Dictionaries printed locally are readily available in shops, but are not particularly good; it is better to bring your own. You may also come across *Streamline* and *Chatterbox* for sale, as well as some Penguin books. However, these books are all very expensive and it is therefore essential to bring a selection of books and tapes and some supplementary material with you (see p 19 for suggestions).

As was mentioned above, it is rather hit or miss whether your school will provide a tape-recorder and it is very unlikely you will have access to a photocopier in the school. However all towns generally have a shop where photocopies can be made. There may be an overhead projector, although this will not necessarily be in working order, and the school may have a video locked away in a room somewhere. It is worth noting that satellite and cable TV is becoming more popular. Basic stationery is readily available and cheap.

Health and insurance

Most of the organizations which send teachers to Romania provide health insurance; however it is very important to check this before you arrive. The important thing is to be covered for repatriation should you be in need of hospital treatment. If your organization does not provide this you will have to take out your own health insurance before you come. It is also advisable to take out some travel insurance to cover your luggage, etc (see p 19). Check with the school to make sure you are covered locally for health care.

Hospitals in Romania suffer from a shortage of money and subsequently a shortage of drugs, quality nursing staff and modern equipment. They tend to be very basic to say the least and a stay in one is not an experience you will wish to repeat.

Nearly all doctors have their own private practice so find out a good one from colleagues.

Romania currently has an AIDS problem, due mainly to shared needles, and for this reason bringing a supply of your own is recommended. However, this problem is rapidly improving.

In hospitals foreigners are likely to get preferential treatment, and, even though you may be covered by insurance, an extra fee is common. If you are in Bucharest get addresses of English-speaking doctors and dentists from the embassy. In emergencies call 061.

Language

The Romanian language has its roots in Classical Latin and uses a Latin script. It is spelt phonetically and stress is usually on the penultimate syllable although it does tend to shift.

Speakers of Italian, French and to some extent Spanish will find they recognize certain words and phrases, especially in their written form. In areas of Transylvania and Banat, Hungarian is spoken by ethnic Hungarians. German is also spoken in certain areas.

Although not a particularly easy language to learn (the grammar is quite complicated), time spent learning some Romanian will make your stay much more rewarding. A good book is *Romanian With or Without a Teacher* by Liana Popp. This can be purchased in a lot of bookshops in Romania. Another option is *Teach Yourself Romanian*.

Money – expenses and how much to take

Romania is still a very cheap country compared to Western countries, although salaries can't keep up with inflation which is currently around 30% a month (1994). If you are having to survive simply on a local salary without any supplement, you may find it hard to make ends meet. Bring a minimum of $500 to tide you over and for use in emergencies. One thing you will want to do if you are staying in Romania for any length of time is to have a holiday outside the country. You will therefore need to have money in reserve for this purpose.

Credit cards are not accepted, except in the large hotels, and although traveller's cheques are safe, they are difficult to cash. The preferred currencies are the US dollar and the German Deutschmark. The unit of currency is the lei which is not yet convertible.

Exchange rates (early 1995):

$	1 800 lei
DM	1 200 lei
£	2 800 lei

Visas

Visas are currently required for all EU nationals as well as citizens of the USA, Canada, Australia and New Zealand. These can be obtained from consulates and embassies abroad (see p 246). It is possible to get visas on the train at the border or at Bucharest airport, but it is advisable to get one before coming – for one thing it may be cheaper. A visa is valid for three months from the date of issue. Ask for the longest time possible. They are usually issued for 30 days, but 60-day visas are possible, especially when coming by train from Hungary.

Work permits and residence status

Work permits will usually be sorted out by your place of employment. You should, however, be aware that the ease with which these can be obtained varies from place to place.

Your residence status will normally be sorted out by your place of employment and is normally a formality once your work papers have been arranged.

Arriving and finding your feet

Travel preparations

Flights from the UK. There are regular flights on Tarom, the national carrier, to Bucharest from London's Heathrow Airport although not everyday. There is also a direct flight to Timisoara at least once a week. Alternatively you can fly to Budapest and take a train or bus from there. Some of the best deals can be found from:

> **STA Travel**, 86 Old Brompton Road, London SW7 3LH. Tel: (0171) 581 9921.
> **East European Travel**. Tel: (0171) 837 2811.

The UK office of Tarom is:

> **Tarom Romanian Airline**, 17 Nottingham Street, London W1M 3RD. Tel: (0171) 224 3693.

Flights from the USA and Canada. There are regular flights on

Tarom from New York to Bucharest. The STA and Tarom addresses are:

> **STA**, 48 E 11th Street, Suite 805, New York, NY 10003. Tel: (212) 477 7166.
>
> **Tarom Romanian Airline**, 342 Madison Avenue, Suite 213, New York, NY 10173. Tel: (212) 687 6013/(212) 687 6014/(212) 687 6242.

Arrival

Transport from the airport (Bucharest). You should avoid taking a taxi from the airport unless you can afford to pay around $30 for the trip into the city. The best thing to do is to take the bus outside the arrivals hall which will take you into the centre. This runs every half an hour from around 6am to 9.30pm. You will need to change a bit of money first in order to buy your ticket (100 lei) which can be purchased on board.

Arriving without a job

Very few people go to Romania without having a pre-arranged job to go to attached to some organization and this is by far the best way of working in the country. If you want to try your luck and find work on the spot your best bet is to look for work outside Bucharest, where accommodation is cheaper and the cost of living is lower.

Whichever town you choose, the best thing to do once you are there is to contact schools direct. They will be more than happy to have a native English speaker teacher, but obviously employment will depend on what terms and conditions they will be able to offer you. For example, will they be able to provide free accommodation? Will your salary be enough to live on? If possible try to contact the local schools' inspector (*inspectorat scolar*) who will be able to help place you in a school. The best time to arrive is late August just before the start of the school term.

Where to teach English

You are more limited in Romania than, say, in Hungary, Poland or the Czech Republic as to where you can teach, and most people tend to work in state secondary or primary schools. There are opportunities in a few colleges, universities and bilingual schools, and these posts are usually filled through one of the organizations mentioned above. You may in addition take on some private students.

The only private language school of any note is the International

House/Soros school in Timisoara. Apart from this there are no private language schools to speak of, although in the cities and larger towns you may come across teachers who rent out rooms and teach English privately. These courses are sometimes attached to a cultural centre or college, but are not organized 'schools' as such.

International House has around 10 native English speaker teachers in Romania, alongside a handful of locally employed teachers. The school is very well equipped and teachers receive a dollar supplement in addition to their local salary. Contracts are normally for one year. The minimum qualification is the RSA/UCLES CTEFLA with a good pass grade, or equivalent. Applications should be made through Teacher Selection International House (see p 13).

Private students are easy to find and it is common for teachers to supplement their income this way. The rate usually depends on the means of the student.

Useful organizations and addresses

British Council, Calea Dorobantilor 14, Bucharest. Tel: 210 0314. Fax: 210 0310.

International House/Soros, Bd Republicii 9, 1990 Timisoara. Tel/Fax: (56) 19 05 93.

Ministry of Education and Science, Str Berthelot 30, 70749 Bucharest.

Soros, Bucuresti, Calea Victoriei 133, CP22 – 196, 71102. Tel: (90) 506 325/597 427. Fax: 120 284.

PART 2
LIVING IN ROMANIA

How expensive is Romania?

While Romania is still a cheap country for the Western traveller and US dollars can go a long way on a day-to-day basis, you may still find yourself digging into reserves; especially if you are having to live on a local salary. For example, Western goods are expensive, as is drinking imported beer, though these are not really necessary; Romanian equivalents are usually available and substantially cheaper. Shopping in the local markets is inexpensive and, after accommodation, between $80 and $100 a month will be enough to give you a reasonable standard of living.

Everyday living

Accommodation

Urgent accommodation. Should you arrive in Bucharest in need of urgent accommodation for a night or two, be careful; it is not cheap and the selection is limited. Avoid the large hotels as you will end up paying Western prices. Go for something much more downmarket. One place which is relatively cheap and central is the hotel Rahova in Strada Rahova. Here you can get a single room for about $10 a night. Take the bus from the airport to the last stop, piata Unirii, which is close to the Hanul Manuc. Strada Rahova runs off from that.

Long-term accommodation. An acute flat shortage exists throughout Romania, and very few new ones are being built. As a result, if you are having to find accommodation on your own this will be difficult. Agencies usually charge way over the odds and prices go up even more if they know you are a Westerner. You will definitely need to get a Romanian to help you do the negotiating.

Generally accommodation in some form or other is provided with the job, and if not the school will undoubtedly help you find a place in order to keep you. A number of teachers, especially those coming out for short periods, live with families. While this is a wonderful way for you to integrate into the way of life, it can also have its problems which you should at least be aware of.

The family putting you up will no doubt to be over the moon to have a native speaker living with them and will soon 'adopt' you into their family, showering you with hospitality. One of the consequences of this, however, is that you may get very little, if any privacy, and little things like not being able to use the bathroom when you want can be frustrating. If you are a woman, you may also be asked to account for your movements, not because the family is nosey, but out of concern for your well-being. Any horror stories about dangers should be taken with a pinch of salt as these tend to be exaggerated. While the family will feed you, the food may not always be to your liking, and you may not get a proper balanced diet. Finally you may be expected to teach one or more of the family English, which again may be a problem if you are already working full-time.

Teachers renting a flat on their own will find the accommodation small and very basic; it usually comprises one room, a hall and a small kitchen as well as a bathroom. The cooker is normally gas which may be from the mains or from a refillable tank. Some buildings are without heating or hot water for certain periods and if you live on the top of a four-storey towerblock the water pressure is substantially reduced. As a rule avoid the top floor of anything, the roof may leak and the lift may not work.

Power cuts can also occur, although these are less regular than they were a few years ago. If anything goes wrong in the flat, which it invariably will, getting it fixed can be a mammoth task. You are best asking someone from your workplace for help.

If your flat comes with a washing machine it will probably be the twin tub sort; if you do not have one, ask your landlady whether she or someone she knows will do your washing for a small sum.

Telephones are slightly less of a problem here than in some of the other countries mentioned in this book, but even if you have a telephone in your flat it does not necessarily mean you can make international calls. These are expensive in any case, so you are better getting people to call you.

Rents vary, and can be anything from $60–100 a month up for one room ($500 a month for a two-room flat in Bucharest), with most landlords/landladies preferring payment in hard currency. It is common for the landlord/landlady not to give you a formal contract so as to avoid paying tax; you may have to negotiate some form of alternative agreement.

Eating

In general, food shortages are a thing of the past and most food-stuffs can be bought, although there is still a limited variety. Fruit and vegetables are seasonal and anything imported is expensive. Meat, while readily available, is also expensive.

The food in restaurants does not compare to meals you may find yourself treated to in a Romanian home, which might consist of several dishes, starting with soup, possibly followed by *sarmale* (cabbage leaves stuffed with mince), and then by a roast of sorts. Dessert may be pancakes or pastries. All this is usually washed down with a bottle of wine or a plum brandy or even both!

Restaurants. Restaurants tend to offer little choice and, even if they have a menu, it is worth asking before ordering to check they have what is listed. Unfortunately Romanian specialities can rarely be found and the usual dishes on offer will be pork, beef cutlets or chicken served with chips. Note that meat will be charged by the weight in a lot of places.

Most restaurants serve soup, and these are quite tasty. Service on the whole is poor and generally restaurants will close at 10pm.

A number of restaurants have now been privatized, although there is still very little variety. You may find the odd pizzeria in the larger towns although not a lot else. There are some very good Chinese restaurants in Bucharest, although these are expensive.

For vegetarians there isn't a great deal of choice. Even the stuffed peppers (*ardei umpluti*), usually contain meat. You are basically limited to fried cheese in breadcrumbs and bean dishes. It is not really advisable for vegans to work in Romania for any extended period.

Romanians tend not to eat out a lot preferring to eat at home. The main meal is in the middle of the day and for this reason restaurants usually offer a more extensive menu at midday. Cheap food can be found in the *expres* or self-service *auto-servire* restaurants. The food in these places is meaty and fatty served with lots of beans and cabbage. Ask the locals for the best places.

Drinking and nightlife

The beer (*bere*) is like lager and is sold in bottles in most restaurants. Apart from local brews such as 'Urus', there are a number of more expensive imported beers. Insist on the local brew if they try to palm you off with some expensive imported beer.

You can find some nice Romanian wines and these are generally sold by the bottle. You are better off paying a bit more and getting a good wine rather than a cheap one as these can be a bit rough. Look out for homemade wine which can also be very good.

If you are feeling brave there are several strong spirits available which if you are not careful could leave you with a sore head. One to try is *tuica*, a sort of fruit brandy; the most popular is the plum variety. Romanians drink it before meals as it is said to stimulate the appetite! Do not buy it in the supermarkets. Let your Romanian friends know that you want to try it, and some will appear!

There is not a lot in the way of nightlife in Romania and at most you may find the odd disco which stays open after all the bars are closed. Some bars stay open all night, *bar de zi*. In winter there is not a lot to do but in summer you can sit outside open-air bars, although these usually close around 10pm. You will find that you are invited around to people's houses where most of the socialising goes on. Students and other young people occasionally hold parties and are keen to invite foreign guests.

Transport

Public transport is run-down, dirty, overcrowded, inefficient but relatively inexpensive. Having said that, within towns and cities you can get around relatively easily. Transport connecting the main towns is generally good; however, getting to smaller towns is not always so simple and will generally involve changing.

Trains. Trains are a popular way of getting around the country due to high petrol prices. However, this means that they are usually crowded and reserving a seat is essential. The Romanian National Railways (CFR) run a network which covers nearly all parts of the country. Although local services are slow, they are generally reliable. Long distance trains have sleeping compartments which must be booked up to 10 days in advance.

Buses. Buses between towns and cities do not run very often and in rural areas the service is worse still. Within towns and cities themselves public transport is generally good although crowded. Tickets can be purchased from kiosks, tobacconists and sometimes bookshops and should be punched when on board. In some places it is possible to buy tickets on the bus.

Driving. It is not advisable to take a reasonably good foreign car to Romania. On one hand there is the shortage of petrol (although this is improving), and you may also have problems getting spare parts. There is always the chance that your car may be stolen. Unleaded petrol is not easy to get hold of in many parts of the country. Roads in the cities are not in a particularly good condition and in rural areas they are full of pot holes. The real advantage of having a car, however, is the chance to to see parts of the country which are difficult to reach by public transport.

Hitching. Hitching is safe and popular, especially in the rural areas where there are very few cars. However, the cars are usually small and full and you may have to wait a long time for a lift. A small tip is usually expected equivalent to the bus fare for the same journey. However, foreigners are often not expected to pay, but the offer should be made anyway.

Shopping

Shopping is time consuming and on occasions frustrating. The shops are much more well-stocked now than they were prior to 1989, and Western products can be found on the shelves. One of the problems, however, is knowing where to buy the particular item you want. Some shops do not specialize and sell whatever they can. If you are looking for something in particular, it is quite likely to be in a shop where you would least expect it to be! While there are no shortages now, some items are not always available all the time. If you see something you need, as a rule buy it, as it may not be there tomorrow. *Deschis* means open and *inchis* closed. Shops open at either 9am or 10am and usually close at 6pm. Shops close at 2pm on Saturdays and all day Sunday.

You should make an effort to find the local market as soon as possible for your fruit and vegetables. Markets open early and are fun to visit, full of life and bustle and will give you a slice of local life. Remember to take a bag!

Banks and financial matters

Banks are open 8am–12 noon, Monday–Friday. Nearly all banks accept recognized traveller's cheques and the larger hotels and expensive restaurants will generally accept credit cards. It is possible to have money transferred from abroad.

Libraries and bookshops

You will not find very many shops selling books in English, either for general reading or teaching purposes. It is therefore worth bringing a few books to read with you, and you will usually find someone to swap them with. The British Council has well stocked libraries in Bucharest and Ijasi with large ELT sections, and there are plans to open other resource centres in other towns. University libraries are also a good source for English books.

Post

Post offices are open 7.30am–8pm, Monday–Friday and Saturdays until 12 noon. Post boxes are yellow. Stamps can be bought at tobacconists, bookshops and hotels. Unfortunately the post is sometimes slow and unreliable. Letters from the UK take around a week and from the USA a minimum of two weeks. Sending parcels home can sometimes be a problem although having them sent to Romania is not a problem. DHL is also available.

The country and the people

Romanians are on the whole a warm and hospitable people. Apart from the ethnic Romanians, you will come across a range of various cultures and traditions; other groups that make up the population include the estimated 2 million ethnic Hungarians living in the region of Transylvania, by far the greatest ethnic minority; ethnic Germans; and smaller groups of Ukrainians, Serbs, Turks and gypsies.

Romanians are by and large a religious people (orthodox) and extremely helpful and honest. On the other hand, they are also a spontaneous people ready to enjoy life to the full. Westerners are still somewhat of a novelty in Romania, and though people may appear to be slightly cautious at first (a throwback to the old regime) they will make you feel very welcome.

Geography

Covering an area of 237 500 square kilometres, Romania is a country of varied landscapes. The River Danube winds its way through eight countries as it flows into the Danube Delta, and approximately one-third of the country is flood plain. The other main features are rolling hillsides and the Carpathian Mountains which cover the Central and Northern part of the country and offer some of the most beautiful and largely untouched countryside in Europe. For those who enjoy walking there is some wonderful countryside to explore.

Climate

Most of Romania has a continental climate. Winters are severe with icy winds and snow covering many areas of the country. Summers are hot with temperatures rising to 40°C on the Black Sea coast, but can still be cold in the mountains. Spring is usually wet, with most of the rain falling in the mountainous regions.

PART 3
TEACHING ENGLISH

The Romanian education system

For all children from the age of six to sixteen education in general education schools (*şcoala de cultură generala de zece ani*) is compulsory.

Following this, secondary level pupils have a number of possibilities. If they are successful in the entrance exam they can go to a general secondary school (*liceul*). These schools prepare students for university or college. There are also specialized secondary schools, which put the emphasis on industrial, agricultural, teacher training or art studies, as well as general education. Finally there are vocational secondary schools (*şcoli profesionale de ucenici*), which give training in a specialized field towards a career. Provision is made for tuition in minority languages such as Hungarian and German.

There are also a number of bilingual schools which specialize in one or more languages. In such schools a number of the subjects are taught, for example, in English.

No state exams in English exist, although students take exams in a number of subjects to complete secondary school, and English may be one of their chosen subjects. International exams such as TOEFL are only now becoming known.

Methods used in the classroom

English language teachers in Romania have had very little exposure to new methodologies and as a result are prone to using old grammar translation methods. They tend to be very textbook orientated, and focus is put on reading comprehension and writing.

Students are usually required to read a text, perhaps repeat parts of it, and complete certain exercises which follow. There are very rarely any actual communication activities that take place in the classroom.

The kind of language needed

After years of grammar translation style of teaching where the students are obliged to sit back and take a passive role in the classroom, the need now is for more active communication.

Romanian students need to be encouraged to speak, activating their passive knowledge and using everyday English. They also need to widen their vocabulary. They will be interested in you and keen to learn about your country. At first they will be unsure of communicative methodology, but once they see the rationale behind it, and get used to it, they generally respond well. As those who have studied English before will have been taught a more formal English, they need more informal and colloquial language.

Romanian students

Romanian students are some of the most motivated students you will come across. They are also very good learners and generally well behaved. On the whole they accept anything the teacher gives them and are not terribly critical. It is, however, necessary to spell out the purpose of activities so they see a reason for doing something. Because of their experience of a more formal approach to teaching, ideas such as pair and group work may seem quite novel to them at first.

These ideas should, however, be introduced slowly; do not start your first few lessons with your wackiest activities. Students are not very good at listening to each other in class and see the teacher as the fountain of all knowledge. You will find them hard working and they generally want and expect homework, which they do.

Although not immediately friendly, over time they will open up and soon start inviting you out. Do not expect this to happen initially; you may want to suggest something first. You can also expect them to bring in music tapes for you to transcribe, etc.

Specific Romanian problems

Prepositions. It is difficult for Romanian students to use prepositions correctly and mistakes are often made.

> **I'm going at the mountains. (x)**

Countable v uncountable. Certain nouns in English are uncountable whereas the same word in Romanian is countable:

> **I lost my luggages. (x)**
> **Please give me the informations. (x)**

Some/any. Some and any are determiners and are used with uncountable and plural nouns. Some is generally used in affirmative sentences and 'any' is used in questions and negatives. Common mistakes by Romanians include:

> **I've got any money. (x)**
> **No I don't need some help. (x)**

False friends. The following are common words which Romanian students confuse. Some sound very similar to a Romanian word but the meaning is different.

Sensible – sensitive: **She's a sensitive child and she comes straight home from school. (x)**
Let – leaves: **Just let the dishes – I'll do them later. (x)**
Stay – stand – sit – rest: **I rested at the Hotel Apollo. (x)**
Announce – tell somebody something: **I'll announce him that you are here. (x)**
Actual – at the moment: **Actual I'm working in Timisoara. (x)**
Lose – miss: **Oh no! I've lost my train. (x)**
Serious – solid: **We bought a serious table for the dining room. (x)**

Other common errors include overuse of 'of course' and:

> **I have emotion. (x)**
> **I am agree. (x)**

Gender. Romanian has a gender for inanimate objects and this is sometimes transferred to English, eg using 'he' when talking about a computer.

APPENDICES

Appendix 1. Case history

Kaye Anderson is from New Zealand and went to Romania in 1993.

When I announced to family and friends that I was going to work in Romania, the reactions varied from raised eyebrows to 'you must be crazy' to real fears for my welfare. But there were good reasons for my decision: the DoS, with whom I had worked before, had chosen to spend a second year there, so I figured living conditions couldn't be *too* bad; I fancied some small-city living after working in Istanbul; I knew the school was well-resourced with plenty of books, photocopiers and a networked computer system; and a US$ supplement, which could be saved, promised the opportunity to take the Diploma the following year.

My arrival at Arad railway station at 10.30 at night raised all the doubts planted in my mind by the 'well-wishers' in New Zealand. It was dirty, badly lit and the people were very poorly dressed. I expect they were curious rather than unfriendly, because I felt extraordinarily conspicuous with my suitcase, backpack and bag of books, so different to their motley collections of plastic bags and striped carry-alls.

My flat in Timişoara, on the other hand, was a wonderful surprise! Sunny, well-furnished, separate living room and bedroom, balcony, telephone and 10 minutes walk to the school, market and town centre.

One-stop shopping is not a feature of Romanian life. Instead it is necessary to shop for fruit and vegetables at the market, for bread at the baker's, for cheese and yogurt (bring your own jars) at the cheese shop and so on. A ferret and squirrel mentality was the answer: sniff out the matches, toilet paper and light bulbs, then buy as many as you could afford or carry. The most common reply to your question '*Aveti . . . ?*' ('Have you got any . . . ?) was '*Nu există*' (literally translated, 'It doesn't exist'!). In winter the variety of vegetables was not fantastic, so I was glad of my 'imported' supply of lentils, split peas and vitamin pills. Even eggs disappear at times, and a tomato could cost as much as a trip to the cinema!

Although comparatively new, my school was well established and had a strong body of loyal, faithful and enthusiastic students. Romanians are good language learners and most are highly-motivated, often because emigration is their main goal. Because Romanian is a Romance language and its Latin roots are still very evident, there are many 'false friends'.

As a teacher, there are many opportunities for genuine friendships among the students, who will indulge you with large quantities of food, homemade wine and *tuica* (*sweka*), the extremely potent national drink made from plums.

For me, the school with its 600 students, both adults and younger learners, provided lots of opportunities for professional development and a social life which was a pleasant change from the bars and restaurants of a larger city. I also appreciated the opportunity to acquire a small understanding of the problems which face a country in the process of transition from a regime of cruel oppression to some kind of democracy. All in all, an unforgettable experience.

Appendix 2. Classroom Romanian

Verb *Verb*
Noun *Substantiv*
Adjective *Adjectiv*
Preposition *Prepozitie*
Article *Articol*
Pronoun *Pronume*

Present *Prezent*
Present Continuous *Prezentul continuu*
Past *Trecut*
Future *Viitor*
Singular *Singular*
Plural *Plural*

Syllable *Silabă*
Consonant *Consonă*
Vowel *Vocală*
Question *Intrebare*
Answer *Răspuns*

Polite *Politicos*
Impolite *Nepoliticos*
Questionnaire *Chestionar*
Opposite *Opus*
Clue/hint *Aluzie/idee*
Classroom *Sală de clasa*
Staffroom *Caracelarie*
Homework *Tema*

Appendix 3. Festivals and public holidays

Principal national holidays

1 and 2 January	New Year
March/April	Easter Monday
1 and 2 May	Labour Days
1 December	National Day
25 December	Christmas Day (celebrations start on 24th)

On 1 March women receive flowers (snowdrops) and 8 March is women's day. There are many local festivals throughout the year, especially in Transylvania and Moldavia.

Appendix 4. Embassies

Selected Romanian embassies abroad
Canada: 655 Rideau Street, Ottawa ON K1N 683. Tel: (613) 232 5345.
UK: 4 Palace Green, London W8 4QD. Tel: 0171 937 9666.
USA: 1607 23rd Street NW, Washington DC 20008. Tel: (202) 232 4749.

Selected embassies in Bucharest
UK: 24 Strada Jules Michelet, 70154 Bucharest. Tel: 31 20 303/4.
USA: 7–9 Str Tudor Arghezi, Bucharest. Tel: 12 40 40.

7 | Bulgaria

Bulgaria has had English language teachers working in the country for many years, but the numbers have always been low, and it has not had anything like the influx seen in Hungary, Poland and the Czech Republic; nor does such a development seem likely for some years to come.

Nearly all the teachers come through one organization or another, working in conjunction with the Bulgarian Ministry of Education and Science to provide English teachers and teacher trainers for schools and institutes of higher education. These include: the British Council, EEP, The Central Bureau, European Post to Post Teacher Exchange, Peace Corps and Soros (see pp 9–15) for further details on these organizations).

These organizations all provide fairly comprehensive briefings for teachers, as well as language and other training. The British Council also provides training courses and seminars for their staff while they are in Bulgaria. The British Council recruits teachers with a degree, PGCE or TEFL qualifications plus experience to work in state schools. To work in an institute of higher education a higher degree and experience are needed depending on the post. For the East European Partnership (EEP), experienced and qualified teachers are recruited, some with specialist qualifications. Among other initiatives, EEP has volunteer teachers working in provincial high schools in south-west Bulgaria. EEP works closely with the British Council.

Although there is a huge demand for EFL teachers and teacher trainers, it is very difficult to find work in the country on your own without the backing of an organization, especially for young inexperienced teachers.

All job applications have in theory to be approved by the Ministry of Education, making it difficult for teachers to arrange work on their own. Nevertheless, ELT within Bulgaria is quite developed, although the private sector has not really been established yet.

The standard of living is low, and there are hardships to cope with if you live in Bulgaria. It is, however, a beautiful country, with both summer and winter resorts, attracting tourists all year round.

For more information on the country contact:

Balkan Holidays, 19 Conduit Street, London W1R 9TD. Tel: (0171) 491 4499.

Bulgarian National Tourist Office, 161 East 86th Street, New York, NY 10028. Tel: (212) 722 1110.

PART 1
PREPARING YOUR TRIP
AND FINDING TEACHING JOBS

Before you go

Essentials

Western products are available in the large cities but are very expensive. Tampons and condoms are available but as they are imported they are expensive; it is better to bring your own supply. Film is expensive, as is getting it processed, so pick up some before you come.

You should definitely bring a small medical kit with you, which should include any prescribed medicines you are taking, as well as a supply of multi-vitamins.

Teaching materials

Several of the major publishers have representatives in Sofia including Cambridge University Press (CUP), Oxford University Press (OUP) and Longman, making it possible to buy and order books, although at prices comparable to the West. The high cost makes it difficult for many parents to buy books for their children, but some schools are now using Western books such as the *Headway* series. However, you are more likely to come across the *Discoveries* series (which is used in secondary schools) or locally printed text books. In some schools you may not have access to a textbook of any description. Bring lots of authentic and supplementary material, and a selection of your favourite books.

Facilities and materials in schools vary widely; whereas some may have nothing but a blackboard (you will not find any white boards), in others you may well find a tape-recorder or overhead projector hidden away somewhere. Again, the school may have a video, but actually having access to it is a different matter. You are unlikely to have photocopying facilities, although all towns have a shop where photocopying can be done. You will, however, have to pay for this yourself, which can be expensive. Photocopying is generally of poor quality.

Basic stationery is available and cheap. It is also worth noting that the British Council has a number of resource centres in certain cities (Sofia, Stara Zagora Plovdiv, Varna) which stock a good selection of ELT materials, newspapers and journals. For a full list of addresses write to the British Council in Sofia. More and more people have access to satellite TV (see p 19 for more suggestions on teaching materials).

Health and insurance

You do not need any special inoculations to enter Bulgaria, although you might find yourself getting ill more often than at home. Diarrhoea is a common complaint, as are colds, so bring along the necessary medicines.

The UK has a reciprocal agreement with Bulgaria regarding emergency health care, though it is advisable to take out health insurance before you come. Organized programmes often include health insurance but check this out first (you might also want to take out additional insurance to cover your luggage). You will be entitled to use the health system free of charge, although you still have to pay for medicines. Doctors will not usually speak English, and the hospitals are outdated and sometimes horrific. They lack equipment and medicines and can be health hazards in themselves.

You can contact the US or UK embassies for a list of English speaking doctors in Sofia, and there is also a special clinic for foreigners in the Mladost I suburb (1, Ul. Evgeni Pavlovski. Tel: 75 361).

Tax

Teachers are required to pay tax on local salaries which is worked out on a progressive system.

Language

Bulgarian is a south slavonic tongue closely related to Slovenian and Serbo-Croat, and, more distantly, Russian. It uses a Cyrillic alphabet, although road signs are in roman letters. Knowledge of Russian will help you when learning the language. It is worth at least learning the alphabet before you come and a few basic expressions, so you are not at a complete loss when you arrive. Unfortunately, apart from the odd phrase book, there are very few books around to help you learn Bulgarian.

Money – expenses and how much to take

Bulgaria is still a cheap country by Western standards, although if you are only receiving a local salary you will definitely need some money in reserve. You should take about $200 to help tide you over for the first few weeks and also have some more in reserve should you want to travel around the country or outside it, or in case you need to fly home in an emergency. The best currencies to take and most popular are the US dollar or the German Deutschmark (pound sterling is not too popular but can be changed in banks). Traveller's cheques are a safe way to carry your money, but few places apart from some banks in large cities accept them. The same applies to credit cards.

The unit of currency is the lev (plural, leva), which is made up of stotinki (singular, stotinka). Leva can be exchanged for US dollars or Deutschmarks at bureau de change offices (usually recognizable by 'change' signs) in most major cities.

Exchange rates (early 1995):

DM	40 leva
$	70 leva
£	105 leva

Visas

British, US, Canadian, Australian, and Irish citizens all need a visa to enter Bulgaria. These are issued from Bulgarian embassies and consulates abroad (see p 256). You can also buy them on the train at the border when entering the country, although it is always advisable to get one before you come.

If you intend to leave the country during your stay, it is advisable to get a multi-entry visa before you come. Again, these can be obtained from the Bulgarian embassy in your country. Apart from several passport photos, you will be required to show evidence of a specific post in Bulgaria, ie a contract from the school. Multi-entry visas can be obtained in Bulgaria, but it is a tedious process. Because visas are expensive you may want to try and arrange for the money to be reimbursed by the school in lev (Bulgarian currency) when you get there. Once in the country foreigners are required to register with the local police within 48 hours.

Work and residence permits

Work permits can only be issued in your home country, therefore you need to obtain one before coming. This will be sorted out for you if you come through an organized programme. However, if you deal directly with a school or institute you need a signed contract by both parties guaranteeing you work, and this has to be sent to the Bulgarian embassy/consulate in your home country. Permits are then normally issued for a year. Before this the school will need to see evidence of your degree and EFL certificate.

Once you are in Bulgaria with your work permit, the residence permit is usually just a formality and is normally arranged by your employer.

Internal passports

An internal passport is essential if you intend to travel in Bulgaria, as it entitles you to reduced entry fees to museums, galleries, etc. More importantly it secures hotel acommodation at about one-fifth to one-eighth of the tourist rate.

You may be told you must be resident for six months before you are eligible for this, but put your case forward strongly and you will receive one in a matter of weeks. Ask your school how to apply for one.

Arriving and finding your feet

Travel preparations

Flights from the UK. There are regular flights from London's Heathrow to Sofia. The Bulgarian airline Balkan offers Apex tickets. There are also flights to Varna and Burgas but these are mainly for package tours.

> **Balkan Airlines**, 322 Regent Street, London WC1. Tel: (0171) 637 7637. Fax: (0171) 637 2481.

Flights from the USA. There are no direct flights to Sofia from the USA. You will therefore have to make a stopover first. Currently one of the cheapest ways of getting there is with KLM via Amsterdam. Tickets can be booked through the Bulgarian tourist office in New York (see p 249).

Arriving without a job

It is virtually impossible to arrive in Bulgaria and find work legally, as jobs have to be arranged through the Bulgarian Ministry of Education, or at least have their seal of approval, and work papers are only issued through the embassy or consulate of your home country. So, unless you want to make a speedy return trip home, you are better off organizing a job before you go through one of the organizations recruiting teachers and trainers for Bulgaria.

Working for a school without the backing of an organization is difficult, and you will receive no sterling or dollar supplement. This will almost certainly mean you have to pay for your own travel costs.

If you do try and arrange work on your own you must ensure that you receive a good local salary (with paid holidays) and that it will be adjusted in accordance with rising inflation. British teachers usually receive a tax free salary in Bulgaria.

Although schools will pay you as much as they possibly can, and far more than the Bulgarian staff are paid, do consider carefully whether a private contract with a Bulgarian school makes economic sense in your own case. The Bulgarians will give all they possibly can, but even so, you could find yourself out of pocket due to travel and other costs.

You also need to bear in mind that unless you are with an organization that offers support throughout your stay in the country you may feel isolated, especially if you do not speak the language.

Finding work. For information on job opportunities contact the organizations listed at the front of this book (pp 9–15) or the Ministry of Education or the Ministry for Higher Education, both of which recruit 'lektors' for specialized secondary schools and institutes of higher education:

> **Ministry of Education and Science**, Boulevard A. Stamboliiski 18, 1540 Sofia.
> **Ministry for Higher Education**, Chapaev 55a, Sofia.

Where to teach

The places you can teach in Bulgaria are limited. There are a number of private language schools, but these are mainly in Sofia.

There are a number of state language schools (*Ezikovi Uchilista*) and English Language Medium Schools (ELMS) throughout the country and they offer a general education alongside an intensive language programme. Although schools usually offer more than one language, eg French and German, English is by far the most popular. The students usually study English for between 25 and 30 hours (45 minute periods) a week, with the other subjects mainly taught in Bulgarian.

You will probably receive little or no help from the Bulgarian staff, as schools make no provision for, or indeed have little conception of, in-service training.

There are several posts as lektors in one of the many universities and colleges in Bulgaria. These positions are usually filled through the British Council.

Useful organizations and addresses

British Council, 7 Tulovo Street, 1504 Sofia. Tel: (02) 463 346/443 394.
Ministry of Education, 18 Boulevard Stamboliiski, 11540 Sofia.

PART 2
LIVING IN BULGARIA

How expensive is Bulgaria?

In the state sector the low salary usually comes with assistance in the form of accommodation and free heating. In some cases a sterling supplement of about £3000 will be paid, or a portion of your salary (usually half) will be paid in sterling at the official bank exchange rate. The British Council and Soros pay sterling or dollar supplements and offer free accommodation.

Everyday living

Accommodation

Accommodation is usually provided by the employer and more than likely will be in an apartment block. These often look as they are about to collapse, and are generally in a very poor condition. Flats normally have two rooms, a bedroom and living room, plus a small kitchen and bathroom. All bathrooms have showers rather than baths (often without curtains), and the plumbing is one of several things that normally go wrong. To make matters worse it is difficult to get things fixed, at least quickly. Outside Sofia flats are rarely centrally heated and have an electric heater which means you can only heat one room at a time. In winter flats can be cold. Hot water comes from an electric boiler. Most flats will have a telephone though not a washing machine, which can be an inconvenience as there are no laundries either!

If you are having to negotiate a flat with your school you need to ensure that the school will not only pay the rent, but also the heating, electricity and water. In winter the fuel bills are high and increase with inflation. Obviously if you have a telephone you will have to pay the bills.

Eating

Eating and drinking are relatively cheap. Restaurants have limited menus and most serve pork or chicken. There are local beers which are cheap and a number of more expensive imported ones.

Bulgaria is a major wine producer and there are some excellent local labels. The best places to buy food are the open markets, and vegetables are not in short supply, although they are seasonal.

Newspapers

A number of Western papers can be found in Sofia or Varna at the large hotels. These include the *Times* and the *Herald Tribune*. They are very expensive. *Newsweek* and *Time* are more easily available in other cities. There is also a monthly newspaper called *English for Everyone* which is aimed at both English teachers and students. This is printed in Bulgaria and is available everywhere.

Libraries

The British Council can be found at:

> **British Council**, 7 Tulovo Street, 1504 Sofia. Tel: (02) 463 346/443 394.

The American Centre (1 Stamboliiski Boulevard next to the US Embassy), has a library with a wide range of books and news-papers.

Help lines

The following are help numbers: ambulance (150); police (160); and airport information (72-24-14).

PART 3
TEACHING ENGLISH

The Bulgarian education system

Education is compulsory between the ages of six to sixteen. Schools are not separated into primary and secondary level, rather they are unified secondary polytechnic schools, which offer an 11-year course which includes primary, general secondary and vocational education. Students may then continue at semi-higher or higher education institutes. Higher education is currently going through major reorganization.

The kind of language needed

Students usually have a sound grammar base, and emphasis is put on reading and writing skills in the classroom. Students have little exposure to actual communication, and it is in this area that students need the most practice.

There are no state exams in English as such, but Oxford, Cambridge, and Pitmans all have exam centres in Sofia. As yet these exams are not very widespread and they do not carry much weight within Bulgaria.

Bulgarian students

While you will come across motivated and disciplined pupils, this is not the case with all students. You may well have disruptive students who show no inclination at all to learn English. One of the reasons for this lies in the status of native speakers in the school. Generally they do not award marks, or when they do the marks are disregarded when deciding final grades.

APPENDICES

Appendix 1. Classroom Bulgarian

Noun *Sashtestvitelno ime*
Verb *Glagol*
Adjective *Prilagatelno*
Preposition *Predlog*
Article *Chlen*
Pronoun *Mestoimenie*

Tenses *Glagolni vremena*

Present *Segashno*
Past *Minalno*
Present perfect *Segashno svarshe-no*
Future *Badeshte*

Question *Vapros*
Answer *Otgovor*
Singular *Edinstveno*
Plural *Mnozhestveno*
Syllable *Srichka*
Consonant *Saglasna*
Vowel *Glasna*

Polite *Uchtiv*
Impolite *Neuchtiv*
Stress *Udarenie*
Intonation *Intonatsya*
Homework *Domashna rabota*
Imagine *Predstavi si*

Appendix 2. Embassies
Selected Bulgarian embassies abroad
UK: 186–188 Queen's Gate, London SW7 5HL. Tel: (0171) 584 9433.
USA: 1028 11 East 84th Street, New York, NY 1028. Tel: (212) 737 4790.
1621 22nd Street NW, Washington, DC 20008. Tel: (202) 387 7969.

Selected embassies in Sofia
Australia, Canada and New Zealand do not have embassies in Sofia.
UK: 65–67 Boulevard Vassil Levski, Sofia 1000. Tel: 885 361/2. (Open Monday–Thursday.)
USA: 1 Stamboliiski Boulevard. Tel: 884 801. (Open 8.30am–1pm, Monday–Friday.)

8 | Teaching children and adolescents

It is quite likely that you will teach children in the six to sixteen age range at some stage during your time in Eastern and Central Europe. Teaching children, of any age, can be very rewarding and enjoyable and different approaches and methods need to be adapted from those used when teaching adults. If you have never taught children before try and observe some lessons first, and talk to your colleagues.

Motivation

Children, unlike most adults, are not necessarily motivated to learn English, and may see it as an irrelevance. The teacher therefore needs to motivate students; using jokes is one example, for the simple reason that children are interested in them. Often jokes which adults feel are awful, kids find funny; hence a joke book can be an invaluable teaching aid. Jokes are also memorable. Children also like drawing and colour, and for the teacher this can be exploited. For example, you may not need to explain something if you are able to draw it or represent it visually, eg MTWTFSS for the days of the week. A picture of a car can be a car or it can mean to drive. Children have very visual minds.

Getting children to draw stories or songs in pairs/groups can likewise be very useful. This exercise can be more motivating than writing the stories because it includes the challenge of having to decipher what other groups have drawn.

To keep your students motivated you need to keep them involved at all times. Teachers should not be lecturers, rather they are facilitators, encouraging their students to do things.

Staging

Staging lessons is very important. Because children generally have a limited concentration span they need diversity in activity types. You can use the same activities time and time again, and like bedtime stories, kids never get fed up with them. Adults on the other hand would soon get bored. You can repeat activities, but they need to be kept quite short.

You also need to change the focus and pace of a lesson. Two types of activities to consider are 'stirring' activities and 'settling' activities, and you need to be adaptable in the use of these. For example, sometimes kids get over-excited and over-active, and before long you will have mayhem in the classroom. You would then need a 'settling' activity. This could be a short reading describing somebody, whom the students then have to draw. At other times you may need a 'stirring' activity which may for example involve physical movement.

Projects

Projects can be multi-various and provide an excellent way of integrating skills work as well as providing motivation for students.

For example, give your class a crossword puzzle based on six or seven items of vocabulary you taught them the previous week, but deliberately make it a bad crossword puzzle. Ask them what they think of it, which will probably be not a lot, and then challenge them to make a better one, which they probably will do.

Project work can be especially useful with adolescents as you can cater more for the individual. Other projects could be on sports, pop stars, producing information booklets on their own town, or writing and taping a radio programme. Projects are also a good way for you to find out what they like so you can select material accordingly. Projects do not have to be for the whole lesson but can be from 10 to 30 minutes.

Discipline

Children can get fed up and bored very quickly, usually because you are spending too long on something which they do not see as being in anyway relevant to them. It could also be because you have gone outside their experience and outside their knowledge. Remember that anything you do not manage to finish can always be picked up in a later lesson.

When starting a course with a new group you may want to consider 'contracts' which the teacher and the students design together. First the kids work out what the teacher has to do (eg mark homework, prepare lessons carefully, etc). Then they work out their own rules. Classroom rules are much easier to enforce if they have been determined by the students themselves.

When you take on a new class it is usually better to be firmer at the beginning rather than trying to be too friendly. If you lose control from the start it is more difficult to establish it later.

Age group 6–10

When teaching young children it is far better to adopt an 'inductive' approach (ie grammar rules not made explicit), rather than a 'deductive' approach (ie trying to explain rules to them). Young children can't conceptualize language in the way older learners can.

For example if we take the following joke:

A: I've just found this penguin in the street.
B: Have you taken him to the zoo?
A: Yes, and now I'm taking him to the cinema.

In the middle of the joke there is contextualized use of the present perfect, 'have you taken him to the zoo'. Playing around with jokes is one way to teach grammatical points such as the present perfect, without worrying about analysis of the language.

Language can also be viewed 'holistically', ie you do not have to take small discrete items of language and present these individually to children. Rather, for example, when recreating a story attention can be drawn to specific grammar or lexical points. Children have enquiring minds and the best time for the presentation of new language is when they ask 'why?'

Games

For young learners games are important, though it is important to remember what is seen as a game to a child is merely a way of making practice fun. Games need to have aims like any other activities.

Songs and chants

Basic drilling doesn't always work with children. However use of rhythm and songs is generally more successful. For example Carolyn Graham's *Jazz Chants* work well in a limited form. With very young learners action songs are fun and useful (eg head, shoulders, knees and toes).

Memory

Children learn very quickly and forget just as quickly. This is why it is possible to re-do activities again and again using exactly the same lexis or grammar point. For example, you can play hangman every lesson for four weeks with vocabulary on clothing.

Activities also act as memory aids; children remember the activity and consequently the language. Colour, drawings and other visual techniques can be good memory aids.

Rituals

Children like rituals. It is a good idea, for example, to start the lesson in one particular way. This may simply involve getting the students to stand up and sit down, or having a different student each lesson to write the date on the board. This is very effective in terms of bringing the class together and signalling the start of the lesson. Oddly enough kids are negative about the very original. Original ideas need to be incorporated slowly into your classes.

Adolescents

Adolescence is a stage between childhood and adulthood. Young learners are usually a delight to teach and will do anything you ask them to do. However students between the ages of 12 and 16 are probably the hardest age group to teach.

Girls tend to mature more quickly than boys and by the age of 14–15 you are dealing with people who like to think of themselves as 'grown-up'. Games are therefore not always the best approach. Although your students now need to be treated as adults, that does not mean you have to deal with adult topics. Your students' areas of interest should be discovered first before you start planning your lesson topics.

Adolescents are used to sitting back, listening to the teacher and assessing the teacher's ability. If you can interest them and maintain their interest as well as make them work, they will consider you a good teacher. Part of the skill of maintaining interest is the information content and use of whatever experience and knowledge they have.

Motivating adolescents

Whilst most adolescents in Eastern and Central Europe are generally well motivated to learn English the following suggestions may help you with your teaching.

A check-list of questions to ask yourself when planning a lesson for adolescents should include: Do I have sufficient variety of activities in this lesson? Are there enough changes of pace? Have I pitched the level of input sufficiently to make it challenging for them? Will it stimulate interest? Is the topic/content relevant to their world? Will I be bringing their lives into the classroom, calling on their experiences and interests? Over a series of lessons, how much have I varied ways of presenting activities? How much have I recycled language and how often do the students have tests?

It can be very useful at the beginning of a course to sit down with the students, talk about their interests and negotiate the course content and class rules. This appeals to their 'adultness' and can provide motivation if students know, for example, that in exchange for a certain amount of work they will be able to watch a video, listen to a song, etc. Bribery can be a very useful strategy when used in moderation! Thus within a lesson we must consider:

The coursebook and supplementary materials. Unfortunately a lot of the coursebooks available and used in Eastern and Central Europe stimulate neither interest nor imagination, and some expect too much from teenagers with limited experience of the world. Students will easily become bored and de-motivated if books are used for the whole lesson without some supplementary material.

Reading. Authentic materials are very popular with teenagers, eg music magazines or teenage magazines. Opportunities to exploit these texts are endless, eg 15/16-year-old students are usually very keen to produce a photo story with captions after working on one from a teenage magazine. Teenagers are generally eager to learn more about their favourite pop stars and will happily write questions about information they wish to find out from a text.

Listening. As with reading, this needs to be interesting to gain students' attention. Songs are an excellent source of material as they are often the one English language activity in which students are involved outside the classroom. Teenagers will readily bring in songs – get them to bring in a copy of the words too, if possible, and then ask them to design a task for the song. Follow-up work could include a profile or poster about the band.

Writing. Being very sensitive, adolescents are frequently much more adventurous when writing than speaking. Writing activities prompted by visual aids go down well, eg writing a newspaper story which links three unconnected pictures, or where there is a clear task such as writing a quiz. Pen-pals between classes or countries are popular too.

Speaking. Adolescent egos are very delicate and therefore they should not be forced to do something if it is likely to embarrass them. It is a good idea to stick to small group discussions around their interests. Role-play where students take on role models, eg pop stars, which are attractive to them generally work well, although adequate time is needed for preparation.

Vocabulary. Lexical input is usually well-received, especially slang/colloquial language. One idea is for students to have an 'alternative dictionary' in which expressions are collected. They can then select, say, four expressions, write dialogues set in the disco/coffee bar, etc and then act them out.

Video. As with readings and listenings, authentic material is very popular in Eastern and Central Europe. Clips from 'soaps' and pop videos go down very well. Another stimulus for students to read a book (easy reader) is the knowledge that they will watch the film when they have finished the book.

Exams. Whether you agree with them or not, exams seem to be very important to adolescents and are therefore a source of long-term motivation. One variation is to get your class to write end-of-term exams for other classes at the same level. A great form of revision and a writing exercise!

Peer-teaching. As well as writing exams for each other, teenagers will often take great pleasure in teaching grammatical structures to each other. They will need some time to prepare this but the results are often worth the time spent on it. It is also a good way of increasing the use of English in the classroom and giving students more responsibility for their learning.

Games. These appeal to the 'childishness' of teenagers and can also be a good way to provide short-term motivation, ie 'finish this and we'll have a game!'

You. Finally, whatever wealth of material available to you, you will only really stimulate adolescents if you show a genuine interest in them and enthusiasm in your teaching. Although it may be difficult at times not to take their sullenness personally, or to lose your temper with them and resort to doing grammar exercises, when sufficiently motivated teenagers can be one of the most rewarding age groups to teach.

Conclusion

The main thing with children of all ages is to give them a sense of achievement, to make them feel they are doing something with English. You need to get them to produce a product, eg a wall poster or a project. Work should be put up on the walls regularly and taken down regularly. It should be displayed neatly – children are impressed by visual displays. Have texts typed up and pictures mounted.

Do not be too worried if your students are not speaking all the time. A lot of learning goes on in a passive way. Teenagers, for example, may feel embarrassed about speaking English in front of their colleagues.

Finally, if they are available, the Macmillan *Dossier* series and Mary Glasgow Publications (magazines for children) are good source material.

9 | Teaching business people

A growing amount of the teaching in Eastern and Central Europe is to business people, and involves an increasing amount of English for specific purposes (ESP), for example teaching hotel staff the type of language that will be useful to them professionally, or teaching the language of law to lawyers. However, while these specialist areas are still developing, it is still more likely that you will find yourself teaching general English to professional people, or teaching business content and skills through the medium of English to pre-professionals. A lot of teachers have initial fears about teaching 'business English', arguing they have had no experience in the field. While a knowledge of business is very useful, it is definitely not a prerequisite to teaching English to business people, which is more a case of adapting a different approach from the one you would use if you were teaching a general English class in the school. The type of language learners need is often in areas such as telephoning, introductions, presentations, etc.

Teaching can take place in a number of ways:

- *One-to-one.* Teaching one-to-one requires a different approach to working with a group (see below).
- *In-company group.* An in-company group may study before work starts, during the day or after work.
- *In-school group.* A group of business people from the same company or from different companies may come to the school to study.

For all of the above, 'clients' (a common term when referring to learners from a company) may study intensively or over a longer period of time.

Clients

The type of clients you are likely to meet can vary immensely. Ages can range from early 20s to mid-50s, and quite often the older generation have had little or no previous language learning experience. Younger learners not only tend to pick things up more quickly, they have usually learned some English at school. Often groups are small, around four to six, although you may get groups of up to 12 and of course one-to-one (see p 268).

One of the problems of teaching business people is that they are often tired. If you are teaching them in the evening after they have been working all day (in some cases from as early as 7am), it is unreasonable to expect to cover the same amount of material as you would normally do. You may have to compromise and make the material less challenging, or cut down on input or even, in extreme cases, scrap your lesson plan altogether and turn it into a conversation class.

Attendance is sometimes sporadic with company courses, and if the course is at the company there is always a chance your clients may be pulled out of a lesson at any time. Homework may also be difficult for them to do due to pressure of work, family, etc.

Another of the problems you will come across is the diversity of levels within a group. Groups are often put together according to job type, or for economic reasons; not necessarily according to language ability.

In such cases you need to challenge the stronger learners so that they don't get bored, and at the same time try not to lose the weaker ones. A secretary may well be in the same group as her boss, and you have to be careful not to make him look stupid in front of his employees. Group dynamics are very important.

Not all learners will be motivated to study English, although the vast majority will be. A number of them will have been 'required' to learn. Failure to do so could well result in them losing their job or not getting promotion. Commonly lessons are held outside work hours and eat into clients' free time, and often motivation can depend on the attitude and support of the company itself.

The balance of business people learning English is pretty evenly split between men and women, although this obviously varies from company to company.

What they need

Before you can begin any course you have to find out what the students want and what they need. There is often a difference. You also have to balance the clients' wants and needs with those of the company.

A lot of business people still need basic grounding in English rather than anything too specific; but this doesn't mean you cannot draw on their own work environment to make the course relevant to them. Often they will know the terminology and vocabulary directly related to their work, but are unable to put it into a proper sentence, or do not know how to use it. You need to have a general understanding of the client's job; it is not up to you to teach content, rather to input language with which he can express himself in an area in which he is familiar. Any interest you show will be much appreciated.

Needs analysis and planning the course

After initially testing your clients to get an idea of their level, your next step should be to give them a 'needs analysis'. This can be in the form of a written questionnaire for the clients to complete, or simply an informal chat with the clients and/or training manager.

A written questionnaire to be filled in by both you and the client will ideally include not only the client's details and past learning experience, but will ask clients to identify specific objectives of the course and get them to prioritize them. For example, Ms Horvath, a marketing manager, may want to prepare herself for a presentation of her company's new product at an international sales conference.

It is a good idea to include a 'Needs Negotiation' session in the Day 1 lesson plan (plus time for introductions and some language input, eg question forms and an intonation/diagnostic activity to test for skills fluency and language gaps). Explain to the group the rationale behind the Needs Negotiation and that, although you have their details individually, the group as a whole needs to establish priorities. Being able to discuss the course content sometimes comes as a surprise to clients who are simply happy to accept what the teacher gives them, thinking the teacher knows best. It can be therefore difficult to get clients to define their own needs. (NB The 'needs analysis' may take place in the learner's native language and be translated if the clients are of a very low level.)

A needs negotiation session should:

- get each participant to note down (1) precisely what they use English for in their jobs and (2) what they will need it for in the future;
- run a feedback session where everyone shares this information publicly;
- discuss the findings and agree on common needs; and
- tell them you will give them a plan next lesson with as much attention to individual needs as possible, but obviously focusing on overlaps.

Planning the programme

After the pre-course assessment of needs and ability from the questionnaire responses and negotiation with the group, begin listing suitable situations, language and published materials, eg:

Situation/topic	Language	Material
1. Socialising with clients	Offers, requests, small talk	*In at the Deep End* (Unit 16)
2. Presentations	Introducing oneself, dealing with questions	*Business Objectives* (Unit 1)

Having given your group a draft timetable for the next lesson, usually covering the first 15–20 hours (don't plan too far ahead), you need to demonstrate to them the relevance of each activity/topic to their individual needs.

Stress that the timetable is flexible and extra needs should be stated as the course goes on. Any individual whose needs are not satisfied within the programme (eg only one student might need business letter practice) can be catered for with extra self-study. However long the course is, recap on objectives, highlight the aims of each activity, evaluate progress and *ask for feedback*.

Mid-course evaluation

About half-way through the course, set some work that participants can get on with individually. Take each student out for five minutes to elicit their reactions so far and their needs for the remainder of the course. This gives credibility to your claim to take individual needs seriously, and gives you a double check on how the learners feel about the course.

Materials

There is an abundance of material on the market for teaching business English and a lot is now widely available in Eastern and Central Europe. This varies from general business English books to very specific books, for example English for banking. A high proportion of these also come with accompanying tapes. A number of videos specifically made for teaching business people are now available, and although very expensive, can add variety to a course.

Authentic materials are invaluable when teaching business groups. Anything you can obtain from the company – eg faxes, letters, company reports, publicity material – will prove very useful. Other sorts of authentic material such as articles from business magazines and newspapers are a good source and Eastern and Central Europe now has a wide variety of such magazines, eg *The Economist, Business Central Europe*, as well as the local English language papers. Finally the students themselves are an invaluable source of material.

Note that any material presented to your students should ideally be typed and professional-looking. It is a good idea to hole-punch it first so they can add it to their file (see p 272 for books).

One-to-one

Teaching one-to-one is very intensive for both the client and teacher; hence it is essential to establish a good working relationship with him and build a rapport. If you can do this, the experience can be highly productive, rewarding and enjoyable for both parties.

Motivation. Ensure you know why the client is learning, ie whose decision: his or the company's? Draw on information in the needs analysis – focus on those language points and negotiate the course with the client. One-to-one is very flexible as there are no other clients' needs to consider, and it should therefore be personalized to make it 100% relevant to that person.

Needs and activities. Timing and activities need to be planned very carefully. You also need to timetable short breaks into your plan and periods where the learner can work quietly on his own. Adapt your lessons to the particular needs and interests of your clients. Get the client to suggest the content of the lessons and continually re-negotiate the syllabus. Change the focus of the lesson, eg use cuisennaire rods (coloured rods of different sizes) to deflect attention.

Learner independence. Encourage learner independence by taking grammar books and dictionaries into the class. Get the client to bring in material, eg articles from magazines, letters, etc. Use and exploit the learner as a resource and be an interested and intelligent listener. Always keep an eye/ear out for topics that the learner might be interested in.

Recording. Tape the learner and have him listen/correct at home. You could, for example, record one part of a dialogue and get him to tape the other half at home. Roleplay with teacher and learner playing both roles is also valuable. Practise/record with different levels of formality/attitude, etc.

Recycling. Change the medium of practice, eg from story to dialogue to telephone call to letter/memo to role play.

Correction. Vary your correction techniques. Don't correct all the time. Record the learner and let him pick a couple of areas he would like to improve on. (Rank the importance of mistakes.) Make a note of mistakes/errors, and use for input next time. Try some lessons where fluency is the aim; other lessons can be more accuracy-based.

PRACTICAL IDEAS FOR USE WITH A GROUP OR ONE-TO-ONE

The following are a few suggestions you can adapt for use with either a group or in one-to-one teaching. All of them draw on the learner's own work situation, knowledge and experience, leaving room for teachers to supplement the lesson with other material.

Describing a product or service

Language

- Adjectives describing products or services (eg reliable, effective, expensive, competitive, etc).
- Height/width/depth/shape/colour.
- A thing for . . . plus . . . ing (eg a clip for holding).
- Suitable for . . ./ made of . . .

Description. Ask students whose company produces a particular product, or offers a specific service, to make descriptive notes about the product or service. These can then be discussed with a partner.

Presentation. As a follow-up, get the students to present their product or service to the rest of the group, outlining its uses, benefits, how it has changed, particular features, etc allowing time at the end for the students listening to ask questions. This can also be done with other products.

Advertisements. Finally ask your students to design a TV/radio/magazine advertisement for their product or service (or invent a new product) and discuss how and where they think it should be marketed.

Problems at work

Language

- If we do *x* then *y* will happen.
- If we did *x* then *y* would happen.
- Language of discussion – agreeing/disagreeing.
- Offering suggestions.

Description. Get the students to tell you or a partner a current problem at work. Students then discuss possible solutions and consequences.

Sample problem. Suggest the company needs to cut its costs by 5%. Ask your students to discuss and agree on possible solutions.

Describing a company's history and make-up

Language

- Past tenses/passives/dates.
- Linking words, eg next, following.

Description. Tell your students to describe the origins of the company and how it has grown over the years, highlighting key moments, new products, etc.

Work relationships. Ask the students to draw an organization chart of the company or department, indicating what roles each person/ department plays and the relationship between them.

Job descriptions. Tell the students to choose one or two positions and discuss qualities, qualifications, etc needed to do the job well. As a follow up ask the students to write their own job description.

Describing company progress

Language

- Graph language – increase/decrease (present perfect/past).
- Prepositions: rose by, increased to, stayed at, etc.
- Adjectives/adverbs/figures.

Explaining data. Ask the students to provide data and graphs showing aspects of the company's sales, costs, level of production, etc. Ask the students to explain what the material shows and give reasons for changes.

Functions of the company. Ask the students to think about their company in terms of the product or service they provide, who their customers are, strengths and weaknesses of the company, main competitors, etc.

Company report. Tell the students to follow up by writing a company report.

Discussing working conditions

Language

- Simple present.
- Adverbs of frequency.
- Conditionals.

Improving working conditions. Ask the students to look at their work conditions and to try to find ways of improving them. Ask them to consider, and to make notes, on their working conditions in relation to: pay, hours, holidays, work environment, and perks.

Comparisons. Ask the students to compare the notes they have written. Ask them: how have these conditions changed over the last few years and what aspects would they like changed in the future.

Typical days. Tell the students to describe a typical day and to think of ways in which they could make more effective use of their time, and what aspects of their own work they would like to change.

THINGS TO CONSIDER

Before you begin

Find out as much as you can about the company. What do they do? Who are their competitors? If you are teaching at the company, how do you get there, who should you meet, what facilities do they have (eg whiteboard, chalkboard, taperecorder etc)? What is the contact telephone number and address?

On arrival

On the first day, take everything you need (photocopies, board pens etc) – better to be overprepared than under! It is also worth allowing yourself plenty of time to find the company on the first day; punctuality is important. Don't bank on there being a tape-recorder.

Dress the part. At least until you learn the appropriate dress code, wear formal smart clothes. However good your teaching, you will initially be judged on your appearance as a representative of your school.

If you speak the local language use the formal form of 'you' when you greet reception staff initially. Take your cue from them.

It is always worthwhile establishing a good relationship with reception and administration staff. They can be really helpful with facilities and organizational necessities.

During the course

Keep a record of attendance and material covered, as well as details of lessons cancelled and any problems (eg lateness). Always tell your school if clients want to reschedule lessons or change the programme in any way.

Never gossip about the participants to other people in the company. Casual remarks made to other students or reception staff have a tendency to get distorted and to rebound on you and the school.

Use the opportunity to make the course relevant by seeing the participants at work and using examples of faxes/letters/telephone calls they send or receive.

After the course

You will probably be asked to write a post-course report which should be done promptly. This will normally include details of course content, student evaluation and test/attendance percentages, plus suggestions for further study. Remember companies have high expectations and usually pay more than individuals for their courses.

Suggested materials
Advanced Business Contacts – Upper/Intermediate (Prentice-Hall)
Business Opportunities – Intermediate (OUP)
Business Objectives (OUP)
Business Ventures 1 + 2 – Elementary and Pre-Intermediate (OUP)
Developing Business Contacts – Intermediate (Prentice-Hall)
Getting Ahead – Pre-intermediate (CUP)
In at the Deep End – Intermediate (OUP)
International Business English

Invaluable for the teacher
Business Dictionary (OUP)
Business English Usage (Longman)
Business English Teacher's Resource Book (Longman)

10 Further reading

There are numerous books in English on the countries of Eastern and Central Europe. Below are a few personal recommendations.

POLAND

History/general

Norman Davies, *The Heart of Europe: A Short History of Poland*, OUP, 1984
Norman Davies, *God's Playground: A History of Poland*, Clarendon Press, Oxford, and Columbia Press, New York, 1982
Stewart Stevens, *The Poles*, Collins, 1982
Adam Zamoyski, *The Polish Way*, John Murray, 1987
Lech Wałęsa, *A Path of Hope*, Pan, London
Timothy Garton Ash, *The Polish Revolution: Solidarity 1980–82*, Cape, London

Guidebooks

Slater and McLachlan, *Rough Guide to Poland*, Penguin, 1991
Krzysztof Dydynski, *Poland: A Travel Survival Kit*, Lonely Planet, 1993
Poland, Insight Guides, APA Publications, Singapore
Edith Stohl, *The Golden Pages* (*Gives information, primarily on Warsaw, for ex pats.*)

CZECH REPUBLIC AND SLOVAKIA

History

Ivan Svitek, *The Unbearable Burden of History: History of Czechoslovakia*
Timothy Garton Ash, *We the People: The Revolution of 89*, Granta, Penguin

Literature

Milan Kundera, *The Joke, The Unbearable Lightness of Being, The Book of Laughter and Forgetting*, all published by Faber, London

Guidebooks

Rough Guide to The Czech and Slovak Republics, Penguin

HUNGARY

History

Peter F Sugar, *A History of Hungary*, I.B. Tauris, London

Guidebooks

Bob Dent, *Blue Guide to Hungary*, A&C Black/W Norton, London/New York
Török Andràs, *A Critical Guide to Budapest*, Zephyr Press/Park Publishing, 1993 (*An excellent book for a Hungarian insight into the city. Has useful walks with detailed commentaries.*)
Ex-Pats' Guide to Budapest (*A very practical book written by ex-pats for ex-pats containing detailed information on all you need to know about living in Hungary, and Budapest in particular. Available from* Bestsellers, *see p 197.*)
Dan Richardson, *Rough Guide to Hungary*, Penguin. (*New updated version giving a comprehensive guide on what to see and do.*)

GENERAL

A literary guide to Eastern and Central Europe is due in 1995 from the publishers of this book.

James Naughton, ed, *A Traveller's Literary Companion to Eastern and Central Europe*, In Print, Brighton, UK, forthcoming 1995

Index